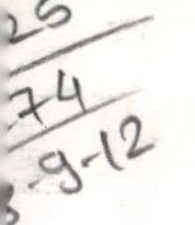

GENERAL INSURANCE IN INDIA

Principles and Practices

GENERAL INSURANCE IN INDIA

Principles and Practices

DR. K.C. SHARMA

Foreword by

DR. A.K. VASHISHT
Professor, University Business School, Panjab University, Chandigarh-160014

REGAL PUBLICATIONS
New Delhi-110027

GENERAL INSURANCE IN INDIA
Principles and Practices

ISBN 978-81-8484-224-1

Typeset by
S.S. COMPOSERS
3190, Mohindra Park, Shakur Basti, Delhi-110034.

Printed in India at
MAYUR ENTERPRISES
WZ Plot No. 3, Gujjar Market, Tihar Village, New Delhi-110018.

Published by
REGAL PUBLICATIONS
F-159, Rajouri Garden, New Delhi-110027.
Phone: +91-11-45546396
E-mail: regalbookspub@yahoo.com

Dedicated Reverentially

to

CA Man Mohan Kamal Mahajan

(Chairman of Dr. IT Group)

Contents

Foreword

It is no denying the fact that Insurance is a cover for risk. The concept of insurance originated as a formal business in the late 17th Century. This business became sophisticated business in post-Renaissance Europe. In the seventeenth century, coffee houses were opened in Europe; people from all walks of life visited those coffee houses and thus such places became meeting venues. People discussed matters of interest to them and exchanged information. Mr. Edward Lloyd also opened a coffee house that became a popular haunt of ship owners, merchants, and ship captains. His coffee house became a reliable source of the latest shipping news. Lloyd's became the meeting place for parties wishing to insure cargoes and ships. Lloyd's of London remains the leading market for marine and other specialist types of insurance even today.

We observe that the Sanskrit term 'yogakshema' or well-being of the society is found in the Rig Veda; it is interpreted as insurance. The 'Joint Family System' practised in India is a form of 'micro insurance' to take care of situations as consequence of calamities.

The British Government appointed S.C. Sen, a well-known solicitor of India in 1934 to study and report on the amendments to insurance legislation. The government set-up an Informal Advisory Committee of leading insurance men, headed by N.N. Sircar who was at the material time Law Member in the British India government. The Committee submitted a bill to the Legislative Assembly in 1937 which resulted in the passage of the Insurance Act, 1938. That Act became the cornerstone of insurance legislation in India.

May 13, 1971 is a historic moment in India when an ordinance was promulgated by the President of India to take over the ownership and management of 107 general insurance companies which were doing business in India at that time. General Insurance Business (Nationalization) Act, 1972 or GIBNA became the guiding act of General Insurance. IRDA Act was passed in 1999 containing all regulations governing insurance and it also established autonomous regulating authority.

History bears testimony to the most disturbing situation when, in 1991, India's forex reserves were barely enough to pay for the imports (including bulk and unavoidable oil imports) for two weeks. As response to such a condition, particularly to avoid default in repayments of external borrowings, extensive and intensive reforms were initiated to restructure economy and socio-economic institutions as well as to introduce changes in the business laws. In that process, Banking and Insurance sectors have also been affected. These sectors have been opened for private sector and global competition by providing level-playing field to the players in the economy. Foreign companies have started operating in India in collaboration with Indian partners.

The book written by Dr. K.C. Sharma on General Insurance (other than Life Insurance), manuscript of which has been studied by me, is a good attempt at codifying the rules, regulations and practices for the benefit of general readers. The book is written in simple language, in lucid style. The book is seemingly a must for the students of management and practitioners of insurance business.

Dr. Sharma is an established writer and I trust he will turn over many more books on management and miscellaneous subjects in due course. I wish him success in his dedicated endeavours in public interest.

DR. A.K. VASHISHT,
Professor and Dean, Faculty of Commerce,
University Business School, Panjab University,
Chandigarh-160014

Preface

All Individuals and business organizations increasingly recognize that high level of professional knowledge and skills are essential to their success. Both of them are increasingly spending on professional education as knowledge and processes change fast in today's scenario due to technology changes as a result of new breakthroughs in science and new dimensions added by research. Expenditure on research and development is considered an investment into a collective future. Investment in human resource, truly called human capital, has thus acquired position in the centre stage of strategies in all the countries to promote economic well-being, better skilled labour forces, social cohesion, team spirit and other positive individual and social benefits. However, investment in professional education is not adequate due to limited public and private resources as identified by 'UNESCO Millennium Goals'. There is a challenge in regard to desired rather needed expansion in professional educational opportunities. The challenge is that of maintaining their quality and ensuring their equitable distribution. This is linked to the questions of harnessing finances in competition with various equally pressing demands on this critical resource.

Reforms have been ushered in the insurance sector and the sector has been opened to foreign competition. We can see that one of the significant gains of insurance sector reforms has been the tremendous increase in the awareness levels of general public about the insurance terms, conditions, privileges of the policyholder, and obligations of the insurer. Deficiency of service can be brought to judicial system to claim damage and compensation. Insurance is sunrise industry; it has tremendous employment opportunities that are growing manifold. A lot of youngsters are coming forward to learn more and more about the insurance subject. Their aim is not only to get a foothold in the employment market but also to improve their knowledge to make informed decisions when they go in for buying insurance and also guide their friends, relatives and kin.

The aim of bringing out this book is to help students, insurance teachers and others interested in the subject to:

(a) become self-reliant, so that they acquire the expertise to determine their own priorities to interpret and use insurance concept effectively;
(b) undertake research, problem-solving and problem formulation, and
(c) sustain capacities to create insurance consciousness.

It has been observed the world over that the Insurers are engaged in a battle to create and maintain high skilled talent in their workforces. There is relentless competition that has led insurers to monitor skills, in particular the training skills, in their executives. This seeks to empower such insurance executives to handle insurance business confidently and to the satisfaction of the insured.

This book would hopefully be found as a gateway enabling individuals to learn new skills in both the classroom and the workplace, while imbibing their learning rights and execution responsibilities.

While life insurance has taken roots and is becoming a need in many literate persons, the business of general insurance is still on a rapid growth path and has to spread to embrace all spheres concerned. General insurers are contributing to corporate risk management and protection of underlying assets of financing banks. There are increased litigations and consumer activism. General insurance is assisting in liability or casualty management of individuals and corporates. Major lines of general insurance are fire, marine, and miscellaneous including motor insurance. General insurance risks are usually managed on an annual basis. Although aspects such as marketing, asset management, survey and adjustment are other technical areas of general insurance yet underwriting and claims management are critical areas for general insurance. This book is an effort to integrate the general insurance principles and practices to present a business model that would possibly work.

This book deals with General Insurance only. I most gratefully acknowledge the debt due by me to my colleagues and friends for their contribution in the completion of the present work. My special gratitude goes to my wife, Vidya and daughters, Anjana and Anupama and grandchildren (Abhimanyu and Utkarsh). While my wife encouraged me, the daughters contributed their ideas, Abhimanyu helped with the computer and Utkarsh fiddled with the computer reminding mc of the work awaiting my attention.

I am particularly thankful to Regal Publications, New Delhi for bringing out this book within a reasonably short time and in a nice get-up.

DR. K.C. SHARMA

1

Introduction

Insurance is neither very old nor so modern concept; it got originated as a formal business in the late 17th Century. Insurance assumed sophistication in post-Renaissance Europe. In the late 1680s, Mr. Edward Lloyd opened a coffee house that became a popular haunt of ship owners, merchants, and ship captains. A reliable source of the latest shipping news, Lloyd's, became the meeting place for parties wishing to insure cargoes and ships. Lloyd's of London remains the leading market for marine and other specialist types of insurance.

Indian scholars, more particularly those having knowledge of Indian scriptures, observe that the Sanskrit term 'yogakshema' or well-being of the society or insurance is found in the Rig Veda. The 'Joint Family System' practised in India is a form of micro insurance to take care of calamitous situations.

In 1934, the then British Government appointed S.C. Sen, a well-known solicitor in India, to study and report on the amendments to insurance legislation. The government set-up an Informal Advisory committee of leading insurance men, headed by N.N. Sircar, the then Law Member, in the British India government. This committee submitted a bill to the Legislative Assembly in 1937. At last, the Insurance Act, 1938 was enacted. The Insurance Act became the cornerstone of Indian insurance legislation.

May 13, 1971 was historic date when an ordinance was promulgated by the President of India to take over the ownership and management of 107 general insurance companies then operating in India, by the Government of India. General insurance Business (Nationalization) Act, 1972 or GIBNA became the guiding act of General Insurance till the IRDA Act was passed in 1999.

Evaluating an insurer's promises to perform certain obligations under certain specified future situations is not an easy task for the customers of insurance. The degree of standardization of general insurance products varies from country to country, from rigidly controlled tariff markets to open markets with minimal controls, compatible with the type of government or state of economy.

Intensive or cut-throat and unregulated competition in marketing general insurance products can produce inadequate rates and insolvency. It also breeds sharp loss adjusting practices, abortive policy language and tendencies towards monopolization. These are recognized to be against public interest.

In answering to the requirements of clients, the insurers need to enter into different types of reinsurance contracts as part of their business. The regulator has to ensure that foreign exchange is not unduly drained off through reckless re-insurance programmes of the insurers. Many regulators specify that the insurers shall cede such percentage of the sum insured on each policy for different classes of insurance written in the country to a national reinsure (s) registered in the country.

Premium rates are crucial to insurance business; these should ensure the survival of the insurance company, achieving optimum strategy positioning, providing quality and value for the service, contributing to the society's well-being and optimizing the returns for a given type of risk.

As the insurance contract is based on utmost faith, any circumstance that is within the knowledge of the insuring person and is likely to influence the insurer in deciding whether he will accept or refuse the risk, or influence him in assessing the premium that he will charge, must be fully disclosed to the insurer before the contract is concluded. The action of the proposer in withholding these vital details from the insurer is not in keeping with the principle of utmost good faith in insurance.

Insurable interest denotes such an interest to the common man, in the object insured, whereby any loss or damage to the object would seriously prejudice the interests of the insured. Insurance thrives on theory of large numbers; insurance covers only the pure risk/loss, not the speculative loss. Only losses covered by insurance are paid as claim by the insurers not all losses; this is the principle of nearest cause in insurance.

Due to lack of innovation, Insurance industry in India is lagging behind its counterparts in the developed countries in such fields as risk management, loss prevention techniques, non-life actuarial studies and arbitration. The industry also lacks credible data for insurance product development by loss modeling.

Indians being conservative, business of general insurance is still in its rapid growth path. Still, the general insurers are contributing to corporate risk management and protection of underlying assets of financing banks. With litigations and consumer activism, general insurance is also assisting in liability or casualty management of individual sand corporate. Fire, marine and miscellaneous including motor insurance are major lines of general insurance.

EVOLUTION OF INSURANCE

It is the relatively modern societies that built-up economies with money and financial instruments and evolved other forms of insurance down the centuries. In the money economy context, Chinese and Babylonian traders evolved some methods of transferring or distributing risk as long ago as the 3rd and 2nd millennia BC, respectively. Chinese merchants traveling treacherous river rapids would redistribute their wares across many vessels to limit the loss due to any single vessel being incidentally capsized. As recorded in the famous code of Hammurabi, the Babylonians developed a system around 1750 BC that was practised by early Mediterranean sailing merchants. Thereby, if a merchant received a loan to fund his shipment, he would pay the lender an additional sum in exchange for the lender's guarantee to cancel the loan should the shipment be stolen. The Code of Hammurabi indicates that ancient Babylon had government insurances for theft and crop as well as an adoption annuity plan. Personal insurance on contribution principle has been found in the Thiasoi of ancient Greece.

Achaemenian monarchs were believed to have been the first to insure their people through an official process by registering donations to the monarch in governmental notary offices. Each year, in Norouz (beginning of the Iranian New year), the heads of different ethnic groups as well as others who were willing to take part in the process, presented gifts to the monarch. When a gift was worth more than 10, 000 Derrik (Achaemenian gold coin weighing 8.35-8.42g), it was registered in a special office so that whenever the person who presented the gift was in trouble, the monarch and the court would help him. As per Jahez, a historian and writer, whenever the donor of the present was in trouble or wanted to construct a building, set-up a fest or have his children married, the court would check the registration and the donor would receive double the amount. The ancient inhabitants of Rhodes invented the concept of the 'general average' whereby merchants whose goods were being shipped together would pay a proportionally divided premium which would be used to reimburse any merchant whose goods were jettisoned (thrown out of a ship to save the ship, lives or other goods) during storm or sinkage.

It is believed that Greeks and Romans introduced the origins of health and life insurance around 600 AD when they organized guilds called benevolent societies that cared for the families and paid funeral expenses of members upon death. Rome evolved the Fund of Collegia of the soldiery. Funds of the Collegia Tenuiorum were used to meet the unexpected expenses, burial expenses and needs of the soldiers' families, guilds in the middle ages served a similar purpose.

Friendly societies existed in England in which people donated amounts of money to a general sum that could be used for emergencies; this arrangement worked before insurance was established in the late 17th century. Stand alone insurance contracts or insurance policies not bundled with loans or other kinds of contracts are believed to have been invented in Genoa in the 14th century. Insurance pools were formed and backed by pledges of landed estates. These new insurance contracts allowed insurance to be separated from investment. Insurance became far more sophisticated in post-renaissance Europe, and specialized varieties of insurance developed.

Commercial activity/hub brought London to the centre stage. London's growing importance as a centre for trade by the end of the seventeenth century created a sudden spurt in demand for marine insurance. In the late 1680s, Mr. Edward Lloyd opened a coffee house that became a popular haunt of ship owners, merchants, and ship-captains, and thereby a reliable source of the latest shipping news. It became the meeting place for parties wishing to insure cargoes and ships, and those willing to underwrite such ventures. Today, Lloyd's of London remains the leading market (note that it is not an insurance company) for marine and other specialised types of insurance, but it works rather differently than the more familiar kinds of insurance.

Regarding insurance legislation, the earliest version of insurance law relates to marine insurance for which the English are indebted to the Lombards, who, driven away from their native states in Northern and Central Italy about the middle of the 13th century, settled in every maritime country in Europe. It appears that laws issued by the magistrates of Barcelona, laws published in Venice in 1468 and other regulations were familiar to the Lombards, and those laws/regulations formed the basis upon which the Lomnbards effected insurance on English merchandise from their residences in Lombard Street. The power of the Lombards was broken by a decree in 1597. Keate and Gurney state that the most important laws came from an unknown French source in a set of regulations published probably at Rouen in the 17th century, and that in British statute books, we find no mention of Marine insurance until 1601 when an act was passed concerning matters of assurance amongst Merchants. An Act of Parliament passed/enforced in 1720 vested monopoly rights of marine insurance in the two companies, Royal Exchange and London Assurance, and Lloyds until repealed in 1824. There was no marked development in British laws until 1756. Lord Mansfield became Lord Chief Justice and devoted himself earnestly to the study of the principles of marine insurance and its application in other countries. From Lord Mansfield's times, till the passage of Marine Insurance Act of 1906, the law of marine insurance was administered by an appeal to precedent.

Concerning the insurance sector, one of the most

momentous events of the century happened in London in June 1861 with the Great Fire (the greatest since 1666) at Tooley Street, Southward. The fire apparently started in stored hemp, spread furiously, could not be fully extinguished for a fortnight, and the fire offices sustained an enormous loss of between pound 1 and 2 million. The companies noted that the situation had gone out of hand due to the high loss and low premiums due to excessive competition. In the aftermath of this Great fire of London, that devoured 13, 200 houses, Nicholas Barbon opened an office to insure buildings. In 1680, he established England's fire insurance company, the Fire Office, to insure brick and frame homes. Insurers came together and to ensure that a repeat of this would not happen in the future, a new institution, the Fire Offices Committee (FOC), a voluntary, autonomous association, was formally created by the various fire (insurance) offices in 1868. Those companies transacting fire insurance agreed to adhere to certain minimum rates. FOC ushered in a new era of cooperation among British insurers and was followed by Accident Offices' Association (AOA), Engineering Offices' Association (EOA) and Aviation Offices' Insurance Association (AOIA). Through this entire process, insurance evolved and established as a subject and profession distinctly different from other branches of financial transactions.

In the United States of America, the first insurance company that underwrote the fire insurance risk was formed in Charles Town (modern day Charleston), South Carolina, in 1732. Benjamin Franklin helped to popularize and make standard the practice of insurance, particularly against fire, in the form of perpetual insurance. In 1752, he founded the Philadelphia Contributionship for the insurance of houses from loss by fire. Franklin's company was the first to make contributions toward fire prevention. His company warned against certain fire hazards. In case of certain buildings where the risk of fire was too great, such as all wooden houses, his company refused insurance.

THE INDIAN SCENARIO

The fundamental principle of insurance, that is a group sharing the losses of a few, had been appreciated in India in some way or other from the very ancient times. Hinduism, like other religions, exhorts man to help his fellow men in distress in the field of commerce in some way or the other. Scholars observe that the Sanskrit term 'Yogakshema' (well-being of the society of which insurance is a tool) is found in the Rig Veda and that some kind of community insurance was practised by the Aryan tribes of India nearly 3000 years ago. Manu Smriti speaks of a system of 'collective co-operation'. Yajnavalkya mentions some transactions akin to insurance. In its earliest and crude forms, insurance was probably perceived as a function of the State. In the ninth chapter of the Magnum Opus, Shrimad Bhagavad Gita, Lord Krishna promises yogakshema to devotees. The kings were expected to look after their people, and praja ranjan (welfare of the subjects) alone could justify their existence according to ancient Sanskrit literature. The 'Joint Family System' practised in India is seen by many as a form of micro-insurance to take care of calamitous situations, including death and sickness within the extended family. In course of time, many monarchs turned despotic and the functions of the State in even advanced countries were limited to the protection of subjects against foreign attacks and maintenance of law and order within. In the Indian context, religion and 'other worldliness' dominated the economic institutions; insurance was intertwined within the warp and well of the special fabric. This state continued until the arrival of the Europeans on the Indian soil and organization of economic activity, as we see it in the modern world, took shape.

In India, life insurance in modern context, started with the British influence. Many English companies extended their branches to India for underwriting European lives and later Parsee and Indian lives too. Sir John Child, who was the Governor of Bombay (now called Mumbai) between 1681 and 1690, was instructed by the Court of Directors to constitute an insurance office on the Mumbai Island, but it is not known what came of this organization. The Bombay Insurance Society was set-up in 1793 on Bombay Island by a few well-known European Merchants. Life Insurance in its present form came to India from the United Kingdom with the establishment of a British firm, Oriental Life Insurance Company in Kolkata in 1818 to help the widows of the European community. This was followed by the formation of the Bombay Life Assurance Company in 1829, and the Oriental Government Security Life Insurance Company in 1874. It has been documented that as early as 1822, when Indian social reformers were opposing the practice of Sati, Raja Ram Mohan Roy appealed through the Calcutta Journal to the good sense of the rich to start a fund for widows and orphans. Round about the decade beginning from 1850, considerable pressure seems to have been brought to bear upon the then Government of India to operate life insurance business under government control through a department of the State. History tells us that the proposal was turned down as the Government did not possess sufficient data on Indian lives, and as the insurance consciousness was not present to an adequate degree. The Princely State of Travancore (part of present Kerala State) was issuing life insurance policies in the late 19th century, and policies of 1896 are still preserved by the Kerala State Insurance Department, Thiruvananthapuram.

In India, the earliest known policy in English (dated 1555) is expressed as on the good ship Santa Crux "from any port in the isles of Indea of Calicut unto lixborne". It is known that members of the East India Company handled Bottomry Bond transactions. The first general insurance company, the Triton Insurance company Limited, was established in Kolkata in 1850. The Indian Mercantile Insurance Company Limited, which was set-up in Mumbai in 1907, was the first Indian company to transact all classes of general insurance business.

Documented information on non-life insurance operations in the country is available from the early 20th century. The Royal Exchange Assurance opened shop in India in 1900, and by 1907, almost 10 per cent of its accident business came from India and 6 other foreign agencies. Royal Exchange Assurance's net marine premium from India for the year 1914 is recorded as pound 40, 000 as against pound 17, 000 from Australia and pound 10, 000 from South Africa.

When Mumbai emerged from World War I as the centre of Indian trade, inspired by the growth of Indian trade and industry, and encouraged by the undercurrent of nationalism, leading businessmen in Mumbai rose to give concrete shape to proposals for meeting the insurance needs of Indian trade. Five offices were established in 1919, almost simultaneously, for transacting general insurance business. The newly formed insurance companies received support from the growth of nationalism in India.

Mahatma Gandhi stated, "The keynote of all our Swaraj is in placing all our insurance with our Indian companies", while Nehru said, "I hope Indians will realize the importance of patronizing only Indian insurance institutions".

The few years after 1922 were critical for Indian insurance when six new Indian offices were pitted against nearly 150 foreign offices, including those of some of the largest insurance groups in the world. The general economic conditions were against them and political agitation was at its zenith. Simultaneously, a powerful combination of American offices began their operations to be followed by a number of French companies a year later. To make matters worse for the Indian companies, an all round reduction in rates was enforced in 1928, depression set in a year later, foreign trade fell immediately, farm prices came done and purchasing power fell, and internal economy collapsed, while serious fire losses in Karachi and heavy riot losses in Mumbai were incurred

However, the industry came to the rescue of Indian insurers and hundreds of Indian businessmen signed a pledge to insure only with Indian offices. By this time, Indian industries such as sugar, paper, matches, paint and cement had gradually begun to take root, aided by a protective tariff system. Indian insurers' share of the total business written in India rose from a mere 11 per cent in 1928 to 22 per cent in 1935 and 32 per cent in 1939, largely at the expense of foreign offices, while the total business itself had registered an increase of only 5 per cent during the period.

EVOLUTION OF THE INDIAN INSURANCE MARKET

The evolution of the market prior to the Insurance Act, 1938 has just been discussed. The second phase of evolution started from the middle of the 1930s. During this period, the Indian market came out of its adolescence and stared addressing problems similar to those faced by the more nature markets. The market and the government were seized by the gravity of the situation, and concerted efforts were made leading to the enactment of the Insurance Act, 1938. The introduction of this Act of 1938 is generally regarded as the turning point for insurance regulation in India and the beginning of the insurance market as it currently exists, and existed some time back too.

THE INSURANCE ACT, 1938

It is considered the bed-rock legislation in India as far as the insurance business is concerned. The Government appointed S.C. Sen, a well-known solicitor, in 1934, as Officer on Special Duty in the Department of Commerce to study and report on the amendments to insurance legislation. Sen propounded the British ideal of minimum statutory control with maximum autonomy. With some modifications, the government set-up an informal Advisory Committee of leading insurance men, headed by N.N. Sircar, the then Law Member. This committee elicited views and suggestions from many stakeholders and submitted a bill to the Legislative Assembly in 1937. The bill stirred up intense public interest in the country. The trade associations submitted memoranda, insurance associations pressed for amendments and a Lloyd's representative flew over from London to watch their interest. Over a thousand amendments were suggested from various quarters and at last the Insurance Act, 1938 was enacted.

However, soon the market started criticizing the Act for its drafting mistakes, contradictions and impractical clauses. Though it was widely conceded that the act wrote a fresh chapter into the history of Indian insurance by attempting to prevent the formation and continuation of mushroom companies and by introducing sound insurance business practices, some authors commented that it became the most controversial law among Indian statutes.

In quick response to the criticism, the government made two amendments to the Act in 1939. To remove certain difficulties in administration, the Act was again amended in 1940. The market situation that cam up with World War II and the insurers' experience of working with the Act necessitated further changes. Further amendments were made in 1941, 1942, 1944, 1946 and 1948.

Despite the flaws, the 1938 Act gave the Indian market a regulatory foundation and amongst other things, provided for the constitution of a Department of Insurance, compulsory registration of insurance companies, provision for deposits, control on investments of funds, filing of returns on investments and financial condition, licensing of agents, control on commission, prohibition of rebates, filing of policy conditions and premium rates duly certified by an actuary (in the case of life business), periodical, valuation of liabilities, and provision for policyholders directors. The Act granted very wide powers to the Controller of Insurance in the matter of insurance regulation. The government visualized that the Controller of Insurance should be a person of extraordinary calibre, be actuarially qualified, having human considerations and broad outlook to administer law tactfully and even-handedly. The Indian insurance legislation was lauded by contemporary commentator as an excellent attempt to penalize the corrupt directors and executive officers, check wild cat schemes and scandals, and to stop acquisition of insurance companies by designing financiers.

The Insurance Act, 1938, became the corner stone of Indian insurance legislation and along with the insurance Rules formed under it, it still remains the most comprehensive legislation on the subject.

THE INSURANCE AMENDMENT ACT, 1950

The introduction of this comprehensive legislation, however, did not prevent the large-scale increase of new companies and the failures of existing companies. In response to the situation, in April 1945 a committee under the chairmanship of Sir Gowasji Jehangir was appointed to enquire into the undesirable developments in the management of the insurance companies and recommend suitable remedial measures. On the basis of this committee's recommendations, a bill was introduced. The bill was thrice referred to a Select Committee and thrice withdrawn on account of various reasons. Again, a committee under the chairmanship of S. Ranganathan was appointed to report on the working of the Indian Insurance Act and to give suggestions for further legislation. The Bill was redrafted, incorporating the suggestions of the committee and passed as the Insurance Amendment Act, 1950.

The salient features of this Act are the requirement of minimum capital, stricter control on investment and submission of periodical returns on investments, ceiling on expenses of management and agency commission, and appointment of administrators for mismanaged companies. The amendment created a statutory Association called the General Insurance Council. The existing Insurance Associations at Bombay, Calcutta and Madras were converted into the Bombay. Calcutta and Madras Regional Councils under the General Insurance Council with powers to frame and enforce tariff rates and regulations. Another statutory body called the Tariff Committee was constituted under the General Insurance Council and vested with powers to control and regulate the rates, advantages, terms and conditions that might be offered by its members and associate members in respect of general insurance business. The Tariff Committee was an All India body controlling and exercising powers over all Regional Councils. Although the actual rates were framed by the Rating Committees of Regional Councils, the Tariff Committee had the power to decide all major outstanding issues and, if necessary, override the Regional Councils.

THE INSURANCE AMENDMENT ACT, 1968

Even after the enactment of the amendment to the Insurance Act, the failure of companies did not stop. As per published reports, during the ten-year period from 1945 (when the Jehangir Committee was constituted) to 1954, 533 valuation reports of insurance companies were submitted to the Controller of Insurance. Of these, 86 valuations showed a deficit, which was not covered by the free paid up capital. Of these, 25 insurers went into liquidation and another 25 insurers had to transfer their business to other companies. This situation created an increased focus on the social security angle of insurance and the hardships that the common people would suffer if an insurance company became bankrupt. In response to the situation, the Insurance Act of 1938 was again amended in 1968 in order to provide for better social control over general insurance business. This amendment is popularly referred to in insurance circles as the 'introduction of social control measures of 1968 or as Social control amendments.

The amendment provided for regulation of investments, minimum solvency margin regulations, payment of premium before commencement of risk, licensing of surveyors, empowered the controller to carry out inspection, investigation and search, and seizure of books. These amendments, which came into force in June, 1969, renamed the Tariff Committee of the General Insurance Council as the 'Tariff Advisory Committee' and established it as a body corporate with perpetual succession and made the Controller of Insurance its Chairman.

THE GENERAL INSURANCE BUSINESS (NATIONALIZATION) ACT, 1972 (GIBNA)

On January 19, 1956, the Central Government took over the 154 Indian Life insurance companies, 75 provident societies and 16 non-Indian insurance companies then operating in India. These were nationalized and the Life Insurance Corporation of India (LIC) was formed on September 1, 1956 by the enactment of the Life Insurance Corporation of India Act, 1956. The persistent problem of insolvency of life insurers was possibly the most compelling reason leading to the nationalization of the life insurance business. Corresponding changes on the general insurance side were also being contemplated by the government.

On May 13, 1971, an ordinance was promulgated by the President of India to take over the management of the existing 107 general insurance companies by the Government of India. Vide the General Insurance Business (Nationalization) Act, 1972, the General Insurance Corporation of India (GIC) and its four nationalized subsidiaries were formed with effect from January 1, 1973 and all the existing 107 general insurance companies were merged with these four companies. The four nationalized general insurance companies thus formed were the National Insurance Company Limited with its head office at Kolkatta, the New India Assurance Company Limited, headquartered at Mumbai, the Oriental Insurance Company with New Delhi as its head office, and the Untied India Insurance Company Limited with its head quarters at Chennai. A small segment comprising a few state government Insurance Departments insuring properties owned by the respective states had substantial financial interests, Crop Insurance Departments of State Governments, the Calcutta

Hospital and Nursing Home Benefits Association Limited, Export Credit and Guarantee Corporation Limited, and the Deposit Insurance Corporation were excepted from the scope of the takeover. These insurance entities are referred to as exempted insurers in the market. The cumulative effect of all these successive developments was that the Indian general insurance industry was changed into a state monopoly from January 1, 1973. (As explained earlier, the life insurance industry had already become a state monopoly).

The general insurance market was thus left with four public sector insurers who sold the same products at the same rates, either under tariffs formed by the Tariff Advisory Committee or under market agreement entered among the four companies and competition was limited only to the quality of service. Nationalization was generally successful in generating more confidence in the insured, as contracts signed with government owned companies were perceived as backed by a sovereign assurance. The new public sector companies inherited a diversified portfolio, talented personnel and strategic business connections on which they could build on. Insurance penetration increased, ancillary services got organized and employment opportunities grew rather consistently for 15 to 20 years.

Nationalization, however, had its own share of weaknesses. Problems arose due to overstaffing, governmental interference in management, lack of freedom in decision-making, inability of the management to nurture feelings of company loyalty, as well as deficiencies in the system, which could neither provide enough motivation for meritorious employees nor effectively penalize employees for non-performance or lethargy. Professionalism started waning and market penetration stagnated. Growth in the balance sheet was largely limited to the country's inflation and the returns that companies could earn by investing their surplus funds. The report of the Advisory Group on Insurance Regulation (AGIR) of the Standing Committee on International Financial Standards and Codes set-up by the Reserve Bank of India describe the national market situation with one holding company and four subsidiaries as follows:

The "phased" globalization of the Indian economy that started in the early nineties began having its impact on this monopolistic structure. Further, the liberalization of insurance markets was among the objectives of the Uruguay round negotiations conducted under the auspices of GATT. These negotiations included trade in services; insurance had been included in the context of financial services (Para 59 of UNCTAD Report, January 19, 1993)

MACHINERY OF THE INSURANCE SYSTEM

The legal entity (company) that assumes the risk is the insurer. An entity seeking to transfer risk (an individual, corporation, association of any type, etc.) becomes the insured party. Once risk is assumed by an insurer, (the insuring party) by means of a contract called as insurance policy. The fee paid by the insured to the insurer for assuming the risk is called the premium. Generally, an insurance contract includes, at a minimum, some elements like the parties (the insurer, the insured, and the beneficiaries), the premium, the period of coverage, the particular loss event covered and the amount of coverage (i.e. the amount to be paid to the insured or beneficiary in the event of a loss). The policy also states the kind of loss events (perils) that it covers either as an active statement or by a set of exclusions (events not covered).

When insured parties experience a loss for a specified peril, the coverage entitles the policyholders to make a claim against the insurer for the covered amount of loss as specified by the policy. When an insurer makes a payment on the claim, the insured is said to be indemnified against the loss events covered in the policy. Insurance premiums from many insured are used to fund accounts reserved for later payment of claims, theoretically, for a relatively few claimants and for over head costs. An insurer has to set aside and maintain adequate funds for anticipated losses (i.e. reserves) and for the expenses in running the establishment and servicing the insured. The remaining margin (surplus) is an insurer's profit.

Agents (now called counsellers)

Apart from the above, there are insurance agents who represent the insurer to the insured and procure the business on behalf of their principals. Agents are given a commission on the business that they bring in. Agents are sometimes referred to as insurance advisors.

Brokers

Insurance Brokers form another component of the insurance system. As the agent represents the insurer to the insured, the broker represents his client, someone in need of insurance, to one or more insurance houses. An insurance broker shops around amongst many companies for the best insurance policy.

However, with insurance brokers, the fee is usually paid in the form of commission from the insurer that is selected for insurance, rather than directly from the client. There are also companies known as insurance consultants. Similar to an insurance broker, an insurance consultant also shops around amongst many companies for the best insurance policy. However, in this context, the customers cause these consultants to shop around amongst many companies for the best of the insurance policies. Neither insurance consultants nor insurance brokers are insurance companies and no risks are transferred to them during insurance transactions.

Third Party Administrators

Third party administrators are certain expert companies in particular field that are contracted by insurance companies to perform claims handling service for a group or category of clients. These companies often have special expertise that the insurance companies do not have.

Co-insurance

Cases do exist where the insurers do not want to keep (or retain) the entire risk with them. In such cases, the insurers agree to share the risk and the premium proportionately. This arrangement is referred to as co-insurance.

Re-insurance

In many cases, the insurers may feel that retaining a particular risk or group of risks could be too risky for them. In other words, they may not like over-exposure to a particular risk or type of risk. Often, they retain a part of the risk up to the level at which they feel comfortable, and transfer the remaining risk to another insurer called reinsurer. Thus, reinsurers provide insurance to insurance companies. Reinsurance is a means by which an insurance company can protect itself against the risk of losses by transferring their risk to other entities.

To sum up, reinsurance companies are insurance companies that sell policies to other insurance companies, allowing them to reduce their risk and protect them selves from very large losses. The reinsurance market is dominated by a few very large companies with huge reserves. A reinsurer may also be a direct writer of insurance risks as well.

Insurance surveyors and claims adjusters are terms used to describe someone who evaluates the damage caused to property of people when an insurance-related accident occurs. In both the United Kingdom and the Republic of Ireland the term Loss Adjuster is used. They verify the extent of loss, examine the loss *vis-à-vis* the coverage of the insurance policy, investigate liability for the damages caused, and assess the liability under the policy. These professionals handle properly the claims involving damage to buildings and structures, or liability claims involving personal injuries or third person property damage from liability situations, such as motor vehicle accidents, or damage to ships or cargo on board, as the case may be. Some specialize in a particular type of claims, while some surveyors and adjusters handle multiple types of claims and are known as Multi Line Adjusters.

HOW IS INSURANCE REGULATED?

Insurers are regulated in different countries through different systems and procedures. However, there are some fundamental philosophies that form the basis of most of the insurance regulatory regimes among various countries. Some of the fundamental philosophies are discussed in this section.

Insurance companies are broadly classified into two: (a) Life insurance companies that sell life insurance, annuities and pension products, and (b) Non-life or General Insurance companies that sell other types of insurance. The main reason for the distinction between the two types of companies is that life, annuity and pension business is long-term in nature, coverage for life assurance or a pension can cover risks over many decades. By contrast, non-life insurance usually covers a shorter period, such as one year. These companies typically insure automobiles, buildings, household items, business, travel risks, merchandise in transit, ships, airplanes, accident risks and the like.

Insurance regulation is distinctly different from regulation in other branches of finance or economics. By virtue of the contract between the insured and the insurer, the premium paid to the insurer stays with him in return for a promise of indemnification in the event of a loss. The insurer needs to act as per his promise only if the fortuitous event happens. Theoretically, this situation arises only for a small number of policies issued by the insurer. Statistically, as the number of policies increases, the proportion of the number of losses to the number of policies actually decreases.

The uniqueness of insurance necessitates that its regulations have to be laid down in an intricate manner. Regulations need to be rigid enough to prevent fraudulent 'fly-by-night' operators, flexible enough to promote genuine business decisions, and delicate enough to foster creative ideas. In contrast to the *laissez faire* or 'let the people do as they choose' philosophy in many other areas of business, concepts of responsible underwriting, clarity of contract terms, transparency of dealings, prudent investments and policyholders' protection have been matters of regulatory concern.

Watch on Funds

The insurer thus has large amounts of public funds under his control and a much larger amount of promises to keep. Because of this unique position, insurance companies holds huge funds in the market. That is the reason why insurers should serve the society through employment of those funds for growth and development. The insurers should be ready to serve the desired social objectives. The insurance mechanism must serve social purpose. As such, insurance regulation has not only been accepted but encouraged by the insurance business as well as by the customers.

Ensuring Long-term Financial Solvency

The insurers have to guarantee performance of a financial obligation in the event of certain contingencies that might affect the insured at various degrees of probability. When such situations arise, if an insurer fails to hold the safety net, the particular insured's trust is betrayed. The larger issue is that the feeling of comfort and confidence that the general public reposes in the insurance industry gets shattered. Financial solvency is the foundation of public confidence in the private insurance mechanism and has historically been the primary objective of regulation. Here, the insurance regulator uses macro-level controls, such as prescribing a high capital base for issuing licenses and ensuring healthy solvency margins so that only deep pocketed players enter the insurance market.

Standardizing Insurance Products

Customers of tangible goods and services can easily evaluate the product and promises made by sellers. However, for customers of insurance, evaluating an insurer's promises to perform certain obligations under certain specified future situations is not an easy task. In contrast to consumable commodities and many financial services, insurance products are not subject to easy evaluation by the customers at the purchase point (POP). One often finds that many insurance products are purchased merely to fulfil conditions set by banks or other financing institutions when loans are sanctioned by them. Many of the contract conditions are sometimes not comprehensible to the common man. Hence, the insurance regulator ensures a considerable degree of standardization of insurance products.

The degree of standardization of products varies from country to country, from rigidly controlled tariff markets, such as India, Taiwan, Thailand, Sri Lanka at one end of the spectrum to open markets with minimal controls, such as Singapore, United Kingdom and many States of USA at the other extreme where insurance products are by and large controlled by the market forces of demand and supply. Self-explanatory terms of standardization, such as 'Prior Approval', 'Modified Prior Approval', Flex Rating', 'File and Use', 'Use and File', 'State Prescribed', etc. are internationally used to denote the degree of control exercised by the regulator on insurance products.

Preventing Fraud and Speculation by Insurers

Because of the fiduciary nature of the policyholder-insurer

relationship and the resulting opportunity for fraud and financial speculation, complete freedom of entry of new insurance firms into the market is not desirable. The situation of a large amount of public money getting pooled up in a few hands for long periods allows the possibility of the insurers mismanaging public funds through imprudent speculative investments, risky money management decisions or even sheer complacency, unless the market is well regulated. On the other hand, unless regulations allow sufficient flexibility, the insurers will not be able to make prudent innovative decisions to ensure a healthy growth of the funds entrusted to their care and custody. The insurance regulator has to decide how much freedom the insurers should enjoy while managing public funds. Strict norms for investment, transparency in balance sheets, and audit of accounts are some methods that regulators employ for enforcing discipline in financial management.

Creating a Level-playing Ground

Economists concur that intensive unregulated competition in marketing insurance products can produce inadequate rates and insolvency, sharp loss adjusting practices, abortive policy language, and possible tendencies towards monopolization, all of which are recognized to be against public interest. Here, the regulator has to create a level playing ground for all insurers. Ensuring an equitable and congenial environment for business houses well entrenched in the market, government guaranteed insurers, multinational corporate houses, novice insurers and local tender feet insurers is a daunting task for a regulator. Apart from attempts towards standardizing insurance products, regulators try to ensure a level-playing ground by drawing uniform norms for drawing balance sheets, valuation of assets, actuarial vetting of rates, etc. Also, norms are laid down for ensuring policyholders' protection and fairness in dealings. Standards of ethics are insisted upon in advertising as well as in correctly conveying policy terms to the insured through trained agents. The regulator has to maintain uniform yardsticks of strictness with all insurers whether dealing with violations of regulations or grievances relating to deficiencies in services.

Monitoring Re-insurance

The insurers need to enter into different types of reinsurance contracts as part of their business. The regulator has to ensure that foreign exchange is not unduly drained off through reckless reinsurance programmes of the insurers. Objectives of regulation could include maximizing the country's capacity to retain its insurance business within, or ensuring that local companies do not carry too much of risk, disproportionate to their capacity. Regulations would ensure that the insurers secure the bets possible reinsurance protection, get competitive rates for placing the reinsurance business and simplify the administration of business. Many regulators specify that the insurers shall cede such percentage of the sum insured on each policy for different classes of insurance written in the country to a national reinsurer or reinsures registered in the country.

Other concerns include the financial position of the reinsures, the possibility of the reinsurer becoming insolvent when there is a chain of catastrophes, unequal reinsurance arrangements entered into by inexperienced insurance companies and the possibility that insurance companies use reinsurance contract only as a means of cash transfer abroad. Experts in the field argue that having very low reinsurance limits may result in excessive outflow of foreign exchange and thus, it has to be guarded against. On the contrary, high retention limits may result in erosion of the stability of a company in case of large or catastrophic claims. There are instances of general insurance companies in some developing countries ceding hundred per cent of their business to reinsurers (i.e. zero retention limit), or acting as 'fronting' companies of reinsurers. Such activities are not regarded healthy for the market.

Pricing of Insurance Products

Proper rate fixing or pricing of an insurance product is an area of concerns for the regulator. Stories of rate cutting are not unheard of even in closed markets where only government companies transact insurance business. Under-pricing of insurance products is malady very common to the relatively free markets of insurance. Cutting of rates below the actual cost of the indemnity weakens the industry. In open competition, insurance rates are often dependent on the bargaining strength of the insured than the features of the risk as such. Large buyers, therefore, may obtain their insurance too cheaply, as opposed to others who are not in a position to strike sharp bargain. Effective regulation is needed to ensure that insurance products are priced on sound technical reasons.

An insurance policy should be correctly priced for different reasons. While a high price would bring better profits to the insurer, the insured has to bear the brunt of its cost. Also, potential clients would shy away from the market, thereby limiting the insurers' scope of reaping the advantages of the large numbers. A price less than adequate to meet the risk should no doubt bring joy to policyholder at the sales office. However, lesser price would erode the insurers' 'bottom line' and weaken their capacity to meet their obligations in the event of a loss. Historically, insurance law-makers have dreaded this situation. As per the findings of the 'Joint Committee of the Assembly and Senate of the State of New York as early as 1911, wherever there has been a cutting of rates below the actual cost of the indemnity and the policyholder gets his insurance very cheap, its effect on all companies is weakening. They observe that the mutual character of insurance is so strong that nothing that tends to give inferior protection can be for the public good. An insurer's pricing objectives depend on the overall objectives of the insurer and the state of the insurance market. These pricing objectives may be expressed in three main ways to achieve a specified rate of return on capital, to maximize profits, and to maintain or extend market share.

Regulators address the issue of product pricing based on certain operational principle depending upon the degree of regulation each country decides upon. The guidelines issued by the Motor Accidents Authority (MAA), the regulatory body of the New South Wales State of Australia, for the preparation of the rate filing reports are given below as an example.

"Premiums must be sufficient to pay all acquisition and policy administration costs, provide a sum of money to meet the best estimate of the cost of claims (including management expense), provide a profit margin representing an adequate return on capital invested and compensation for the risk, and provide for other matters a prudent insurer would make provision for" (Hart, Buchanan, and Howe).

Rates should be fixed as to ensure the survival of the insurance company, achieving optimum strategic positioning, providing quality and value for the service, contributing to the society's well-being, and optimizing the returns for a given type of risk. Insurance pricing methods can be divided into three major categories (i) individual rating, (ii) class rating, and (iii) modification rating, usually referred to as merit rating. Principal modification rating methods include schedule rating, experience rating, retrospective rating and premium discount plans. The terms of the insurance contract, the conditions under which losses are payable (the insurance cover), and the past experience of losses in the particular type of insurance are taken into reckoning while fixing rates.

Data Repository and Risk Evaluation

Regulators require insurers to maintain their own internal databases and to create national data warehouses so that the products can be priced scientifically based on statistical data. In places, like Japan, New South Wales of Australia and Massachusetts of USA, the concept of Reference Loss Cost Rate (RLCR) is followed. Here, the insurer compares his past loss experience in a particular segment of insurance with the corresponding overall past loss experience in a particular segment of insurance with the corresponding overall past loss experience of the industry from a national data warehouse. Internationally, there are many accepted standards of pricing insurance products and reserving or making provisions for future payment of claims. Premiums are the main source of income for the insurers from which all the insurer's expenditure has to be met. An insurer's expenditure includes his management expenses, such as rent, office maintenance, salaries, agency commissions, advertisement expense, taxes, etc. on the one hand, and pure claim-costs, assumed liabilities, incidental expenditure, such as surveyor's fees, legal expense, etc. on the other.

Theory of Large Numbers

When a dice is repeated many times, the average outcome is the expected value. The premium that an insured would pay would be minuscule compared to the magnitude of the loss that the insurer is liable to incur in the event of a claim. However, historically, the actual number (frequency) of loss-making policies is very less in comparison to the number of policies issued, and the total quantum of losses payable (severity) is lesser than the total amount of premiums received. Thus, in any given period, the losses of the few are borne by the majority of the policyholders who do not incur losses. Statistically, the insurers know that the probability of incurring losses actually decreases when the number of policies increases. This apparent paradox is referred in insurance parlance as the law or theory of large numbers.

Reserving

Even in the case of yearly policies, the insurer's liabilities go beyond the close of the policy period. The amount of the liability for future claim payments can be very uncertain, particularly for long-term classes and cannot be measured precisely. An insurer's standards for creating reserves or reserving for his liabilities are most important for his security. These liabilities include the insurer's liability to meet payments on claims that have been reported to the insurer (reported claims), payments on claims that have already occurred but have not yet been reported to the insurer called as incurred but not reported (IBNR) claims, payment on claims that have not yet occurred but for which the premium has already been paid, other payments, such as super-annuation, long service leave, holiday pay, and so on. These liabilities have to be assessed for creating sufficient reserves. In countries where procedural delays are inherent in the judicial system, liability claims can take many years for a court judgment. The award may consist of the liability amount plus interest, as well as costs of the claimant. It is important, therefore, for the insurer to estimate his anticipated liabilities accurately and create reserves for settling them. This process, known as reserving, is done using actuarial calculations in many developed markets.

PRESENT DAY TRENDS IN INSURANCE

The insurance industry has grown down the years alongside the economy. Modern day economists consider insurance penetration as a yardstick of economic development.

Most of the developed and developing countries have been taking significant steps in both economic and insurance reform over the last three decades. The reform process is an ongoing process though.

Bodies such as world Trade Organization (WTO), World Bank, Asian Development Bank (ADB), Basel Committee on Banking Supervision (BCBS) and many other international bodies have taken active interest in addressing insurance-related problems at international forum. The International Association of Insurance Supervisors (IAIS) is a full-time body working for the development of insurance through multi-pronged strategies. It has developed core insurance principles relevant to contemporary markets, promoted discussions on areas of common concern, augmented educational endeavors of developing countries, and provided a forum of interaction among the insurance supervisors and professionals all over the world.

SUMMARY

This chapter has provided an overview of insurance and the basic concept of insurance so that the readers can appreciate the importance of insurance in the society and the economy. A brief history of the evolution of insurance as a separate stream of knowledge over the years has been provided in this chapter. The evolution of the Indian market has also been traced. The chapter familiarizes readers with the insurance mechanism and the players in the insurance field. It also touches upon some common terms in the insurance market. The principles of insurance will be discussed in detail in the subsequent chapter. Fundamental aspects of insurance regulation along with their purposes have been discussed. A brief mention of the present day trend in insurance has been given to—

(1) Insurance is an arrangement whereby many other people who also are susceptible to the same type of losses share the financial losses of a few.

(2) The insured and the insurer are the two parties of an insurance contract.

(3) A risk is the uncertainty part of any activity that cannot be reasonably foreseen to happen within a

particular time or in a particular manner. In insurance, the chance or likelihood of a loss to occur is the risk covered.

(4) An objective risk is one that exists in nature and is commonly applicable for all persons or entities facing the same situation. Risks are subjective when it depends on the individual's perception as to how far an objective situation can apply in his particular case.

(5) Risk can be categorized as 'pure' when there is a chance of a loss without any chance of gain. In case, there is a possibility of a gain ensuing from the loss, the risk is called a 'speculative' risk.

(6) Risk perception is the subjective judgement that people make about the characteristics and severity of a risk.

(7) Physical hazards refer to certain physical conditions that create or increase the chance of loss from any peril. Moral hazards denote the dishonesty of the insured that can increase the probability of a claim. Moral hazards refer to an indifferent or callous attitude of the insured that increases or inflates the quantum of loss.

(8) Personal losses such as death and poor health, losses to one's material possession such as houses and vehicles, loss of expected income from one's business consequential to a property loss, and liabilities to third parties are examples of insurable losses.

(9) Chinese merchants travelling treacherous river tides would redistribute their wares across many vessels to limit the loss due to any single vessel's capsizing. Babylonians developed a system around 1750 BC, whereby if a merchant received a loan to fund his shipment, he would pay the lender an additional sum in exchange for the lender's guarantee to cancel the loan, should the shipment be stolen. In Rhodes, there was a system whereby merchants whose goods were being shipped together would pay a proportionally divided premium that would be used to reimburse any merchant whose goods were jettisoned during storm or sinkage.

(10) The Great Fire of London that devoured 13, 200 houses and caused losses of about pound 2 million to insurers, created a new awareness about insurance and increased cooperation among insurers that resulted in the creation of the fire (insurance) offices in 1868 and popularized fire insurance.

(11) The insurance principles of sharing by a group the losses of a few had been appreciated in India from very ancient times. In ancient India, the concept of 'Yogakshem' or insurance is found in the Rig Veda. Manu Smriti speaks of a system of collective co-operation. Yajnavalkya mentions some transactions akin to insurance. The 'Joint Family system' practised in India is seen by many as a form of micro insurance to take care of calamitous situation, including death and sickness within the extended family.

(12) In post-World War I India, encouraged by the spirit of nationalism, businessmen in Mumbai established fire offices to meet the insurance needs of Indian trade. The new insurance companies received support from the growth of nationalism in India, and Mahatma Gandhi and Nehru spoke in favour of Indian insurance institutions. Later on, hundred of Indian businessmen signed a pledge to insure only with Indian offices. As a result, Indian insurers' share of a total business written in India rose from a mere 11 per cent in 1928 to 22 per cent in 1935 and to 31 per cent in 1939, largely at the expense of foreign offices, while the total business itself had increased only by 5 per cent during that period.

(13) The Insurance Act granted very wide powers to the Controller of insurance in the matter of insurance regulation. The government visualized that the Controller of Insurance should be a person of extraordinary calibre, qualified, tactful and even-handed. Compulsory registration of insurance companies, control on investments of funds, licensing of agents, control on commission, prohibition of rebates, and filing of policy conditions and premium rates duly certified by an actuary (in the case of life

business) were made compulsory. The Indian insurance legislation was lauded by contemporary commentators as an excellent attempt to penalize the corrupt directors and executive officers, check wild cat schemes, and to stop acquisition of insurance companies by designing financiers.

(14) The Insurance Act became the corner stone of Indian insurance legislation and, along with the Insurance Rules formed under it, remains the most comprehensive legislation on the subject.

(15) The main changes as result of the amendment were as follows:
  (a) Requirement of minimum capital,
  (b) Stricter control on investments,
  (c) Submission of periodical returns on investments,
  (d) Ceiling on expense of management and agency commission,
  (e) Appointment of administrators for mismanaged companies, and
  (f) Creation of Statutory bodies like General Insurance Council and Tariff Committee to frame and enforce tariff rates and regulations.

(16) Sir Gowasji Jehangir, Chairman of the original committee, and S. Ranganathan, Chairman of the review committee were men of merit and integrity.

(17) The amendment provided for:
  (a) Regulation of investments,
  (b) Minimum solvency, margin regulations,
  (c) Payment of premium before commencement of risk, and
  (d) Licensing of surveyors, and powers to the Controller to carry out inspection, investigation and search and seizure of books.

  Tariff Committee (TC) of the General Insurance Council (GIC) was renamed as Tariff Advisory Committee (TAC) and established as a body corporate with perpetual succession. The Controller of Insurance (COI) was made its Chairman.

(18) After enactment of GIBNA, the general insurance

market was left with four public sector insurers which sold the same products at the same rates, either under tariffs framed by TAC or under market agreements, and competition was limited only to the quality of service. Nationalization improved the confidence of the insured, as contracts signed with government-owned companies were perceived as backed by a sovereign assurance.

(19) The four nationalized general insurance companies formed under GIBNA were the National Insurance Company Limited, the New India Assurance Company Limited, the Oriental Insurance Company Limited, and the United India Insurance Company Limited.

(20) The legal entity that assumes the risk is the insurer. The entity which transfers the risk is the insured party, the fee paid by the insured to the insurer for assuming the risk is called the premium and the evidence of the contract is the insurance policy.

(21) Insurance Regulations are considered different from the Regulations in other branches for various reasons:

(a) The product is bought and premium paid is for the promise of indemnification in the event of a loss.

(b) The insurer needs to act as per his promise only if the fortuitous event happens, which may arise only for a small number of policies.

(c) Regulations need to prevent fraudulent "fly by night" operators and ensure that the companies are there with sufficient funds to pay the claims when a loss occurs.

(In contrast to the *laissez faire* philosophy in other areas of business, policyholders' protection has been the matter of regulatory concern.

(22) In insurance, the premium paid to the insurer is in return for a promise of indemnification in the event of the loss. The uniqueness of insurance necessitates its regulations to be covered under the following aspects:

(23) *Watch on Funds*: The insurer thus has large amounts of public funds under his control and a much larger amount of promises to keep.

(24) *Ensuring Long-Term Financial Solvency*: The insurer has to perform a financial obligation in the event of a loss that might happen at various degrees of probability. Financial solvency of the insurer is the foundation of the insurance mechanism and historically, the primary objective of regulation.

(25) *Standardizing Insurance Products*: Customers of tangible goods and services can easily evaluate the products and promises made. The evaluating of an insurer's promises to perform certain obligations under certain specified future situation is not easy for customers of insurance.

(26) *Preventing Fraud and Speculation by Insurers*: The innovations in the economy have simultaneously created a class of hackers and tricksters. To avoid falling into the trap laid by 'fly by night' operators, regulations and high pitch caution and watch have been prescribed by the Regulating Authority. As a large amount of public money gets pooled up in a few hands for long periods, there is a possibility of insurers' mismanaging public funds through imprudent and speculative investments, making risky money management decisions or being complacent, unless the market is well regulated.

(27) *Creating a Level Playing Ground for all Players in Insurance*: Intensive unregulated competition in marketing of the insurance products can produce inadequate rates and lead to denial of claims, and abortive policy language used, which is against public interest. So, the Regulator has to create a level-playing field for all insurers.

(28) *Regulators have to regulate re-insurance too*: Insurers need to enter into different types of re-insurance contracts as part of their business. The Regulator has to check whether foreign exchange is unduly drained-off through reckless re-insurance programmes. Re-insurance should be for maximizing

the country's capacity to retain its insurance business within and ensuring that local companies do not carry too much of risk, disproportionate to their capacity. Many Regulators insist that a percentage of the sum insured, written within the country, shall be ceded to national reinsure(s) registered in the country.

Regulator should ensure that the insurers secure the best possible re-insurance protection and get competitive rates for placing their re-insurance business. They should prevent unhealthy practices such as ceding hundred per cent of their business to re-insurers (i.e. with zero retention limit), or acting as 'fronting' companies of reinsurers. Such activities are not regarded healthy for the market.

2

Principles of Insurance

INTRODUCTION

Insurance has been evolved by wise men, based on their life experience, as the mantra to broaden the cause of a particular risk over a number of persons who are exposed to it and who agree to insure themselves against it. Conceptualization requires imagination, creativity and quest to explore and devise new methods, ways and systems and procedures. Salute to those who did this marvel of the schematic framework to add one more class of institution in society!

Insurance helps to manage risks of various types. Risk is defined as uncertainty of a financial loss. The main functions of insurance include providing certainty, protection, risk sharing, and prevention of loss and capital formation.

As has been discussed in the previous chapters, the term 'insurance' has been defined as the technique in which a sum of money as premium is paid in consideration for the insurer's undertaking to incur the risk of paying a large sum upon happening of a particular uncertainty.

Insurance is a contract whereby—

(a) Certain sum, called premium, is charged as consideration,

(b) Against the payment of the said premium, a large sum is guaranteed to be paid by the insurer,

(c) The payment will be made in the shape of a certain/ definite sum, i.e. the loss incurred or the policy amount, whichever is less, and

(d) The payment is made only upon the happening of the contingency.

Therefore, insurance may be defined as a contract in which one party (insurer) agrees to pay to the other party (insured or beneficiary under the policy), a certain sum upon a particular unforeseen event (risk) taking place against which insurance was sought.

Every subject or discipline has certain generally accepted and systematically laid down standards or principles to achieve the underlying objectives. Insurance is also not an exception to this general rule. There is a body of doctrines commonly associated with the theory and procedures of insurance, guiding all stakeholders about the explanation and application of current policies and for making the best choice among the available alternatives.

These principles may be defined as the rules of action or code of conduct that are universally accepted by the different stakeholders involved in the business of insurance.

These are given in the table on next page for better and quick understanding due to visual effect.

PRINCIPLES OF INSURANCE

(I) General Principles (or Essentials of Insurance Contract)

All agreements are contracts if they are made by the free consent of parties, competent to contract; for a lawful consideration, for a lawful object and are not expressly declared to be void. As we know, an agreement enforceable by law is called a contract. Like all general contracts, a contract of insurance is also required to fulfil all basic requirements as prescribed under section 10 of the Indian Contract Act, 1872. These requirements are given on next page.

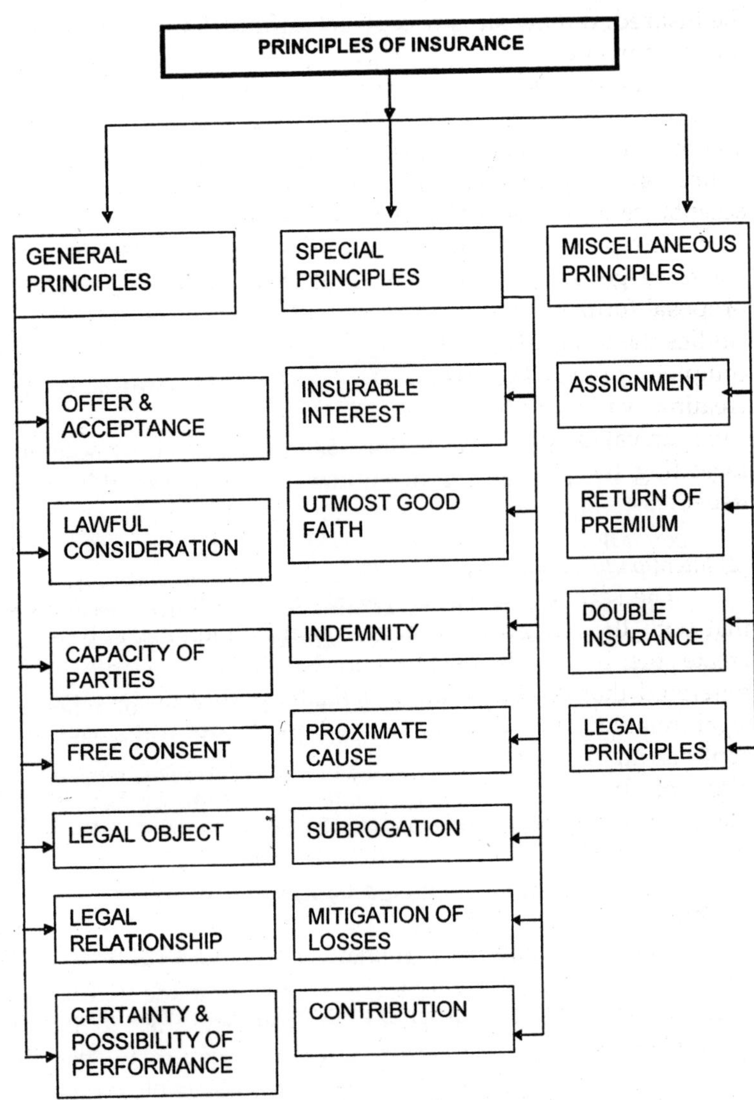

(I) Offer and Acceptance

It is the first requirement in the formation of a valid contract. The offer in insurance is intimation of the proposer's intention to purchase an insurance policy. When the insurer is ready to undertake the stated risk, it is called acceptance. In insurance, 'offer' is known as 'proposal'. It generally comes from the insured. If the insurer accepts the proposal, it is transformed into an agreement.

Therefore, when one party (potential policyholder) makes a proposal to another party (insurance company) and the latter accept it, the proposal is said to be accepted. The moment the notice of acceptance is communicated, it would be a valid acceptance and valid contract is born instantaneously.

The procedure goes like this: potential policyholder who wants to get his risk insured is required to fill a prescribed proposal form in an insurance contract. The insurance company studies the offer made in the proposal form. It may accept it. To complete offer and acceptance as conditions precedent for creating valid contract, the notice of acceptance must be communicated to the insured along with the information regarding the premium payable and first premium receipt is issued.

(2) Intention to Create Legal Relations

The second basic principle of valid insurance contract is that both the parties must have common intention and act to create the legal relationship between them. It needs to be reiterated that the intention of both the parties is to create the legal relationship between themselves. Under the insurance contract, an insured expresses his intention while making a valid offer and the insurer expresses his intention on the acceptance of that offer which will bind both the parties in accordance with the terms and conditions of the insurance policy.

(3) Parties Competent to make Contract

Both the parties to insurance contract should be competent/capable of entering into contract, Section II of Indian Contract Act, 1872, lays down that every person is competent to contract—

Who is of the age of majority according to the law governing majority (under Indian Majority Act);
Who is of sound mind (can understand the full implications of the terms and conditions of contract); and
Who is not disqualified from entering into contract by any law to which he is subject (undischarged insolvent, etc.).

A valid contract requires that both the parties should understand the legal implications of each other's conduct as obligations (rights and duties/obligations) under the contract. A minor is not competent to contract. A person is said to be of sound mind, who can understand the contract at the time of making the contract. An alien enemy, an insolvent and criminal cannot enter into contract. Contract made by incompetent party/ parties will be void. Therefore, minor, persons of unsound mind and those with criminal background cannot take an insurance policy because they cannot enter into valid contract.

(4) Free Consent

It means when both the parties have agreed to a contract on the terms and conditions of the agreement in the same sense and spirit, they are said to have a free consent. Under Section 14 of Indian Contract Act, 1872, the consent is to be free when it is not caused by: coercion; undue influence; fraud; misrepresentation; and mistake.

Contract without free consent is voidable at the option of the party whose consent is not free except when there is fraud. In case of fraud, the contract is void.

(5) Lawful Consideration

It means when a party to an agreement promises to do something, he/she must get something in return. This is called 'consideration' in law. In insurance contract, the payment of premium is the consideration on the part of the insured. The contract of insurance is the contract of indemnity under which an insurance company, in consideration of premium, undertakes to compensate the loss of the stated insured against a specified risk, e.g. fire, marine hazard, accident or death. The consideration for which the insurance company undertakes to compensate the risk of insured is called the 'premium'. Premium may be paid either in lump sum or in periodical instalments spread over the specified period of policy. The insurance contract cannot be initiated without the payment of premium.

(6) Lawful Object

There is another important basic principle of insurance contract and that is the legality (or lawfulness) of objects. The object of the insurance, contract should be lawful. It is lawful when:

It is not forbidden by law, or
It is not immoral, or
It is not opposed to public policy, or
It is not against the provisions of any law

An unlawful object of any contract shall make it unenforceable at law. If the object of insurance, like the consideration, is found to be unlawful, the policy is void.

(7) Certainty and Possibility of Performance

Also important is the factor and that is the parties to a contract must agree on the terms of their mutually arrived agreement. They have to make their intention clear in their contract. The terms of contract must be definite or certain and capable of performance. If the agreement does not make it possible to ascertain its meaning and is impossible to perform, it cannot be enforced.

(II) Specific or Fundamental Principles of Insurance Contracts

Insurance contracts, to whichever category they may belong, they are based on the following fundamental principles:

(1) Principle of Utmost Good Faith

The contracts of insurance are, therefore, included in the category of the contracts uberima fiddie, i.e. those contracts which require absolute and utmost good faith on the part of the parties concerned. In this respect, such contracts are different from the ordinary business contracts; the latter are based on the rule of Caveat Emptor (let the buyer beware). For instance, in an ordinary sale of goods contract, the buyer is expected to take reasonable care to satisfy himself as to the genuineness and quality of goods intended to be purchased. If the goods turn out to be otherwise, the buyer will have no remedy against the seller and will have to bear the loss.

This principle compels both the parties to the contract to make full disclosure of all martial facts. The material facts mean those facts which may affect the decision of either party whether to enter or not to enter into the contract. Both the parties should have the same state of mind when entering into contract, only then the correct risk, rights and obligations can be ascertained. It also means that there should not be any concealment, misrepresentation, half-disclosure or fraud regarding the subject matter to be insured. Otherwise, the contract would be null and void. Under the contract of insurance, greater degree of good faith is expected from the proposer.

Therefore, the insured must disclose the following facts in a life insurance contract:

> Name, address and his occupation; date of birth, age, height, weight, etc.; facts about his life and habits; family history; information about health; quantum and nature of his income; and a certification by the proposer that he has answered all questions truly and correctly and agrees that the proposal and declaration shall be the basis of contract.

The breach of obligation of disclosing material facts may arise in the following:

> Non-disclosure of material facts; intentional non-disclosure of facts; non-disclosure of material facts by negligence or through oversight; and misrepresentation of material facts with fraudulent purposes/intention.
>
> In case of marine insurance, the offer-maker is required to disclose the following information about the subject matter of insurance:
>
> Nature of goods; method of packing; particulars of vessel carrying the goods; the port of shipment and destination along the route of journey; insurance cover required and condition of insurance; sum to be insured; and past claims information and experience.
>
> Section 20 of the Marine Insurance Act prescribes that in the following cases, the insured is not required to disclose the information:
>
> Facts already known to insurer; facts which the insurer is expected to know in the normal course of his business; facts which may tend to reduce the risk; and facts covered under the warranty.

It generally happens, and it begins a controversy and promotes litigation, that the insurance company finds it a better way to cancel the contract or dismiss the claim on account of non-disclosure of material facts and as a consequent breach of utmost good faith. Similarly, the insured may also avoid contract, in case the insurance company does not conduct in good faith in disclosing the scope of insurance.

In the case of fire insurance also, this principle is applicable. But this duty lies more on the offer-maker, who is in possession of all material facts relating to the subject matter to be insured. The insurer is also required to disclose important facts of policy to the prospective offerer also. The following material facts are required to be disclosed in contract of fire insurance:

Location of property; details of construction and description of property; particulars of occupier, i.e. whether used for office, residence, shop, godown, manufacturing unit or service undertaking, etc.; nature of goods or material; and particulars of previous loss, if any, suffered.

(2) Principle of Insurable Interest

No person can enter into a valid contract of insurance unless he had insurable interest in the object to be insured. If it were not so, and if everyone were at liberty to take out an insurance policy on any object or life in the world, irrespective of his insurable interest, the contracts of insurance would have been reduced to mere gambling. In such conditions, insurance contract would be reduced to wagering contracts, which are not valid and cannot be enforced in a court of law as wagering is unlawful activity.

It is important to understand insurable interest. It is understood as an interest in the preservation of a thing, or continuation of a life, recognized by law. Whoever has such interest in an object or a life may insure that object or life. Truly speaking, insurable interest is in the nature of pecuniary or financial interest in an object or a life. It follows that a person can have an insurable interest only when he would stand to benefit financially by the continuation of object or life insured. In other words, he would be put to a financial loss by the happening of the event against which an object or the life of the person has been insured. Moreover, insurable interest is not a mere sentimental interest in the object insured. It is a pecuniary interest and it follows that the loss caused by the risk insured against must be capable of measurement in term of money. It is important to know the views expressed by Prof. Mehr, "If the happening of the event insured cannot cost the insured in terms of money, then there is no insurable interest".

Essentials of Insurable Interest

The essentials of a valid insurable interest are as under:

There must be a specific subject matter to be insured; the insured should have the monetary benefit in the subject matter; the insured should have the legal relationship with the subject matter and it must be recognized by law; the insured must be the owner or possess the legal right or interest in the subject matter; the insured should be economically benefited by the existence of the subject matter; and the insurance-maker should suffer an economic loss on its non-existence or at the death of the insured thing/person.

Insurable interest in a life insurance should exist when a policy is purchased. In a life insurance policy, the insurable interest is as follows:

A child has an insurable interest in the life of his father; a person has unlimited interest in his own life; a husband has an insurable interest in the life of his wife; a wife has an insurable interest in the life of her husband; a creditor has an insurable interest, to the extent of his debt, in the life of his debtor; a partner in a business has an insurable interest in the life or lives of his co-partner or co-partners; a company has an insurable interest in the life of a senior officer whose death may affect the profit of a business; and a servant has an insurable interest in the life of his employer.

Insurable interest in case of fire insurance must exist when insurance is effected as well as when the loss occurs. In fire insurance, however, insurable interest is as under:

The owner of the property has in his property; every partner has an equitable interest in the properties of the firm; and an agent has an insurable interest in the property of his principal.

In marine insurance, insurable interest must exist only when the loss occurs. In Marine Insurance, the following persons have insurable interest:

The owner of a ship has an insurable interest in the ship; the cargo owner has in its cargo; the master and the crew of the ship have it in respect of their wages; a creditor who has advanced money on the security of cargo or ship, upto his claim; a ship owner in the freight to be received on the completion of journey; a mortgagor has an insurable interest to the full value of the property; a mortgagee has it to the extent of the sum due to him; and a trustee holds property in trust up to the extent of value of such property.

(3) Principle of Indemnity

All contracts of insurance, except for life insurance, are contracts of indemnity. The basic principle of insurance is to transfer the loss of a person to the insurance company which can easily be spread over a large number of policyholders. It is, therefore, necessary that a person will get exactly the same amount as he has lost due to the loss of his goods or damage to the property. The insured cannot be permitted to make profit out of his loss. If insurance company were to agree to compensate a higher sum than the actual loss, there would be a constant temptation on the part of the insured to destroy his goods or property intentionally and thus to reap profit out of insurance. If it is so, it will be against the basic principle and also an anti-social act. For example, if the goods are insured for Rs. 10, 000 and the insured suffers a loss of Rs. 5000, he will be compensated for Rs. 5000 only. But if the insured has taken a policy for a smaller value than the actual loss, the insurance company is bound to pay only the amount of policy and not the actual loss (assuming that average clause is not applicable). This is so because by insuring his goods for a lesser value, the insured has expressed his intention of transferring only a part of his actual loss to the insurance company. The balance of loss will justifiably be met by the insured himself. Thus, for a policy of Rs. 4000 instead of Rs. 10, 000 and the actual loss being Rs. 6000, insurance company will pay only Rs. 4000 and no more.

Merits of Principle of Indemnity

There are merits in the principle of indemnity which are as follows:

(1) Avoidance of Under or Over-Insurance

If this principle were not there, there would be tendency on the part of the insured to get things over-valued and then intentionally cause a loss and gain profit through enforcing insurance claim. Since in insurance only the actual loss is compensated, the insured would be discouraged to under or over value the policy's amount.

(2) To Avoid Anti-social Activity

This principle avoids anti social act on the part of the insured. If the insured is allowed to make profit (which is against the principle of indemnity), there would be a constant temptation to destroy the property after it is insured. Therefore, the whole society will be doing only anti-social act to get easy money. But in insurance, only the cash value of loss of the insured is compensated even if it might have been insured for a greater amount.

(3) To Maintain Premium at Low Level

This principle helps the insurance company to maintain premium at low level because very few claims will be made and those will be genuine (within the actual value). If this principle is not made applicable, large amount of compensation will be required to be paid for a small loss. This will increase the cost of insurance and the companies would be forced to raise the premium. This will defeat the purpose of insurance.

Main Features of Indemnity

The following are the main features of the principle of indemnity:

(1) All contracts of insurance are contracts of indemnity except life insurance.

(2) There is an indirect relationship between the principle of indemnity and insurable interest because

the insured is required to prove the amount of his actual loss and his interest therein in order to get compensation.

(3) The amount of compensation cannot exceed the amount of actual loss or the value of policy, whichever is less.

(4) After the compensation of loss, the insured cannot hold the ownership right on the things insured, i.e. the ownership right will shift to the insurance company.

(5) Valued policies are not covered under the principle of indemnity.

Conditions for Indemnity

The following conditions are required to be satisfied in full for the application of the principle of indemnity:

Insured has to prove that he has suffered a loss on the subject matter insured and it is the actual monetary loss; the compensation cannot exceed the amount insured; insurer has a right to get back the extra amount, if any, paid to the insured; the insurer has a right to get back all amount received by the insured from the third party if the loss is fully indemnified by the insurer; and the principle of indemnity is not applicable in case of life insurance as the actual loss on death cannot be calculated.

Liability of Insurer to Pay Compensation

According to the application of the principle of indemnity, the insured can get only the actual loss of goods or property destroyed, or the insured amount, whichever is less. The loss payable is calculated after considering the following factors:

(a) Sum Insured or the Value of Policy

Every insurance policy is issued for a specific sum, called sum insured, which is the maximum limit or liability of the insurer in respect of goods insured. But the actual amount payable is calculated with reference to his actual loss or the sum insured, whichever is less.

(b) Excess and Franchise Clause

It is a practice that certain insurance polices are issued subject to excess or franchise clause. This clause says that under certain conditions a part of the loss shall be borne by the insured himself. The liability of insurer is limited by the imposition of excess or franchise clause. In case of imposition of this clause, if the loss does not exceed the limit, it is not paid at all and if it exceeds the limit, only excess is paid under 'Excess clause' and total loss is indemnified under the franchise clause.

(c) Pro-Rata Average

Sometimes, the policy contains an average clause. This condition is incorporated with two objectives, i.e. to penalize the insured for taking a policy for a lesser sum than the actual value of property and secondly, to limit the liability of insurer. According to the provision contained in this clause, the compensation payable by the insurer is proportionately reduced in case of under-insurance of goods or property. For example, a person may insure his property for Rs. 75, 000. While the actual loss is assessed at Rs. 40, 000 and the market value of the property at the time of loss is Rs. 10, 000, the claim will be settled at Rs. 40000 × 75, 000/1, 00, 000 = Rs. 30, 000. Obviously, in this case, the insured is penalized for Rs. 10, 000 for under-insurance of his property. Formula is as under:

Liability of Insurer =

$$\text{Actual Loss} \times \frac{\text{Insurance Policy Taken}}{\text{Market value of property at the time of loss}}$$

(d) Salvage

In the event of loss of insured property, it may be partially destroyed, not completely. Anything left after the occurrence of loss is known as 'Salvage'. The salvage or scrap left of the damaged or destroyed goods or property is to be reduced from the amount of indemnity payable to the insured.

(e) Subrogation

The doctrine of subrogation is an extension and corollary of the principle of indemnity. According to the principle of indemnity, the insurer steps into the shoes of the insured and becomes entitled to all the rights of the insured regarding the subject matter of insurance after the claim of the insured has been fully and finally settled. In some cases, there may a possibility of his getting something in addition to what he has received from the insurer. If the goods are not fully destroyed, the insured may try to obtain some amount of scrap in addition to what to the money received by him in the settlement of his claim. This will be against the principle of indemnity because the insured will get more than what he lost. Therefore, whatever is left of the damaged or destroyed goods or property will automatically pass on to the insurance company after the claim of the insured has been settled.

(f) Contribution

Sometimes, the insured may get his goods or property insured with more than one insurer. This is referred to as 'Double Insurance'. In the event of loss, the insured will be indemnified only against actual loss incurred against the risk insured. In such cases, the companies concerned will follow the principle of contribution for the payment of compensation. According to this principle, each insurance company will contribute that proportion of the loss which the policy insured by it bears to the total amount for which insurance has been effected with all the insurance companies. But in case where the insured chooses to get the amount of loss from one particular company or two of them, the paying company or companies can later on adjust loss paid with other insurer by receiving their contribution according to the proportion of their insured amount.

Methods of Indemnifying

There are four alternative methods to indemnify an insured in the event of loss, damage or destruction of subject matter insured. These are as follows:

Cash Payment

Cash payment of the amount of claim of insurance is the easiest and a very common method of indemnification. After making proper enquiries of loss, the insurer accepts the claim by making cash payment through cheque to the insured.

Repairs

In some cases, where the subject matter of insurance is partially damaged and is capable of being repaired, the insurer, instead of making cash payment, prefers to settle claim of the loss or damage by means of getting the damaged subject matter, repaired. The repair is authorized to the insured and the insured has to submit bill of repairs alongwith a note of satisfaction and then the repair bill is paid by the insurer.

Replacement

In case the subject of the insurance policy is damaged, lost or destroyed to such an extent that it is not possible and feasible to get it repaired, the insurance company may arrange the replacement of the property. Generally, this practice is followed in case of theft of property.

Reinstatement

Reinstatement is a method rarely used. In this case, the property damaged is reinstalled in its original position.

Principle of Subrogation

This principle is also known as 'Doctrine of Rights Substitution'. It is an extension of the principle of indemnity. Subrogation is the transfer of rights and remedies of the insured in the subject matter (property) to the insurer after indemnification.

In other words, the insurer steps into the shoes of the insured and becomes entitled to all rights of action against the third party to cover the loss from the responsible person regarding the subject matter of insurance after the claim of the insured has been fully settled and paid.

The principle of subrogation refers to the right of the insurer to stand in the place of the insured after the settlement of a claim. The insurer can recover the loss from the third party. There always exists a possibility of getting something in addition to the claim received from the insurer by the insured, e.g. value of scrap, damages from the person responsible for the loss and several other alternatives.

Definition of Subrogation

According to Federation of insurance Institutes, "Subrogation is the transfer of rights and remedies of the insured to the insurer who has indemnified the insured in respect of the loss".

According to Dinsdale—

> "Subrogation may be defined as the insurer's right to receive the benefit of all the rights of the insured against third parties which, if satisfied, will extinguish or diminish the ultimate loss sustained".

Essentials of Subrogation

(i) Extension of Principle of Indemnity

It is the extension and corollary of the principle of indemnity. According to principle of indemnity, only the actual loss is compensated to the insured. If the goods or property are partially damaged or destroyed, the insurer can recover some amount after the claim is fully and finally settled with the insured. The loss to property may be caused by an act of a third party. Accordingly, the insured is required to subrogate all his rights in favour of the insurer to reduce his paid compensation.

(ii) Subrogation is the Substitution

All rights and remeidies available to the insured are transferred to the insurer after the settlement of claim. Insurance company is substituted in place of insured for all matters concerning the loss.

(iii) Subrogation is only up to the Amount of Payment

The insurer is substituted only up to the amount of compensation paid to the insured. If the insured has been compensated by the third party after he has been indemnified by his insurer, he (insured) is liable to compensate the insurer for the amount received by him from the third party.

(iv) Subrogation may be Applied before Payment

If the insured is compensated to some extent by the third party before being fully indemnified by the insurer, then the insurer can pay only the balance amount of the loss.

(v) Personal Insurance

The principle of subrogation is not applicable in case of personal insurance.

Need of Subrogation

The principle of subrogation has been introduced with the aim to protect the interest of insurers. In case of loss without it, the insured may be in a position to collect more money than his actual loss by selling the salvage. According to this principle, since the insured is required to subrogate all his rights in favour of the insurer after the loss is settled, cannot make profit out of insurance policy. Moreover, the insurer has a right to claim loss if it is caused by the act of third party.

Features of Subrogation

Subrogation has the following features:

(a) It is a corollary to and outcome of the principle of indemnity and is applicable in all contracts of indemnity.
(b) It is applicable only after the payment of loss by the insurer.
(c) It may also arise even before indemnification of loss except in case of marine insurance policies.
(d) The insured is required to provide all help to insurer while enforcing the claim against the defaulters.
(e) The insurer has a right to sue the third party in the name of the insured. But all expenses of litigation are to be borne by the insurer.
(f) The insured will hold the amount of compensation received from the third party in trust for the insurer if he has already been compensated by the insurer.
(g) The right of subrogation arises from the acts of torts, contract, salvage, etc.
(h) The principle of subrogation is automatically applied even without any express condition in the contract in this regard.
(i) Under this principle, the insurer cannot recover from the defaulter party anything more than the amount of compensation paid to the insured. The right of recovery is limited to the amount of claim paid to the insured.

How Right of Subrogation Arises?

Subrogation rights arise in the following ways:

Tort

Where the insured has sustained some damage, lost right or incurred liability due to atrocious acts of some other person and the insurer has indemnified the loss, the insured is entitled to take action to recover the loss from the wrong doer.

Contract

Subrogation relates to rights, which arise out of certain contracts. This may arise where there is a custom of the trade to which the contract applies. Subrogation right may arise from contract where a person has contractual right to compensation regardless of fault.

Subject Matter of Insurance

Sometimes, a situation may arise, where an insured has been indemnified and the subject matter treated as lost. Once the claim has been compensated, the insured cannot claim the salvage or scarp.

Principle of Causa Proxima (Immediate and the Nearest Cause)

The principle of proximate cause is also called 'causa proxima'. The term causa proxima is a Latin term which means, the nearest cause or proximate cause or immediate cause. Causa proxima is the real cause of loss and not the distant cause. It is helpful in deciding the actual cause of loss when a number of causes have contributed to the occurrence of loss. The maxim used in this regard is 'Sed Causa proxima non-remote spectator' which means that 'see the nearest or direct cause and not the remote or distant cause'. The real, nearest and direct cause of loss must be seen while making payment of the loss. If the real cause of loss is insured, the insurer is liable to compensate the loss, otherwise the insurer may not be responsible for loss.

In other words, while deciding the liability of the insurer, the direct, nearest or proximate cause and not the remote or indirect cause of the loss is to be taken into account.

Meaning and Definition of the Doctrine of Causa Proxima

The doctrine of causa proxima is in fact based on the law of cause and effect which means that having proved the cause and effect thereof, there remains no need to proceed further.

In case of *Pawsey* Vs. *South Union and National Insurance Co.*, it was observed that:

> "Proximate cause means the active and efficient cause that sets in motion a train of events which bring about result, without the intervention of any force started and working actively from new and independent source".

Thus, the cause must be 'immediate cause' to be 'proximate'. The expression 'immediate' should be understood in terms of effectiveness or efficiency. In other words, proximate cause is the cause, which is effectual in producing that result.

The proximate cause means that direct, the most dominant and most effective cause of which the loss is the natural consequence. It is the cause, which is most closely and directly connected with the loss, not necessarily in time but in efficiency and effectiveness.

Practical Aspects of Doctrine of Causa Proxima

There is no problem in deciding the question of liability of the insurer if the loss is the outcome of only one event. But the loss may be the result of two or more events or causes. It becomes necessary to locate the effective and most powerful cause of loss. It is not easy to decide the proximate cause when it is caused by a large number of events.

Events or causes for the purpose of determining the practical use of doctrine of causa proxima may be divided into three categories:

(1) Operation of a Single Cause

Where there is a single event which causes the loss, it will be a clear case of proximate cause and the insurer will be held liable for the event if it is insured under the policy, e.g. if a person dies in road accident, the accident will be the proximate cause under the personal accident policy.

(2) Concurrent Causes

In case of concurrent causes, i.e. causes occurring simultaneously, and the policy has not excluded perils, there arises liability of insurer if one of the causes is 'insured peril' and other causes may be ignored. The concurrent causes may be separable and inseparable causes. Separable causes are those causes which can be separated from each other. The loss caused by a particular separable cause, if insured against peril, will be compensated by the insurer. In case the circumstances are such that causes are inseparable, then the insurer is not liable at all when there exists any expected event.

(3) Successive Causes

Where there is a chain of events causing a loss to the subject matter insured, the liability of insurer would arise if the original cause event is an 'insured peril'.

Principle of Mitigation of Loss

Mitigation of loss means to minimize or to decrease the severity of the loss. Under this doctrine, it is prescribed that whenever the event insured against occurs, it will be the duty of the insured to take all such steps to minimize the loss as he would have taken when the subject matter was not insured. The logic behind the principle of mitigation of loss is that the insured should not become careless and passive at the time of loss simply because his property had been insured. He must act like any uninsured prudent person.

Accordingly to this principle, the insured must act reasonably to make the loss less severe and try to make each and every effort and arrangement to minimize the loss in the event of loss occurring.

Principle of Contribution

Sometime, the same subject matter of insurance could be covered by different policies. It is possible that these policies are taken in different contexts under different portfolios or even multiple policies for extra protection. Here, as we saw in the case of subrogation, there is a possibility that the insured might get compensated more than once from different sources for the same loss, thereby making a profit. The principle of contribution is relevant in this context.

In the event of multiple policies covering the same subject matter of insurance, the principle of contribution provides for an equitable sharing of any loss between all the insurers according to their respective insurances (Denis Riley, 1967). When a loss is insured under more than one insurance policy, for example, a travel policy and a household policy, in the event of a claim the two insurers share the cost. The principle of contribution like that of subrogation seeks to prevent the insured from getting compensations from different sources for the same loss, thereby violating the principles of indemnity.

Contribution is the right of an insurer who has paid claim under a policy, to call upon others insurer for the same loss, to contribute. This principle is applicable to all contracts of indemnity except the life insurance.

Definition of Contribution

According to the Federation of Insurance Institutes, Mumbai—

> "Principle of contribution refers to the right of an insurer who has paid for a loss under a policy to cover a proportionate amount from other insurers who are liable for the loss".

Therefore, contribution is the right of an insurer, to call upon other insurers liable for the same loss to contribute the payment to the one who has paid the loss under a policy. This doctrine ensures an equitable distribution of losses between different insurers.

Need of Principle of Contribution

Sometimes, a person may get his goods insured with more than one insures. This is known as double insurance. In the event of loss if he got his loss indemnified from all insures, he will receive more compensation than his actual loss. It is against the principle of indemnity. In case of loss, he may choose to get his loss compensated by one or more insurers taken together. In such a case when an insured chooses to collect his loss from one or two of them, the paying company or companies can later claim proportionate amount from other insurers.

Pre-Requisites of the Principle of Contribution

The principle of contribution is not applicable in all cases of 'double insurance'. The following are the pre-requistes for the application of principle of contribution:

(a) The subject matter or property of insurance must be common to all insurers. In simple words, it means that the goods or properties to be insured must be the same in case of all policies issued.

(b) The risk event which causes the loss must be common to all policies in order to attract the principle of contribution.

(c) The policies must be legally enforceable which means that the policies must be valid. These/none of these must not be invalid, void, null or defective at the time of loss.

(d) The policies must be in force at the time of loss. The principle of contribution is applicable only to those polices which shall be in force at the time of occurrence of loss.

(e) The insurable interest must be the same under all policies. All policies must be effected in favour of an insured.

Miscellaneous Principles

There are also certain miscellaneous principles of insurance beside the general and specific principles. These are as under:

(i) Principle of Assignment

Principle of assignment is also known as transfer of interest. It is necessary to distinguish between assignment of the subject matter of property of insurance; the policy and the policy money when payable.

In case of marine and life insurance policies, assignments can be made freely without the prior consent of the insurer. But in case of fire insurance and accident insurance policies, assignment without advance consent of insurer is not valid.

The life insurance policy can be assigned freely for a legal consideration or even without consideration in case of love and affection.

Assignment refers to transfer of interest of policy to third party by the insured. The assignment shall be complete and effective only on the execution of such endorsement either on the policy itself or on a separate deed. Notice for this purpose must be given to the insurer who will acknowledge the assignment. Once the assignment is complete, it cannot be revoked by the assignor. The life policies are the only polices, which can be assigned whether the assignee has an insurable interest or not. A marine cargo policy is freely assignable unless it contains conditions expressly prohibiting assignment. It may be assigned either before or after loss. It may be assigned through endorsement or in any other customary manner.

Assignment of fire insurance cannot be done without prior consent of insurer. Change in insurable interest in fire insurance policies is not valid unless the consent of the insurer has been obtained.

(II) Principle of Return of Premium

The amount of premium once paid cannot ordinarily be refunded. However, in the following cases the premium paid is returnable.

By Agreement in the Policy

The insured may pay full premium while effecting the insurance but it may be agreed in policy to return it wholly or partly on the happening of certain events.

For Reasons of Equity

Equity implies a condition that the insured shall not receive the price of running a risk he bears. So, the contract does not come into effete in this case or it is held to be void. It can be established by the following points.

Non-attachment of Risk

Where the subject matter insured or part thereof, has never been imperiled, e.g. such policy is term insurance with returnable premium. Again, the premium is returned to the policyholder if death does not occur during the period of insurance.

Undeclared Balance of an Open Policy

Policy may be cancelled and premium may be returned for short interest allowed provided there was no further interest in the policy.

(i) Payment of Premium is Apportional

The apportioned part of the consideration is refundable when a part of policy interest is not involved. For example, insurance may be taken for a voyage in stages, each stage being rated separately. In such a case if some stages are not completed, the premium, relating to the journey not completed, is returnable.

Where the assured has no insurable interest throughout the currency of risk, the premium is returnable provided the policy was not attached by way of wagering.

Unreasonable delay in commencing the voyage may also entitle the insurer to cancel the insurance by returning the premium.

(ii) Principle of Over-insurance by Double Insurance

If there is over insurance by way of double insurance, a propitiate part of several premiums is returnable provided that if the policies are taken at different times and any earlier policy has at any time borne the whole risk or if a claim has been paid, premium on the first policy cannot be returned. When double insurance is effected knowingly by the insured, no premium is returnable.

(iii) Legal Principles

Life insurance is a contract and, therefore, the provisions of the Contract Act, 1872 are applicable. The provisions of other Acts like Transfer of Property Act, Estate Duty Act, Indian Stamp Act, Law of Limitation, Succession Act, etc. are also applicable to life insurance.

New for Old Part(s) Principle

When a part of a machine or a vehicle is replaced following an accident, the insurer pays for the cost of a new part to see that the machine is reinstated to its working condition. Here, indemnity is seen as the process of putting the machinery back to working condition and not like replacement of the old part with another old part. In the bargain, the insured gets a new part instead of the old part and the insurer would be meeting the cost of new spare parts.

It is a term used to describe a basis of cover, usually within property insurance. Whereby the insurer agrees to pay the full replacement cost of the damaged insured item and not what the actual item is valued at the time of the loss. This principle is used in areas such as marine hull, machinery parts, vehicle parts and the like.

In other words, it denotes replacing old damaged parts or equipment with new ones rather than repairing them. In an insurance cover for property or equipment, an item cost if destroyed is replaced by the equivalent new item without deduction for age or wear and tear of the old item and regardless of price inflation. Items lost or damaged beyond repair will be at the present purchase price. The advantage is that the insured will not be left out of pocket when replacing items. However, new for old does not apply to item like clothing, household linen and pedal-cycles where wear and tear needs to be taken into consideration. New for old or replacement cost option is usually offered at the proposal stage of arranging insurance and will carry a higher premium charge than a strict indemnity only policy, which will take into account a deduction for wear and tear.

Reinstatement

Reinstatement is a claim settled on option agreed between the insured and the insurers, stating that the insurer would make good the damaged property of the insured, rather than pay a monetary amount. Reinstatement valid is the cost of making good the insured damaged property. Accordingly, the reinstatement clause or memorandum is usually used within a property policy that states the duty of the insurer if they decide to reinstate the property in the event of an insured loss. For this benefit, the insurer would usually charge a policyholder an additional premium.

However, reinstatement of the loss by the insurer is not followed strictly due to various practical issues. Reinstatement would be a costly exercise for the insurer. Again, if he were not able to reinstate to the satisfaction of the insured, his work would have to be abandoned. The insured may not practically prefer reinstatement, as he would like to have better buildings or newer technology or higher capacity equipment to replace the loss. In practical terms, the insured would prefer receiving the full cost of reinstatement in lieu of actual reinstatement. This cost would comprise of: (i) the indemnity per se, (ii) wear and tear, depreciation, and (iii) cost of inflation between date of loss and probable time of reinstatement. This clause helps in bringing the insured closer to his stat prior to the loss, instead of getting a lump sum in the event of the loss. However, there is a possibility of an insured getting away with a lower sum insured (and lower premium) utilizing this clause. Hence, the condition of average (or adjusting the claim payable to the sum insured chosen by the insured) is applied. Reinstatement at 85 per cent average is only applied to a claim settlement, if the building's sum insured is less than 85 per cent of the reinstatement value.

Apart from the above reinstatement that is applied in the case of a loss, there is a concept of reinstatement of premium. Under property insurance, reinstatement premium is the amount of premium payable by the policyholder to restore the sum insured to its original level, following an insured loss.

Agreed Value

Agreed value policies or valued policies are considered a practical way out in many cases where assessing the value of a loss post the event can pose problems. There could be different reasons for such situations and in the context of different types of policies. Moral and morale hazards may be involved in areas such as health insurance. In case of marine cargo, there could be difficulty in finding out the value at the location of the loss. In such cases, the value would be the invoice price plus some other objective measure such as freight, which seldom violate the principle of indemnity. In fire and engineering project insurance, the value of stock may have changed due to some processes involved, or by market conditions, inflation or currency fluctuations. In the case of rarities and personal possessions such as paintings, fitted items or prizes, sentimental reasons would make objective evaluation unacceptable. Values of such items can be extremely difficult to assess post loss. In areas like personal accident, measuring personal losses post event may be painful.

As situations of over insurance and total losses can cause overpayments, the reasonableness of fixing the agreed value becomes important. The agreed value concept has pitfalls as well. If the value reduces between the date of agreeing and the date of loss causing an over indemnification, the valuation in case of partial losses can be difficult. In some cases, partial losses may have to be treated on a different basis. In total losses, the value of salvage may vary widely between the insured and an objective assessor.

Material Fact

Any information that could affect the underwriter's assessment of the risk is regarded as a material fact. The underwriter's assessment can include fixing the insurance premium, framing the condition that would operate in the event of a claim, or even the decision to accept the risk itself. The Marine Insurance Act, 1906 defines the concept as follows:

> "Every circumstance is material which would influence the judgment of a prudent insurer in fixing the premium or determining whether he will take the risk".

Failure by the policyholder or proposer to inform insurers of all relevant material facts that affect the insured risk is referred to as non-disclosure. Non-disclosure of material facts could normally result in a reduced indemnity depending on the level of non-disclosure. However, if the material facts that were not disclosed are found to be very crucial or if there is any serious misrepresentation of facts, insurers are entitled to treat it as a serious matter and refuse to deal with any claims or void the policy from the start of cover.

Reciprocal Duty

Reciprocity is another guiding principle in insurance. Fundamental principles that are binding on one party call for reciprocal behaviour from the other party as well, whether stated or otherwise. While the insured is expected to disclose all material facts, the insurer should also disclose to him benefits under the policy that the insured normally may not know about. For instance, an insured has to inform the insurer that the old wiring in a block of the factory has caused short circuits in the recent past and due to insufficient budget allocation, rewiring has not been done yet. Reciprocally, the insurer should inform the insured that the automatic fire protection system he has installed in the block would entitle him to a discount, or that as a fire safe door had been fixed in the block, the loading for improper electrical installations would be applicable only to that block and not to other communicating blocks.

Condition of Average

The principle of average requires the amount of a claim payment to be reduced proportionately if a policyholder has not insured his property for its full value, or full replacement cost. The insurer has to meet the losses of a few persons from the money pooled from many. If an insured opts for a lesser sum insured and consequently pays a less than adequate amount as premium, it is only logical that the loss also gets reduced proportionally. An insured who contributes less to the common pool is allowed to reap only lesser benefits from the pool. If a policy is subject to average and if the sum insured at the time of a loss is less than the actual value of the property insured, the amount of claim under the policy will also be reduced in proportion to the under-insurance. In mathematical terms:

$$\text{Allowable Claim} = \frac{\text{Loss} \times \text{Sum Insured}}{\text{Value at Risk}}$$

The concept of average is applied by dividing the sum insured by the actual value at risk and applying the same proportion on the loss by multiplying the amount of loss by the result, making the loss proportionate to the sum insured. The remaining part of the sum insured is treated as actually covered by the insured himself who has retained the premium with him. Hence, he has to pay to himself the proportionate amount of the loss as well.

General Average

Concepts of general and particular averages are not to be confused with the condition of average stated above.

General average is a contribution made by all parties involved (usually) in a sea adventure, towards a loss occasioned by the sacrifice of the property of some of the parties in the common interest for the benefit of all. In order to save a ship in peril of sinking during a storm, some of the cargo may have to be thrown overboard. In the exigencies of hazards faced at sea, crewmembers often have precious little time to determine precisely whose cargo they are jettisoning. Thus, to avoid quartering that could waste valuable tie, there arose the equitable practice whereby all the merchants whose cargo was on board would be called on to contribute a portion, based upon a share or percentage, to the merchant or merchants whose goods had been tossed overboard to avert imminent peril. The ship owner and the owners of the saved cargo obviously benefit at the expense of the owners of the jettisoned cargo. It is called general average, because the loss is applicable in general to all the ship, the cargo and the freight at risk saved by the sacrifice. This was unfair demand and the principle of general average evolved so that all parties would contribute in such a situation.

It is believed that the inhabitants of Rhodes invented the concept of the general average. Merchants whose goods were being shipped together would pay a proportionally divided premium that would be used to reimburse any merchant whose goods were jettisoned during storm or sinkage. While general average traces its origins in ancient maritime law, it still remains a part of the admiralty law of most countries. The first condition of general average was the York Antwerp Rules of 1890. American companies accepted it in 1949. General average requires three elements as stated by Justice Grier in *Barnard* Vs. *Adams*.

- "*A common danger*: A danger in which vessel, cargo and crew all participate, a danger imminent and apparently inevitable, except by voluntarily incurring the loss of a portion of the whole to save the remainder".
- "There must be a voluntary jettison, jactus, or casting away, of some portion of the joint corner for the purpose of avoiding this imminent peril, periculi imminent is evitandi causa, or in other words, a

transfer of the peril from the whole to a particular portion of the whole".
- "This attempt to avoid the imminent common peril must be successful".

In simple words, the law of general average is a legal principle of maritime law, according to which all parties in a sea venture proportionally share any loss resulting from a voluntary sacrifice of a part of the ship or cargo to save the whole in an emergency. Thus, if one ships cargo on a vessel that is involved in a loss, he may face a claim against him even though his goods are not damaged. This aspect is questioned by some insured as unfair. However, actually it is not unfair because all the insured are part of the same marine venture, went through the same situations, and anyone could have suffered the loss.

Particular Average

Particular average is the damage or partial loss happening to the ship or cargo or freight, in consequence of some fortuitous or unavoidable accident, and it is borne by the individual owners of the articles damaged or by their insurers. The term is usually used in marine insurance. In contrast to general average, particular average does not deal with damage voluntarily incurred in case of a cargo consignment, the measure of indemnity varies depending on whether there was a total loss to some of the cartons sent, or whether damage was sustained by some part of the consignment. The value is derived as an average of the CIF invoice value (comprising cost, insurance and freight) for the entire consignment. As particular average means a partial loss insurance cover, policies issued on total loss cover are said to be on free of particular average (FPA) which means excluding partial losses (or total loss only). FPA is a set of marine insurance conditions providing a very narrow cover. Another term relating to average that is used in marine insurance is petty averages that are sundry small charges, which occur regularly, and are necessarily defrayed by the master in the usual course of a voyage. These include port charges, common pilotage, and the like, which could be borne partly by the ship and/or partly by the cargo.

Sue and Labour/Particular Charges

Sue and labour/particular charges are charges incurred by or on behalf of the insured for the safety and preservation of the subject matter insured. These are different from general average, particular average and salvage charges. In practice, particular average is treated synonymously with sue and labour.

The principles stem from the theory that the insured should at all times, act as if he/she were uninsured. That is, he should take all reasonable care that he would have taken had the subject matter been uninsured. The sue and labour clause requires the ship owner to make every attempt to reduce or save the exposed interest from loss. Under the terms of the values, the insurer pays for any necessary costs incurred in carrying out the retirements of the sue and labour clause. Thus, if a ship is stranded, under the sue and labour clause, the hull owner would be required to hire salvers and get it towed to the nearest port. In case of fragile cargo such as bottles of jam, this logic applies in taking due care of the consignment, say, with adequate packing and proper labelling. If a heavy machine tilts and damages the cartons containing the jam bottles, the cartons may have to be shifted to a safer place on the ship. Also, the damaged cartons may have to be opened and broken bottles removed so that the leaking contents do not rot and damage the remaining jam bottles by spoiling the labels or by attracting ants and insects. Such ensuring costs reasonably and incurred short of destination. In averting or minimizing the loss are termed sue and labour charges and are payable by the insure if these costs are incurred after the goods reach their destination, such as some additional costs are incurred for cleaning up the remaining bottles and re-labelling them to make them saleable, these are treated as particular charges. Sue and labour follows a loss or damage making incident, whereas particular average can be incurred to avoid or avert the threat of an imminent loss. Differences like these are treated as academic by many authors, and in actual practice both the terms are treated almost synonymously.

Excess and Deductibles

In an insurance policy, the deductible or excess is the portion of any claim that is not covered by the insurance provider. That is, only the amount that is in excess of the deductible is recoverable. It is normally quoted as a fixed amount and is a part of most policies covering losses to the policyholder. The deductibles must be met by the insured, or in other words, paid by the insured before the benefits of the policy can apply. An excess can apply is two ways: either as a voluntary excess at the instance of the insured to obtain a discount on the premium, or as a compulsory excess imposed by the insurer for underwriting reason such as avoiding larger numbers of small claims and their associated administration costs. Often, the second case is specifically referred to as a deductible.

Either way, the excess or deductible is the amount of a claim that is the responsibility of the insured or where he is his own insurer. In simple terms, it is the amount of the claim that you have to pay out of your own pocket. In a typical automobile insurance policy, a deductible will apply to claims arising from damage to or loss of the vehicle, caused by accidents for which the holder is responsible, or by theft. If a person has an insurance policy for his car with Rs. 5000 as deductible for damages, in the event of an accident costing Rs. 8000 worth of damage to the car, the insurance company would pay not Rs. 8000 but Rs. 3000 only. The insured is responsible for the first Rs. 5000 worth of damage (the deductible). Most health insurance policies and some travel insurance policies have deductibles as well. Generally, for a higher deductible, the premium is lower and *vice versa*. Some medical insurance policies have a deductible that does not cover the cost of routine outpatient visits (e.g. to a doctor's clinic). The concept can operate on per event (per condition) basis or a per year basis, explained below:

Per Event Basis

This most common form of deductible is applied on a per event basis. The deductible amount is agreed upon between the insurance company and the policyholder on each occasion that a claim arises for each medical condition that requires treatment, the insured will be required to pay a percentage over fixed sum of the treatment costs. For example, a deductible of Rs. 1000 is applied for the treatment of an illness. If the total bill comes to Rs. 5000, then the insurance company reimburses Rs. 4000. If the total bill from three occasions of treatment comes to Rs. 15, 000 in a year, the insurance company reimburses Rs. 12, 000 (Rs. 15,

000 less Rs. 3000 as deductibles for three occasions @ Rs. 1000 per occasion).

Per Year Basis

In a per year form of deductible, an annual limit for deduction applies instead of a per event basis. The insurance company and the policyholder agree upon an annual limit of deductible and not a claim by claim deductible. Once the claims have reached this limit, the insurance company reimburses all further expenses in full. The insured will be required to pay for their treatment up to the agreed annual limit and the insurance company will be responsible for all further costs. In the above case, if Rs. 1000 is agreed as the deductible, the insured will be required to bear the first Rs. 1000 for the treatment he receives in the year. If the total bill comes to Rs. 5000 for the first occasion of treatment, the insurance company reimburses Rs. 4000. If there are two more occasions of treatment of Rs. 5000 each in the same year, the insurance company does not make any further deductions and the full claim is reimbursed on these subsequent two occasions.

Co-insurance or Co-pay

This is a form of excess used in some markets, where the insurance company requires the policyholder to pay a certain amount, most often expressed as percentage of the total cost. Co-insurance usually applies for dental, maternity treatments and outpatient treatment where the client will bear a percentage of the total expenses. For example, if an insurance company requires 20 per cent co-insurance and the total bill comes to Rs. 1000 the policyholder will bear Rs. 200 and then the insurance company will pay the remaining Rs. 800.

Franchise

This concept is similar to excess and deductibles in that the insurer makes no settlement if the total claim is below the franchise figure. In case of excess, deduction is made when a loss crosses an agreed figure. Franchise is different from excess in that no deduction is made once the loss crosses the agreed figure. This figure, however, applies as a threshold level for a claim to be considered. If the claim is more than the franchise figure, the claim is paid in full. In the above example, if the franchise figure is Rs. 1000, no claim under Rs. 1000 is payable, just as in the case of excess. However, if a loss exceeds Rs. 1000, the entire amount is paid without any deduction. Franchisees are becoming less and less common in modern insurance practice though machinery breakdown covers sometimes use time franchise.

First Loss

First loss denotes a policy where the sum insured is accepted to be less than the value of the property but the insurer undertakes to pay claims up to the sum insured, without application of average. It is a contract written on such an amount as to cover only an insured's expected loss during the policy period with no other insurance in existence. It is a type of partial insurance (which covers less than the full value of goods or property at risk) where both the insured and the insurer acknowledge that the 'subject to average (see average) rule' does not apply. 'First Loss Policies' cover only the estimated largest possible loss and are often used in theft insurance, covering high value goods that would be physically impossible to steal in a single burglary, that is where the possibility of total loss is extremely remote (such as in case of a large store).

In other words, it is an accepted form of partial insurance where the insured decides he would not suffer a total loss and selects a maximum insured sum for any loss that is problem. The sum insured is often decided by calculating the maximum probable loss (MPL) or probable maximum loss (PML). The PML of a particular risk is the estimate of the maximum loss that would occur as a result of damage caused by the most destructive peril to be insured, in regard to the location, construction, occupation and protection of the risk. PML is usually expressed as a percentage of the sum insured. It is important that first loss sums insured are used only on first loss policies where average does not apply. In the usual insurances if the sum insured does not represent the full value, the insured will not get a full settlement of any loss. In some markets, first loss is used to refer to a policy whose limits are reduced (and not reinstated) by loss payments. There are also contexts where the term first loss is used to denote a policy that covers only a single loss during the policy period or that provides coverage of multiple locations for only the first loss at each location during the policy period.

Performance Ratios

Insurance companies have to constantly assess and reassess the effectiveness of their various strategies and readjust them based on their findings. The assessments have to be objective, scientific and based on quantifiable parameters so that they are reliable. Performance is assessed essentially from three angles, the company's exposure, the company's actions, and its results.

(I) Exposure Ratios

These ratios essentially assess where the company is placed in the insurance market and in comparison to the other companies. In other words, it indicates the relative position of the insurer in the environment in which it operates.

Market Share

It indicates the insurer's share in the total pie (market). That is considering the total market as 100, how much of it the company has been able to capture for itself. This is often expressed as line graph or in table or in pie chart.

$$\text{Market Share} = \frac{\text{GDP of the particular company}}{\text{Total GDP of the market}} \times 100$$

The pie chart enables an insurance company to visualize its standing in terms of the share of the market that it controls.

Relative Market Share is another term used for comparison purposes. The comparison can be with the share of the biggest player or with an average share.

Relative Market Share (against biggest share)

$$\text{RMS} = \frac{\text{GDP of the particular company}}{\text{Total GDP of the market}} \times 100$$

In the line graph given in figure, the market share of the company with the largest market share (the highest market share) is taken to be 100 per cent. The company that wants to compare itself with the largest company works out its share as compared to that of the largest company's share.

Similarly, an average company is taken as 100 for comparison to find out where the company comparing its share stands as compared to the Average Company:

$$\text{Average GDP share} = \frac{\text{Total GDP of the market}}{\text{Number of Players}}$$

Relative market share (Against average shares)

$$= \frac{\text{GDP of the particular company}}{\text{Average GDP share}} \times 100$$

Persistence Ratio is considered a yard-stick to evaluate the market performance of the company *vis-à-vis* a past period. The most common comparison is between the premium collection of the current month and the premium collection of the corresponding month of the previous year, i.e. premium amount of January 2008 vs. premium amount of January 2007. Comparison is also made between the current month's premium incomes as a percentage of the total Gross Direct Premium (GDP) vs. the corresponding month's premium of the previous year as a percentage of that year's total GDP. For example, only 5 per cent of this year's GDP came from this January premium, whereas 15 per cent of last year's GDP had come from the business done in last January.

Premium Persistence Ratio refers to the tendency of the policyholders to renew the insurance with the same company. It is taken as an indication of the trust the market reposes in the company. It represents a level of satisfaction of policyholders towards their policies. This indicator is often used as an important reference when evaluating the potential growth of business. As most general insurance policies are one-year policies, substantial thrust is given on the ability of the company to retain existing customers. Customers often seek best rates and services at the point of renewal. Hence, retaining customers is taken as a barometer for the company's ability to keep its rates reasonable, give good service and maintain a healthy level of credibility in the market. It is often indicated as the amount of the premium coming from renewed business vs. the premium expectation as per the company's renewal register.

Premium Persistence Ratio (PPR) works as under:

$$PPR = \frac{\text{Premium in respect of renewed business}}{\text{Premium expected as per renewal register}} \times 100$$

Insurers take pride in stating that they have a premium/policy persistence ratio of 95 per cent, indicating a high level of satisfaction among its customers. In some markets, the terms Policy Persistence Ratio/Policy Retention Ratio are used to make similar comparisons between the number of policies issued in a given period and those issued in a previous period (same season). The gap between the policy retention ratio and the ideal ratio of 100 per cent is referred to as the Policy Lapse Ratio. That is, if 98 per cent of the policies due for renewal have been renewed, it indicates a policy retention ratio of 98 per cent and a policy lapse ratio of 2 per cent.

Policy Lapse Ratio (PLR):

$$PLR = \frac{\text{Number of Policies not renewed as per renewal register}}{\text{Number of Policies expected to be renewed as per renewal register}} \times 100$$

Reinsurance Retention Ratio (net premiums/gross premiums) is different from the policy retention ratio mentioned above. This retention ratio indicates a company's dependence on reinsurers and the potential scope of reinsurance cover purchased. This is done by comparing the amount of premium paid for reinsurance protection *vis-à-vis* the gross amount received by the company.

$$\text{Re-insurance Retention Ratio} = \frac{\text{Net Premium Written}}{\text{Gross Premium Written}} \times 100$$

It is a rough measure of how much of the risk is being carried by an insurer rather than being passed on to reinsurers.

Loss Retention Ratio (LRR) is calculated by dividing net claims incurred by gross claims incurred. If this ratio is materially lower than the premium retention ratio, for consecutive years, it indicates a potential excessive reliance upon reinsurers' support for generating underwriting profits. Heavy dependence on re-insurance support for meeting claims for continuous period can impact an insurer's reputation among reinsures.

$$\text{Loss Retention Ratio} = \frac{\text{Net Claim Incurred}}{\text{Gross Claim Incurred}} \times 100$$

(2) Action Performance Ratios

These ratios relate to the various activities carried out by the insurers as part of their business actions or activities. These are often direct indicators of the company's efficiency and customer satisfaction. Ratios relating to the expeditious settling of claims, claim amount carried forward from previous years, the company's preparedness for settling claims by maintaining solvency margins, keeping sufficient liquid reserves, etc. are often considered indicators of the company's efficiency. An insurer's underwriting performance is measured by a set of ratios. Some such ratios are discussed below.

Claims Ratio is one of the most commonly used ratios. Claims ratio is often used synonymously with loss ratio. It is the percentage of the premium paid towards settlement of claims. In other words, the total losses of the company are divided by the premium collected during the same period; it is expressed as a percentage. This is worked out as under:

$$\text{Claims Ratio} = \frac{\text{Claims}}{\text{Gross Premium}} \times 100$$

A loss ratio of 60% indicates that out of Rs. 10, 000 premium collected, Rs. 6000 has been paid towards claims in the particular period. This ratio does not reflect the costs or expenses that are necessarily incurred by the insurers, and refers purely only to the premium and claim, this is more appropriately called as burning cost or pure risk cost.

Incurred Claims Ratio is an accounting mechanism of apportioning the claims ratio to a particular year as closely as possible. As the insurer continues with the process of settling claims all through the year and claims constantly spill over to one or more future years, it becomes difficult to apportion claims to a particular period and calculate such ratios. Incurred claims ratio is an accounting mechanism of appropriating claims to a year. The amount of claims paid in a year and the amount of claims outstanding at the end of the year are added, from which the amount of claims outstanding at the beginning of the year is deducted. This figure is called incurred claims.

Incurred Claims = claims paid during the year
+ Claims outstanding at the end of the year
– Claims outstanding at the beginning of the year

Gross Premium is the total amount of premium that comes in from the policies issued. Net written premium or net premium prefers to gross premium less premium on re-insurance ceded to re-insurers plus premium on re-insurance accepted.

Net Premium = Gross Premium
+ Premium on reinsurance accepted
– Premium on reinsurance ceded.

When amount of incurred claims is divided by the net written premium, we get the incurred claims ratio that gives a closer picture of the insurer's performance.

$$\text{Incurred Claims Ratio} = \frac{\text{Incurred Claims}}{\text{Net Premium}} \times 100$$

This exercise primarily tries to allocate claims to a particular year to ensure that the claims are more or less matched to the premiums received during the period. In other words, there is no mis-match between assets and liabilities (or tolerable mis-match).

Claims Coverage Ratio is a relative term that seeks to compare the company's claim experience *vis-à-vis* the industry's claim experience in a particular portfolio or a given market segment. This analysis would give insight into having a disproportionate share of claims *vis-à-vis* the market share, if such be the case. For instance, a company can find that it has only 10 per cent share of the industry's own damage insurance in respect of goods carrying vehicles, whereas it is paying 20 per cent of the claims paid by the industry on the particular segment.

Claims Duration Ratio helps in finding out the company's internal effectiveness in settling claims. Claims due to certain occupations and use of certain products take a long time to get noticed. In some cases, the courts take long periods of time, for instance 10-15 years, for settling liability claims (when there is litigation). The types of claims that get settled fast are called short tailed claims and those that take a longer settlement time are referred to as long tailed claims. While making provisions and allocating reserves, actuaries deal with these claims differently based on their devolvement period and duration ratios.

Complaints Ratio of a company is another core indicator. This figure indicates how a company's track record for satisfied customers stacks up against the competition. The common practice is that a ratio less than 0.3 indicates good performance *vis-à-vis* the median for a particular insurance market (marked by a score of "1"). A number higher than 1 suggests a relatively large number of complaints per customer served. Another thumb rule is to count the number of established complaints for every 1, 00, 000 customers served.

Capital Risks Ratio or Solvency Ratio tries to assess whether an insurer is solvent. In other words, if an insurer has adequate assets (over its liabilities) that can be utilized to pay the claims that can arise, it is solvent. It should have adequate technical reserves to meet the obligations entered into, and adequate capital as security. In simple terms, solvency margin can be defined as the surplus of assets over liabilities. A company's ability to pay claims denotes its solvency. Regulators expect that a certain minimum level of solvency margin is maintained so that the fluctuations in the overall results of a year are sufficiently cushioned without directly affecting the company. Solvency ratio from the Indian regulatory perspective is dealt with as a separate topic a little aftrerwards.

(3) Result Performance Ratios

These ratios indicate the end-product or the final result of all the performance parameters of the insurers. This includes concepts such as management expenses ratio and combined ratio. However, before dealing with them directly, we have to be clear about a few more terms.

Net Claims Paid is worked out by adding the claims paid on the re-insurances accepted and reducing the claims received on reinsurance ceded, to the gross claims paid. (Gross Claims paid refers to the total claims paid, including all claim-related expense and interest). When net claim paid is adjusted to the current accounting year, by reducing the effect of the previous year's accumulated claims, we get Net Incurred Claims.

Net incurred claims = Net claim paid
+ Amount of claims outstanding at the end of the year
– Amount of claims outstanding at the beginning of the year

Net Earned Premium

In respect of almost all policies, (other than those effective from April 1 of the year), some part of the premium received and accounted in a particular year would relate to the same accounting year while the remaining part would relate to the un-expired part of the policy falling in the next accounting year. Claims on the un-expired part of these policies would fall in the next year whereas the premium would not. Insurers use the term Earned Premium to refer to the proportion of the premium pertaining to the policy period in which it was received. The part of the premium proportionate to the un-expired period which would fall in the next accounting year is called Unearned Premium (or premium received in advance). The net premium received in a year is apportioned on a 1/365 days basis to take care of the risks that the company is exposed to within the same year, i.e. excluding the premium on the un-expired part of the policies that would spill over to the next accounting year. This share is called net earned premium. On a thumb rule basis, instead of the 1/365 days basis, insurers usually apportion 50 per cent of the previous year's net written premium and the current year's net written premium to work out the current year's net earned premium. (There is a view that as the company continues in business for many years and premiums keep coming every year, the simple written premium and incurred claims are good enough indictors for all practical purposes, as the premium and claims experience tend to even out over long periods, even without such apportionments. However, such simplistic stands do not find favour with actuaries who find that these indicators do not support the kind of precise calculations required in the modern day's competitive environment).

NIC NEP Ratio tries to give a more accurate ratio than the ones seen above. However, one needs to understand the following concepts to appreciate this ratio. Net incurred claims (NIC) divided by net earned premium (NEP) is referred to as Loss ratio or NIC – NEP ratio in common parlance. It may be observed that both the denominator and numerator in this calculation are business figures duly appropriated to a specific year. (It may be noted that loss adjustment expenses are considered part of incurred losses for such calculations).

$$\text{NIC} - \text{NEP Ratio} = \frac{\text{Net Incurred Claims}}{\text{Net Earned Premium}} \times 100$$

Insurers have to take care of various overheads other than settlement of claims. They incur business promotion expenses, agency commissions, administrative expenses, establishment costs, etc. The main variable costs having a direct bearing the insurer's performance are management expenses and agency commissions. The sum total of all such expenses incurred in a year is compared with the net written premium of a given year to assess the insurer's performance. Expense ratio is a commonly accepted term indicating the sum total of management expenses plus commissions, divided by net written premium. Here, it may be borne in mind that as the expenses relate to the payments made in the current year only, the net written premium, i.e. the premium received in the current year is taken into consideration. Both the denominator and numerator are, therefore, actual figures relating to the inflow/outflow in the particular year.

$$\text{Management Expenses Ratio} = \frac{\text{Management Expense}}{\text{Net Written Premium}} \times 100$$

In some markets, expenses ratio refers specifically to management expenses divided by net written premium, while commission ratio is calculated separately as commissions divided by net written premium.

Combined Ratio is obtained when

NIC – NEP ratio + Expense Ratio

The combined ratio is a reflection of the company's overall underwriting profits ability. A combined ratio of less than 100 per cent indicates profitability, while anything over 100 indicates a loss. These ratios are used to assess an insurance company's performance. Over and above these performance indicators, insurers make reserves/provisions for catastrophic losses as well. The insurer has to provide for his company's profit as well. The insurer's profit in the simplest terms can be stated in the form of the following equation:

Profit = Earned premium + Investment Income – Incurred Loss – Underwriting Expenses – Provisions

Solvency Margin

Solvency margin is important for an insurance company. It explains as having sufficient assets in terms of capital, surplus and reserves, and being able to satisfy financial requirements to be eligible to transact insurance business and meet liabilities. Certain mathematical comparisons of differenı components of an entity's financial statement have been prescribed to determine its solvency. Solvency ratios are calculated in India by a three-step method as prescribed by the regulator (IRDA) in the IRDA (Assets, Liabilities and Solvency Margin of Insurers) Regulations, 2000.

The first step that is prescribed for the calculation of the Required Solvency Margin (RSM) is based on (a) net premiums, termed RSM-1, and (b) net incurred claims, termed RSM-2. RSM on net premiums (i.e. RSM-1) is determined as 20 per cent of the amount, which is the higher of (i) the gross premiums multiplied by a set of factors prescribed for the purpose, and (ii) the net premium. In other words, the RSM on net incurred claims (i.e. RSM-2) is determined as 20 per cent of the amount, which is the higher of (i) the gross net incurred claims multiplied by a set of prescribed factors, and (ii) the net incurred claims. The Required Solvency Margin (RSM) for the company is the higher of the two. The second step is to calculate the Available Solvency Margin (ASM), which is the net assets in the policyholders' funds plus the net assets in the shareholders funds. The third step is to calculate the solvency ratio, which is the total ASM divided by the total RSM.

Stated in simple terms, solvency margin denotes the surplus of assets over liabilities. A company's ability to pay claims denotes its solvency. As already stated, it should have adequate technical reserves to meet the obligations entered into, and adequate capital as security. Regulators expect that a certain minimum level of solvency margin is always maintained so that the fluctuations in the overall results of a year are sufficiently cushioned without directly affecting the company.

IAIS Core Principles

Like other professional associations, the International Association of Insurance Supervisors (IAIS) sets standards that are fundamental to developing effective insurance regulation and supervisory practices. IAIS has prescribed a set of legally accepted standards called Insurance Core Principles that are fundamental in developing effective regulation and supervisory practices for the insurance sector. IAIS principles, standards and guidance papers provide the basis for evaluating insurance legislation, supervisory systems and procedures. The IRDA in India has successfully taken care of most of the 28 core principles (which are in seven clusters). However, in its adherence to standards, India needs to focus on certain perceived gaps that are based on internationalization of the Core Principles (Core Principles by Dr. K.C. Mishra). For a core principle to be regarded as being "observed", the essential criteria must be met without any significant shortcomings. We may refer to the Basel Committee on Banking Supervision (BCBS) which has formulated the Core Principles of Banking Supervision, which ensure best supervisory practices in the area of banking supervision.

Insurance Core Principles and Methodology

(International Association of Insurance Supervisors (IAIS) – October 2003)

ICP-1: Conditions for Effective Insurance Supervision

Insurance supervision relies upon:

- A policy on institutional and legal framework for financial sector supervisions.
- A well developed and effective financial market infrastructure.
- Efficient financial markets.

ICP-2: Supervisory Objectives

The principal objectives of insurance supervision are clearly defined.

ICP-3: Supervisory Authority

The supervisory authority:

- Has adequate powers, legal protection and financial resources to exercise its functions and powers.
- Is operationally independent but accountable in the exercise of its functions and powers.
- Hires, trains and maintains sufficient staff with high professional standards.
- Treats confidential information appropriately.

ICP-4: Supervisory Process

The supervisory authority conducts its functions in a transparent and accountable manner.

ICP-5: Supervisory Cooperation and Information Sharing

The supervisory authority cooperates with other agencies and shares information with other relevant supervisors subject to confidentiality requirements.

ICP-6: Licensing

An insurer must be licensed before it can operate within a jurisdiction. The requirements for licensing are clear, objective and public.

ICP-7: Suitability of Persons

The significant owners, board members, senior

management, auditors and actuaries of an insurer are fit and proper to fulfil their roles. This requires that they possess the appropriate integrity, competency, experience and qualifications.

ICP-8: Change in Control and Portfolio Transfers

The supervisory authority approves or rejects proposals to acquire significant ownership or any other interest in an insurer that results in that person, directly or indirectly, alone or with an associate, exercising control over the insurers.

The supervisory authority approves the portfolio transfer or merger of insurance business.

ICP-9: Corporate Governance

The corporate governance framework recognizes and protects rights of all interested parties. The supervisory authority requires compliance with all applicable corporate governance standards.

ICP-10: Internal Control

The supervisory authority requires insurers to have in place internal controls that are adequate for the nature and scale of the business. The oversight and reporting systems allow the board and management to monitor and control the operations.

ICP-11: Market Analysis

Making use of all available sources, the supervisory authority monitors and analyses all factors that may have an impact on insurers and insurance markets. It draws conclusions and takes action as appropriate.

ICP-12: Reporting to Supervisors and Offsite Monitoring

The supervisory authority receives necessary information to contact effective offsite monitoring and to evaluate the condition of each insurer as well as the insurance market.

ICP-13: Onsite Inspection

The supervisory authority carries out onsite inspections to examine the business of an insurer and its compliance with legislation and supervisory requirements.

ICP-14: Preventive and Corrective Measures

The supervisory authority takes preventive and corrective measures that are timely, suitable and necessary to achieve the objectives of insurance supervision.

ICP-15: Enforcement or Sanctions

The supervisory authority enforces corrective action and, where needed, imposes sanctions based on clear and objective criteria that are publicly disclosed.

ICP-16: Winding-up and exit from the market

The legal and regulatory framework defines a range of options for the orderly exit of insurers from the marketplace. It defines insolvency and establishes the criteria and procedure for dealing with insolvency. In the event of winding-up proceedings, the legal framework gives priority to the protection of policyholders.

ICP-17: Group-wide Supervision

The supervisory authority supervises its insurers on a solo and a group wide basis.

ICP-18: Risk Assessment and Management

The supervisory authority requires insures to recognize the range of risks that they faced and to assess and manage them effectively.

ICP-19: Insurance Activity

Since insurance is a risk taking activity, the supervisory authority requires insurers to evaluate and manage the risks that they underwrite, in particular, through re-insurance, and to have the tools to establish an adequate level of premiums.

ICP-20: Liabilities

The supervisory authority requires insurers to comply with standards for establishing adequate technical provisions and other liabilities, and making allowance for re-insurance receivables. The supervisory authority has both the authority and the ability to assess the adequacy of the technical provisions and to require that these provisions be increased, if necessary.

ICP-21: Investments

The supervisory authority requires insurers to comply with standards on investment activates. These standards include requirements on investment policy, assets-mix, valuation, diversification, asset-liability matching, and risk management.

ICP-22: Derivatives and Similar Commitments

The supervisory authority requires insurers to comply with standards on the use of derivatives and similar commitments. These standards address restrictions in their use and disclosure requirements, as well as internal controls and monitoring of the related positions.

ICP-23: Capital Adequacy and Solvency

The supervisory authority requires insurers to comply with the prescribed solvency regime. This regime includes capital adequacy requirements and requires suitable forms of capital that enable the insurers to absorb significant unforeseen losses.

ICP-24: Intermediaries

The supervisory authority sets requirements, directly or through the supervision of insurers, for the conduct of intermediaries.

ICP-25: Consumer Protection

The supervisory authority sets minimum requirements for insurers and intermediaries in dealing with consumers in its jurisdiction, including foreign insurers selling products on a cross-border basis. The requirements include provision of timely, complete and relevant information to consumers both before a contract is entered into to the point at which all obligations under a contract have been satisfied.

ICP-26: Information, Disclosure and Transparency Towards the Market

The supervisory authority requires insurers to disclose relevant information on a timely basis in order to give stakeholders a clear view of their business activities and financial position and to facilitate the understanding of the risk to which they are exposed.

ICP-27: Fraud

The supervisory authority requires that insurers and intermediaries take the necessary measure to prevent, detect and remedy insurance fraud.

ICP-28: Anti-Money Laundering, Combating the Financing of Terrorism (AML/CFT)

The supervisory authority requires insurers and intermediaries, at a minimum those insurers and intermediaries offering life insurance products or other investment-related insurance, to take effective measures to deter, detect and report money-laundering and the financing of terrorism consistent with the Recommendations of the Financial Action Task Force on Money Laundering (FATF).

Summary

The foregoing description has provided the reader/student with a detailed understanding of the fundamental principles of insurance. It would have been realized that insurance as a branch of learning uses its own set of terms and principles. The terms used are numerous and it may not be possible to cover them here. Suffice it to say that this account has familiarized readers with a good number of principles and terms used in the insurance market so that a reasonably good understanding of all the important aspects of insurance is obtained. Effort has been made to give a brief idea of the core principles developed by the International Association of Insurance Supervisors (IAIS).

(1) Although trust or good faith is cardinal to all financial transactions yet the position in insurance emphasizes greatly the importance of trust. As the underwriter knows nothing of the risk and the proposer knows everything about it, it is the duty of the proposer to make a full disclosure of all the material circumstances and facts to the underwriter without being asked. That is expressed by saying that it is a contract of utmost good faith.

(2) When a ship is proposed for insurance, if the proposer does not state the factual negative details

such as the ship's machinery being worn out, or that repairs are needed to make it seaworthy, or that it is carrying hazardous goods that it is not designed to carry, the insurer will not be reasonably expected to know of these. If the insurer had come to know of these details, he might have insured it only with some additional conditions or with an additional premium or he might not have insured the ship at all. In such cases, the withholding of these vital details from the insurer is a breach of the principle of utmost good faith.

(3) Insurance does not allow anyone to insure or get an insurance claim on any risk. It is important that the insured has a real interest on the subject offered for insurance. This is termed 'insurable interest' and is a prime requirement for an insurance contract to be valid.

(4) The requirement of 'insurable interest' is to ensure that the insured does not insure the risk with an intention of speculation, i.e. to make a profit out of the loss.

(5) The importance of 'insurable interest' can be made clearer by the following example. If a person insures his neighbourer's car, he is not at any financial loss if some damage happens to that car. Primarily, he has no financial interest in the car and his contract can only be a bet or wager on someone else's property. Further, as any damage happening to the car is to his advantage (with no loss to him). It is possible that he causes to become instrumental in causing damage to the car. The requirement of insurable interest is to ensure that the insured does not indulge in wagering or making a profit out of the loss.

(6) The principle of indemnity goes hand in hand with insurable interest and implies that the insured will be compensated only to the extent of the financial loss he has suffered or only up to the value previously agreed as the cost of the loss. The principle ensures that an insured should get a full indemnity and that he should get no more, i.e. he does not make a profit from the transaction.

(7) In the cases of health and personal accident insurance where the principle of indemnity does not strictly apply, the insurer promises to pay a predetermined amount to the insured on account of a disability due to an accident and/or to reimburse his medical expenditure. Although indemnity can not be possible for physical suffering yet the unfortunate or their families are moved closer to their former economic position.

(8) Subrogation is a provision by which the insurer is placed in the position of the assured to ensure that the assured is prevented from recovering more than the indemnity from any source. By this principle, on payment of the loss, the insurer is entitled to be placed in the position of the insured and success to all his rights and remedies against third parties in respect of the subject matter of insurance.

(9) In a road accident, if an insured vehicle gets totally damaged beyond repair, the insurer would pay the full sum insured of the vehicle to the insured. However, if the accident was caused entirely due to the fault of another vehicle, the insured has the legal right to claim compensation from the owner of the vehicle that caused the accident. The debris of the damaged vehicle can also be sold as scrap for some amount of money. Such as situation can give opportunity to the insured to recover more money than his loss. By the principle of subrogation, on payment of the loss, the insurer takes over the right of the insured to sue and to recover from any third party in respect of the loss that occurred.

(10) Proximate cause is explained as the active, efficient cause that sets in motion a chain of incidents which brings consequences without the intervention of any force and working actively from a new and independent source. It indicates the proximity or closeness of a loss to its cause or *vice versa*. It refers to the most dominant and most effective cause from which the loss emanated.

(11) A vessel was insured for marine perils but not against war like operations. The vessel was torpedoed and had to berth at a neighboring harbour. When the tide fell, she grounded in the shallow waters and later became a total wreck. The assured claimed for a loss of perils of the sea. As the proximate cause of the loss was the torpedoing, which was not covered under the policy, the claim was not paid.

(12) When a part of a machine or a vehicle is replaced following an accident, the insurer pays for the cost of a new part to see that the machine is re-instated to its working condition. Here, indemnity is seen as the process of putting the machine back to its working condition and not for a like replacement of the old part with another old part. In the bargain, the insured gets a new part instead of the old part and the insurer would be meeting the cost of new spare parts.

(13) 'New for old' is a term used to describe a basis of cover, usually within property insurance, whereby the insurer agrees to pay the full replacement cost of the damaged insured item and not what the actual item is valued at the time of the loss. This principle is used in area such as marine hull, machinery parts, vehicle parts, and the like.

(14) Sometimes, the same subject matter of insurance could be covered by different policies. Here, there is a possibility that the insured might get compensated more than once from different sources for the same loss, thereby making a profit. In the event of multiple policies covering the same subject matter of insurance, the principle of contribution provides for an equitable sharing of any loss between all the insurers according to their respective insurance amount.

(15) Re-instatement is a claim settlement option agreed between the insured and the insurer, stating that the insurer would make good the insured damaged property, rather than pay a monetary amount. For this benefit, the insurer would usually charge the policyholder an additional premium.

(16) Re-instatement of the loss by the insurer is not strictly followed due to various practical issues. Re-instatement would be costly for the insurer. Again, if he were not able to re-instate to the satisfaction of the insured, his work would have to be abandoned. The insured may not practically prefer reinstatement, as he would like to have better buildings or newer technology or higher capacity equipment to replace the loss. In practical terms, the insured would prefer receiving the full cost of re-instatement in lieu of actual re-instatement. This cost would comprise: (i) the indemnity *per se*, (ii) wear and tear and depreciation, and (iii) cost of inflation between date of loss and probate time of re-instatement.

(17) In some contexts, there can be practical difficulties in finding out the value of the loss due to change of value of stock due to processing, market conditions, location of the goods (especially in cargo insurances), inflation or currency fluctuations. In the case of rare objects and personal possessions, objective evaluation values can be extremely difficult to assess post-loss. In areas such as personal accident, measuring personal losses post-event may be offending and painful. Agreed value policies or valued policies are considered a practical way out in many cases where assessing the value of a loss post the event can create difficulties.

(18) Any information that could affect the underwriters' assessment of the risk is regarded a material fact. The underwriter's assessment can include fixing the insurance premium, framing the conditions of acceptance. Framing the conditions that would operate in the event of a claim or the decision to accept the risk itself.

(19) Reciprocity means that principles that are binding on one party call for reciprocal behaviour from the other party also whether stated or otherwise. While the insured is expected to disclose all material facts, the insurer should also disclose the benefits under the policy that the insured normally may not know.

(20) The principle of 'average' requires the amount of a claim payment to be reduced proportionately if a policyholder has not insured the property for its full value. If an insured opts for a lesser sum insured and consequently pays a less than adequate amount as premium, the loss also gets reduced proportionately. The concept of average is applied by dividing the sum insured by the actual value multiplied by the loss incurred. If the sum insured is only 50 per cent of the value, the loss will also be reduced to 50 per cent.

(21) General average is a contribution made by all parties involved (usually) in a sea adventure towards a loss occasioned by the sacrifice of the property of some of the parties in the common interest for the benefit of all.

(22) The law of general average is a legal principle of maritime law according to which all parties in a sea venture proportionally share any loss resulting from a voluntary sacrifice of part of the ship or cargo to save the whole in an emergency. Thus, if an insured ships' cargo on a vessel that is involved in sea hazard/unworthy sea and meets with a loss, he may face a claim from the insurer against him even though he was lucky that his goods were not damaged. This aspect is criticized by some insured as unfair. However, actually it is not unfair because all the insured were also part of the same venture, went through the same situation and all could have suffered the loss.

(23) Particular average means a partial loss. Insurance cover is taken and policies issued on total loss cover only are said to be free of particular average, which means excusing partial losses. 'Sue and Labour' denotes charges incurred by or on behalf of the insured for the safety and preservation of the subject-matter insured.

(24) In an insurance policy, the deductible or excess is the portion of any claim that is not covered by the insurance provider. That is, only the amount that is

in excess of the deductible is recoverable from the insurer.

(25) This most common form of deductible is applied on a per event basis. The deductible amount is agreed upon between the insurance company and the policyholder on each occasion that a claim arises.

(26) In a per year form of deductible, an annual limit is applied instead of per event basis. The insurance company and the policyholder agree upon an annual limit of deductible and not go by claim deductible.

(27) This concept is similar to the excess/deductible, in that the insurer makes no settlement if the total claim is below the franchise figure. In the case of excess, a deduction is made when a loss crosses an agreed figure. The difference is that in franchise, no deduction is made once the loss crosses the agreed figure. It rather applies as a threshold level for a claim to be considered.

(28) Usually the sum insured is the limit of indemnity and in case of under-insurance, the condition of average applies. The Probable Maximum Loss (PML) of a particular risk is the estimate of the maximum loss that would occur as a result of damage caused by the most destructive peril to be insured with regard to the location, construction, occupation and protection of the risk. PML is usually expressed as a percentage of the sum insured. Where the sum insured is decided based on the PML, as in the case of First Loss Policies, the sum insured is accepted to be less than the value of the property, but the insurer undertakes to pay claim up to the sum insured, without application of average.

(29) The simplest form of loss ratio or claims ratio is the total loss divided by net premium. It is expressed as a percentage. As this ratio does not reflect all the costs or expenses that are necessarily incurred by the insurers, this is more appropriately called as the burning cost or pure risk cost.

(30) Incurred claims ratio is an accounting mechanism of appropriating claims to a year. The amount of claims

paid in a year and the amount of claims outstanding at the end of the year are added, from which the amount of claims outstanding at the beginning of the year is deducted. This figure is called the incurred claims which are divided by the net premium to get the incurred claims ratio.

(31) The loss ratio (incurred losses and loss adjustment expenses divided by net earned premium) is added to the expense ratio (underwriting expenses plus commissions divided by net premium written) to determine the company's combined ratio. Thus, combined ratio = loss ratio + expense ratio.

3

General Insurance Market

INTRODUCTION

This topic has assumed great significance in view of the internationalization of economy and open competition. Banking and insurance sectors are the fastest emerging sectors of economy in India. This subject gives awareness about the general insurance market as it exists now. We have discussed the evolution of the market till the point of enactment of the General Insurance Nationalization Act in 1973. In this chapter, we deal with the appointment of the Committee on Reforms in Insurance Sector, which signaled a new era of liberalization and is generally regarded as the advent of the present day insurance market in India. A set of figures that indicate the nation's progress from both the economic and insurance angles are eye-openers and encouraging.

A brief mention about the current trends in the insurance market was made before. Having acquired a basic understanding of the principles and terms of insurance, the reader should be able to understand and appreciate the present day market trends discussed hereinafter.

This chapter will, therefore, familiarize the readers with the legal and economic environment, as well as the systems prevailing in the market.

CHANGES IN THE INDIAN INSURANCE MARKET IN RECENT TIMES

The history and evolution of the Indian general insurance market have already been discussed in detail. It is generally regarded that the market evolved into a fairly modern form by the middle of the 1930s. During this period, the Indian market came out of its adolescence and started addressing problems similar to those faced by more mature markets. We have seen that the combined efforts of the market and the government led to the enactment of the Insurance Act, 1938.

In the early 1990s, the need for further changes in the insurance market was voiced by various segments in both the national and international markets. The consequent changes and the succession of events that have formed the market the way it is today are discussed here. The insurance companies were widely criticized for inefficiencies arising out of overstaffing, governmental interference in management, lack of freedom in decision-making, waning company loyalty, as well as deficiencies in the system, which could neither provide enough motivation for meritorious employees nor effectively penalize employees for non-performance or lethargy. Professionalism in the industry started declining, and the industry's growth rate got largely limited to the rates of inflation and the returns the companies could earn by investing their surplus funds. With market penetration becoming static, the insurers were criticized as indifferent to the country's needs and the Government was criticized for being over protective of the nationalized industry by not allowing competition from private players which could improve matters.

The Malhotra Committee Report on Insurance Reforms, 1994

The Central Government responded to the situation by setting up a high power Committee on Reforms in Insurance Sector on April 7, 1993 headed by R.N. Malhotra, former Governor, Reserve Bank of India, "to examine the reforms required in the insurance sector". This Committee is popularly referred to as the Malhotra Committee. The committee interacted with the insurance companies, their staff unions, various chambers of commerce, trade bodies and a cross-sections of the country's public, and made a detailed analysis of the present Indian insurance industry. It also visualized the shape of things to come in the future and put forward its recommendations for the insurance industry on January 7, 1994.

The Malhotra Committee's report recommended that both life and non-life insurance sectors should be gradually opened for private participation and recommended entry to foreign companies through joint ventures established in India with Indian partners. The Committee prescribed a minimum paid up capital for new insurers as not less than Rs. 100 crore, which would be backed by well-defined solvency standards. The Committee recommended that the regulatory apparatus should be activated even in the present set-up of nationalized insurance sector and, among other things, recommended the establishment of a strong and effective Insurance Regulatory Authority (IRA) in the form of a statutory autonomous board on the lines of Securities and Exchange Board of India (SEBI). By way of detail, the Committee recommended retention of all major tariffs for some period of time, and progressive liberalization therein. The recommendations of the Committee were discussed across the country at different forums, including the managements of the Life Insurance Corporation, the General Insurance Corporation, the subsidiary companies of the latter, trade unions, Chambers of Commerce and various consumer interest groups. The Consultative Committee of the Parliament and the Ministry of Finance also held discussions on the Report of the Committee on Reforms in Insurance Sector with the various stakeholders in the markets. After prolonged deliberations, the government accepted the Committee's recommendation to set-up an autonomous interim Insurance Regulatory Authority (IRA).

The (Interim) Insurance Regulatory Authority, 1996

In his 1995 Budget Speech, the Finance Minister announced the government's views on the subject as follows:

> "As a first step, I propose to establish an independent regulatory authority for the insurance industry. Necessary legislation will be introduced shortly".

An interim Insurance Regulatory authority (IRA) was

formed accordingly on January 23, 1996 by a Government resolution, pending the enactment of comprehensive legislation, which would take time. The IRA came into existence with Mr. N. Rangachari as its full time Chairman, two part time members and a skeletal secretariat. The IRA, through seminars, discussions and press releases, made an attempt to create awareness about modern trends in insurance among various segments of the insured and potential insured. However, it did not have sufficient legislative powers to bring about any significant change in the insurance industry. Although the government had vested the powers of the Controller of Insurance with the Chairman of the IRA yet no serious change could be made in the working of the government-owned public sector insurers.

The then Finance Minister, in his Budget Speech of July 1996, announced that in keeping with the trend of liberalization, the non-statutory insurance regulatory authority would be made statutory and suitably empowered so that it would have sufficient teeth to play an effective regulatory role. In the statement of objects and reasons, necessitating the vesting of the insurance regulatory authority with powers to direct, advise, caution, prohibit, investigate, inspect, prosecute, search, seize, fine, amalgamate, register and regulate insurance companies, it was also conceded that the government was seized of the fact that after the nationalization of the life insurance industry in 1956 and the General insurance industry in 1972, the role of the Controller of Insurance had gradually diminished in its significance.

The Insurance Regulatory Authority Bill was submitted to the Parliament in December, 1996 but had to be withdrawn to incorporate certain changes suggested by the Members of Parliament. With certain amendments, the next government resubmitted the Bill to the Parliament in 1997 when it was shelved once again due to opposition from some quarters. In 1997, the Bill was presented a third time by the new government. The House felt that the Bill needed to be studied by Multi-party Parliamentary Committee under Mr. Murli Deora, then M.P. This Committee made fresh changes to the bill and the same was subsequently cleared by the Council of Ministers. The revised bill termed as the Insurance Regulatory and Development Authority Bill was accordingly submitted to the Parliament for its consideration.

The Insurance Regulatory and Development Authority (IRDA) Act, 1999

The insurance Regulatory and Development Authority Bill was approved by the Lok Sabha on December 1, 1999 and after approval of the Rajya Sabha, it was enacted as the Insurance Regulatory and Development authority (IRDA) Act, . 1999. The IRDA Act, 1999 was notified in the Gazette on April 19, 2000. As per the First Schedule to the IRDA Act, 1999, certain amendments were made to the Insurance Act, 1938, the Life Insurance Corporation Act, 1956 and the General Insurance Business Nationalization Act, 1972 to pave the way for liberalization of the insurance sector.

As per the Preamble of the IRDA Act

> "An Act to provide for the establishment of an authority to protect the interest of holders of insurance policies, to regulate, promote and ensure orderly growth of the insurance industry and for matters connected therewith or incidental thereto ....."

In terms of the IRDA Act and amendments to the Insurance Act, the office of the Controller of Insurance had become redundant under normal circumstances. However, the Central Government has certain powers to appoint a person to be the Controller of Insurance in certain specific situations.

The authority is body corporate having perpetual succession and common seal. It consists of a Chairperson and other members not exceeding nine in number, of whom not more than five would serve full time and not more than four would serve part time, to be appointed by the Central Government from amongst persons of ability, integrity and standing who have knowledge or experience of life insurance, general insurance, actuarial science, finance, economics, law, accountancy, administration or any other discipline which in the opinion of the Central Government shall be useful to the Authority. As per the Act, the Chairperson would hold office for a term of 5 years, or until the age of 65 years. The whole-time members would hold office for a term of 5 years, or until the age of 62. A part-time member would hold office for a term not exceeding 5 years.

The duties of IRDA have been spelt out in the Act as to regulate, promote and ensure orderly growth of the insurance business and re-insurance business. The powers and functions of IRDA have been listed out as follows:

(1) Issue to the applicant a certificate of registration as well as to renew, modify, withdraw, suspend or cancel such registration.
(2) Protection of the interest of the policyholders in matters concerning assigning of policy, nomination by policyholders, insurable interest, settlement of insurance claims, surrender value of policy and other terms and conditions of contracts of insurance.
(3) Specifying the requisite qualifications, code of conduct and practical training for intermediary or insurance intermediaries and agents.
(4) Specifying the code of conduct for surveyors and the loss assessors.
(5) Promoting efficiency requisite in the conduct of insurance business.
(6) Promoting and regulating professional organization connected with the insurance and re-insurance business.
(7) Levying fees and other charges for carrying out the purposes of the IRDA Act.
(8) Calling for information from, undertaking inspection and conducting enquiries and investigations including audit of the insurers, insurance intermediaries and other organizations connected with the insurance business.
(9) Control and regulation of the rates, advantages, terms and conditions that may be offered by insurers in respect of general insurance business not so controlled and regulated by TAC under Section 64U of the Insurance Act, 1938.
(10) Specifying the form and manner in which books of accounts will be maintained and statements of accounts will be rendered by insurers and insurance intermediaries.
(11) Regulating investment of funds by insurance companies.

(12) Regulating maintenance of margins of solvency.
(13) Adjudication of disputes between insurers and intermediary or insurance intermediaries.
(14) Supervising the functioning of the Tariff Advisory Committee.
(15) Specifying the percentage of premium income of the insurer to finance schemes for promoting and regulating professional organizations referred to in clause (f).
(16) Specifying the percentage of life insurance business to be undertaken by the insurers in the rural as well as/or social sector.
(17) Exercising such other powers as may be prescribed.

The IRDA Act, *inter-alia,* allows the issue of necessary regulations consistent with the Act and to carry out the purposes of the Act, IRDA is empowered to constitute an Insurance Advisory Committee to advise it while framing any regulations.

As a sequel to these changes, the General Insurance Business (Nationalization) Amendment Act, 2002 was passed and the General Insurance Corporation ceased to be the holding company of the four public sector insurance companies. The four public sector insurers were given functional autonomy in order to equip them better to face the challenges of liberalization. General Insurance Corporation of India became the national reinsurer and ceased to do direct insurance business. Consequently, Crop insurance, which was one of the major direct lines handled by GIC, got transferred to the newly formed Agricultural Insurance Corporation of India.

Regulations Issued by IRDA

In exercise of its powers under Section 26 of the IRDA Act, IRDA is authorized to make rules and regulations consistent with and to carry out the purposes of the Act in consultation with its Insurance Advisory Committee. The regulations would be notified by IRDA and submitted to the Parliament for its approval.

The IRDA has issued various regulations covering areas such as 'regulation of companies', protection of policyholders, obligations of insurers to rural and social sectors, appointment of actuaries, licensing of insurance agents, maintenance of solvency margins, preparation of financial statements, investment of funds, licensing of brokers, micro-insurance, etc.

Regulations came over various areas, some examples are: fixing financial requirements for licensing companies and intermediaries, specifying professional and academic standards for key-personnel in the insurance sector, setting codes of conduct for intermediaries such as surveyors, brokers and third party administrators, fixing common methodology for working out solvency margins prescribed for insurers, and prescribing uniform formats for submitting financial returns.

Some of the regulations specify standards for the functioning of the insurance regulatory bodies, IRDA itself and the Tariff Advisory Committee (TAC), covering matters such as holding meetings, fixing salaries, and service terms and conditions of the IRDA members and personnel.

Comprehensive Review of the Insurance Law

The Government of India (GOI) initiated a comprehensive review of the insurance regulatory framework through the Law Commission in 2004. This initiative was in response to the market's pleas for review of the laws. The laws relating to the insurance market, as we have seen, are spread beyond the Insurance Act and its amendments, over various acts, regulations, circulars and court judgments. The review process involved removing incongruities and inconsistencies in the present framework and putting in place an integrated set of rules for the country. The Law Commission had a series of discussions with different stakeholders and put up a notice on their website inviting views of the public. After deliberations, it submitted its report to the GOI on June 1, 2004, and suggested that a detailed examination by experts was needed in the following specialized domains of the Insurance Act: (1) Provisions relating to investments, (2) Shareholders' Funds and Policyholders' Funds, (3) Sufficiency of Assets, (4) Insurance Surveyors, and (5) Tariff Advisory Committee. In accordance, the IRDA constituted a Committee of 11 experts chaired by Mr. K.P. Narasimhan, which submitted its Report for the government's consideration. Once the views of the Committee are integrated with the Law Commission's recommendations and the necessary enactments made, the country can hope to be free from the present maze of regulations and have a simplified and efficient regulatory framework for the insurance sector.

BUSINESS INDICATORS

All through the centuries, the insurance industry has grown alongside the growth of the economy. Economists the world over consider insurance penetration a yardstick of economic development. Over the last decade, India has made significant strides in both economic and insurance reforms. The reform process is still going on, as seen in various monitoring/ assessing barometers of the economy.

Snap Shots of the Economy

A student of insurance should have an overview of the external environment, in which the insurers are functioning at present and are expected to function in the future. The trends culled out from contemporary literature give a rough indication of the extent to which the insurers need to prepare themselves to face the challenges.

Economic liberalization has caused cascading effects on various aspects of the Indian economy. The country's transformation from a conventional agricultural economy to an industrialized economy has raised an array of new challenges to the nation's infrastructure, especially in the services sector. India has crossed new milestones in diverse areas such as exploration of oils in the high seas, launching of artificial satellites, creation of state of the art power plants and refineries, acquiring of business processes from different countries, and higher inflow of foreign direct investment to invigorate the backward economy. All these have created a bigger market for the support systems, including insurance.

Growth potential in insurance sector is a well-researched phenomenon anywhere in the world. It depends on several macro-economic parameters. Collectively exhaustive but not mutually exclusive parameters of insurance growth are gross domestic product (GDP) level and growth rate, agricultural production and productivity, energy generation and incremental consumption, infrastructure level and strategy of further implementation, corporate sector and industry, inflation targeting and containment, capital market volume and returns, money and banking, growth rate projections of economy and business confidence level to determine the spirit of times.

Changes in consumer demographic largely determine reorientation of insurance business. The insurance sector has to strive to translate demographic relatives into opportunities for growth. The country's progress in terms of financial knowledge, rapid technological innovation, communication and internet technologies, emerging/evolving business environment, globalization, liberalization, trend to conglomerate, more distribution channels, and increasing education are drivers of change that the insurance sector can tap for its growth.

As per the Swiss Investment Bank 'Credit Suisse', India's Gross Domestic Product (GDP), at around Rs. 41, 00, 000 crore, has crossed the trillion dollar mark for the first time in history in April 2007 when the rupee appreciated to below 41 level against the US dollar. India has thus joined the elite club of 12 countries with a trillion dollar economy. The annual growth rate of 2007 is over 9 per cent and over a period of time hovering around 8 to 9 per cent.

During the first three quarters of 2006-07, the six core infrastructure industries, viz. crude petroleum, petroleum refineries, electricity, finished steel, cement and coal grew approximately at 8.3 per cent as compared to 5.5 per cent in the previous year. The index of industrial production showed a rise of 10.6 per cent as against the 8.3 per cent of the previous fiscal. The three categories of industry—manufacturing, mining and electricity sectors—also fuelled the growth of the economy.

The automobile industry registered a total production of 8.2 million vehicles in the same period with a growth percentage of 15.91 per cent. The number of passenger cars grew by 20.76%, two-wheelers grew by 13.45 per cent, three-wheelers grew by 17.94 per cent and commercial vehicles grew by 37.5 per cent. Automobile exports registered a growth of 28.74 per cent over the previous year. Till December 2006, India had total of nearly 190 million phones.

The responsibility of providing insurance coverage to have these landmark achievements of the nation's progress rests with Indian insurance companies which have to assess and accept the risks for insurance and reinsure the portion of the risk that is beyond their retention capacity in the international market.

Growth in various sectors calls for corresponding regulatory changes as well. In acknowledgement of the scope of regulatory overlap and realizing the increasing need for regulatory convergence, a high level co-ordination committee on capital and financial markets, comprising the heads of the regulatory institutions, meet periodically to ensure a certain degree of effectiveness of supervision, consistency in regulation and harmonization of supervisory practices between the banking, securities and insurance supervisors.

Snap Shots of the Insurance Market

Experts in the industry have forecasted that challenges will emerge in four distinct areas of the insurance industry in the next generation. Challenges can be reasonably expected from the following areas:

(1) New potential hazards resulting from rapid innovation and scientific advancement and the resultant demands on risk management.
(2) New vulnerabilities caused by massive levels of interconnectivity and independency, especially in strategic partnership, electronic networks and supply chains.
(3) New forms of untested insurance such as tsunami, terrorism or even genetic risks including avian flu, SARS and AIDS.
(4) New need of international coverage in many of these areas where risk could be fall out of trans-border occurrences such as terrorist strikes, natural catastrophes, hacking or epidemics.
(5) New liability issues that can arise from areas such as data confidentially, errors, negligence or breaching of deadlines, relating to the business processes outsourcing (BPO) industry that is booming in India.

While the insurance market is growing, the growth has also expanded the scope of training and research in insurance, increased competition in the market, shrunk margins, necessities of new insurance products; these have increased the pressure on insurer' efficiency and performance, blurred boundaries between financial instruments, and institutions, caused international integration/internationalization of financial markets. The emerging situation has increased the need for cross-border financial services, attracted investors from domestic markets to foreign markets and *vice versa*.

TRENDS AND CHALLENGES OF THE INSURANCE MARKET

The Indian general insurance market has mostly been a tariff market for many years. A tariff market is one in which insurance products are standardized along with all related rates, terms and conditions. In the Indian market, the Tariff Advisory Committee is statutory body designated under the Insurance Act to design and regulate the products and their rates. The rates fixed by the Tariff Advisory Committee are mandatory for all insurers; these are the lowest rates. This mechanism of fixing lowest rates is to ensure that insurance companies have sufficient funds at their disposal to settle claims when they arise. In the Indian market, major portfolios such as fire insurance, marine insurance, marine hull, motor insurance, engineering insurance and workmen's compensation have been all through the tariff system. Areas such as crop insurance, cattle insurance and health insurance have been all through the non-tariff system and are controlled by the inter-company arrangements called market agreements. Some portfolios such as personal accident insurance, marine cargo, and insurances of tea, coffee, rubber and cardamom were governed by tariffs for some time but de-terrifed in the 1980s and 1990s.

In essence, the philosophy was that core areas were tariff controlled. Areas where frequent product innovation was called for (e.g. crop and cattle insurance) or where rates had to be entirely re-insurance driven (e.g. aviation and satellite insurance) or where the fortunes of the portfolios did not count much in terms of premium and claims (e.g. pedal cycle insurance, bee-hive or poultry insurance) were left out of the scope of tariffs.

Experts in the field point out that the demise of the tariff in any insurance market is at best an unsetting time and at worst a disastrous path leading to significant losses to major companies. When the UK motor tariff was withdrawn in the late 1960s, the position was compounded by the lack of any reliable data or statistically robust methodologies.

De-tariffing has made the insurers' job more challenging as they have to design more and more products and price them correctly. The provider-scene has changed, more professionalism has come in, the distribution network is getting overhauled, and brokers have come into the market and are expected to add value to services.

Changes have brought with them new challenges for the insurers, the insured and the regulator.

The Organization for Economic Co-operation and Development (OECD), an international body that promotes policies for efficient functioning of markets and encourages convergence of policies, laws and regulations covering financial markets and enterprises, issued twenty guidelines on insurance. The magnitude of the challenges a regulator expects to meet can be visualized from the first of these guidelines, which reads as follows:

> "Adequate prudential and regulatory provision should be enforced in order to ensure the soundness of the insurance markets, the protection of the consumers and the stability of the economy as a whole. Over-regulation should be avoided. The insurance regulatory framework should be adapted to the characteristics of individual countries and encourage the stability, whilst maintaining the necessary flexibility to meet development in the market".

Products Offered to be Offered in Insurance

The Indian market has moved over to a tariff-free regime from January 1, 2007, though in phased manner. The de-tarrifing process has not been effected in the complete sense as only the rates are unfrozen while the products continue to be frozen, i.e. the cover, terms and conditions still continue to be as per the tariffs. Pricing of insurance products in both tariff and tariff-free regimes ideally has to be based on certain actuarial and statistical techniques. Most of this scientific decision-making has to rely heavily on statistical data. For improving the quality of decisions and to provide the industry with correct technical rates and burning costs in a non-tariff regime, the industry needs a national database to bank upon.

Different markets do standardization of products using different methods. Self-explanatory terms of standardization such as 'prior approval', 'modified price approval', 'flex rating', 'file and use', 'use and file', 'no file/record maintenance', 'state prescribed', etc. are internationally used to denote the degree of control exercised by the regulator on insurance products. The Indian tariff products fall under the 'state prescribed' category while the non-tariff products can possibly be categorized as 'no file/record maintenance' type. Some countries have scientific systems such as 'Risk Factor-based Rating Systems' (RFBRS) and 'Risk-based Pricing Models' (RBPM) for pricing their products.

Insurance Information Institute (an international academic body) states that under the 'file and use' mechanism, an insurer has to file a proposed product with the regulator along with all details, terms, conditions and justification for rates. The filing becomes effective immediately or from a future date specified by the filer. The regulator may disapprove a filing at any time if it is not in compliance with the law, after holding a hearing to establish non-compliance. Systems of justification of rates and/or terms are also not uniform and some products need prior re-filing. However, actual implementation of the system varies from product to product and country to country.

The Indian variant of 'file and use' system has a specified waiting period (days) in the case of 'prior approval' category of products, where the products are deemed approved automatically if the regulator does not take any specific action during the waiting period. Usually, rate revisions under 'file and use' are based solely on a change in loss experience, while in terms of modified period approval, rate revision is based on a change in expense relationships and rate classifications. Although guidelines on 'file and use' norms have been set by IRDA in India, the system is still is its nascent stage and yet to crystallize as a full-fledged regulation. The philosophy is that the players will be able to set their own rates and justify them. Also, each company will have to explain whether the rating of the risk is adequate, based on data, and justifiable. When there is no one official fixing rate, there is an increased need for self-regulation and better governance. Probably, the IRDA selected this hybrid 'file and use' system for the Indian market to provide a stable alternate system before removal of tariffs. The hybrid is expected to prevent volatility in the market, promote scientific rating, and usher in a culture of self-regulation with responsibility.

The 'file and use' system makes it mandatory that the wordings of every product sold in the market are legally vetted, the rates actuarially vetted and the product as such certified to be in line with the company's underwriting policy by the Chief Officer or a nominated Compliance Officer..

Providers and Intermediaries

The providers of general insurance (the insurers) in the Indian market are four public sector companies, eight private sector companies, two health insurance companies, one agricultural insurance company, five state government departments, two specialized companies (each on credit guarantee and deposit insurance), and health benefits association.

The State Government Insurance Departments insure properties owned by the respective states or where these states have substantial financial interests. The Calcutta Hospital and Nursing Home Benefits Association Limited provides certain health benefits to its members. Export credit and Guarantee Corporation Limited (ECGC) is the fifth largest credit insurer in the world and provides a set of specialized services for the export industry. The Deposit Insurance Corporation (DICI) and Credit Guarantee Corporation (CGCI) give covers to all bank deposit-holders up to a maximum of Rs. 1, 00, 000 (Rupees one lakh) for principal and interest amount held by him, in case the bank gets liquidated or its licence gets cancelled. The latter guarantees for schematic credit upto a percentage of credit disbursed by banks. A few international insurers have opened liaison offices in India and are waiting with their Indian joint venture partners for the necessary regulatory compliances.

The General Insurance Corporation of India (GICI) is the sole re-insurer in the market and is sometimes referred to as the national re-insurer. There are a few international re-insurers who have also opened representative offices in India for facilitating placement of outward/inward reinsurance business.

The General Insurance Council of India (GICI) and the Life

Insurance Council of India (LICI) are now statutory bodies under the Insurance Act that have recently been revived under the auspices of IRDA. These are intended to function as self-regulatory organizations and reduce the gaps between the insurers, the insured, trade bodies, regulators and the government. The Insurance Association of India (IAI) is another statutory body under the Act, which is yet to be formed.

IRDA has granted licenses to 382 insurance brokers till September 30, 2008. They have set-up offices in different parts of the country. There are a few reinsurance brokers as well in the country which interact between the insures and the reinsurance providers to facilitate placement of risks.

The bancassurance model allows banks to work with the insurers either on a corporate agent model or for referral services. Experts in the field state that regulatory changes have made bancassurance possible and feasible, and find a large untapped growth potential in banks and insurers working together.

Micro insurance groups are also growing as key players in increasing the country's insurance penetration by interacting with rural and sub-urban population. IRDA has brought about regulations to develop and regulate this sector also.

Surveyors are another group of professionals who have got more organized under the initiatives of IRDA. The Indian Institute of Insurance (III), loss surveyors and assessors have been formed to increase professionalism in the field.

The role of independent insurance arbitrators is getting recognized more than ever by the market, as there is an increased interest in 'out of court' settlement of claims and is thus an 'alternative dispute resolution' (ADR) to court cases.

Pricing and Information Technology

For scientific rating to be possible, the market would need a substantial amount of transactional data of reasonable quality and accuracy. Both historical and contemporary data require to be analyzed for making business decisions, product innovations, pricing and effective claims management. Statistical databases for various classes of business, detailing various segments based on nature of risk, type of insurance cover, and probable risk exposure would be needed for proper product pricing. IRDA has taken the initiative for creating a centralized national data repository with the Tariff Advisory Committee (TAC) to cater to the multifarious needs of the industry.

Although the TAC was all along having the powers under Section 64 UE of the Insurance Act to collect this data from the insures yet the power had seldom been effectively exercised. From 2000-01, IRDA and TAC renewed their efforts of colleting data on tariff area of business from both public and private sector players and started a system of charging penalties for non-compliance in submission of the requisitioned data. However, success was limited as the public sector insurers were not able to consolidate the data of their operating offices at their Regional Office or Head Office level.

The new version of software installed by the pubic sector insurers in late 2004 and 2005 gave the PSU insurers the technical capability to consolidate data at their Head Office levels. As a result of this technological breakthrough and the relentless pressure built up by IRDA on the insurers, the insurers have taken up data collection and compilation more seriously. Motor data collation is perceived difficult in terms of numbers and spread, and the insurers require putting in a lot of efforts in culling out and submitting the data, notwithstanding the manifold errors and inconsistencies. Health insurance data available with third Party Administrators and submission thereof is relatively easy to collect. The TAC has been able to collect data in respect of motor and health insurance from 2003-04 onwards and has published certain basic information tables at its website http://www.tac.org.in. The TAC has designed elaborate data format and data dictionaries for fifteen lines of business to streamline the process of data compilation.

In the tariff-free scenario, the TAC is expected to publish technical rates or burning costs, provide the insurers with information on segment-wise claims experience, and analyze data on frequency and severity aspects at a national level. The end objective is that the domestic insurers would develop in-house information technology skills and actuarial systems for more effective pricing and underwriting.

Advanced markets use scientific methods for insurance pricing. Three popular types of pricing are: (i) individual rating, (ii) class or manual rating, and (iii) modification rating, usually referred to as merit rating. Modification rating methods include schedule rating, experience rating, retrospective rating and premium discount plans. These rating methods are dependent on the terms cover and past loss experience of the insurance segment, duly considered. The accuracy of the calculation that goes into rating depends heavily on situational data of the frequency and severity of past losses. The data should be of sizeable quantity, of reasonable quality, creditability and relevance. For large property risks, the Probable Maximum Loss (PML) of the risk is also estimated. The PML of a particular risk is the worst possible scenario that an insurer can estimate in terms of the maximum loss that would occur as a result of damage caused by the most destructive peril to be insured. PML is usually expressed as a percentage of the sum insured.

For the purpose of making reserves or estimating its anticipated liabilities accurately and creating reserves for settling them, the insurer has to go for an actuarial process which, to a large extent, is based on the data.

Although individual insurers have their own data yet they may mot have a comprehensive picture of the entire market. They may not have any legal and ethical means to know how the industry is performing in general and how a particular branch or segment of insurance is behaving. For instance, no single insurer will be able to accurately assess how much money the industry is losing by way of interest on motor liability claims or what the annual payout in maternity claims is or even what the total impact of the Mumbai floods on the insurance industry was. Answer to these and many more questions on the total market or on particular market segment can be derived only from a centralized national data repository.

Beyond the realms of product pricing and reserving, the data repository can be used for many purposes such as claims managements, risk management, fraud detection and finding areas in the market where new products would be required. For instance, if there is a large gap between amounts of claims paid for eye surgeries, the insurers can probably devise a product for the purpose with higher limits. In the life insurance segment, the insurers share data on declined lives, a term used to denote proposals that are uninsurable due to various reasons such as bad health, financial insolvency, moral turpitude, bad habits, or hazardous hobbies or occupations. General insurers are planning to share their data of stolen vehicles so that a vehicle once reported as stolen and paid for as a total loss, doesn't get insured with another insurer. The changed market is expected to usher in more of such co-operative endeavors.

Although a data warehouse is generally regarded a good idea yet one may observe that in the developed nations like the US and the UK, the insurers have been dissuaded from compiling similar data banks owing to issues regarding the insurer's proprietary rights. The insurers are guarded on issues of confidentiality whether company-specific information will get into the hands of competitors, whether their standard of service would get exposed, whether insured entity's rights to confidentiality of personal data get compromised, whether the data will expose the insurers' errors to regulatory scrutiny, etc.

Developments in Related Fields

The changes in the country's business environment have introduced a variety of new activities in the insurance market and those have added to its complexity.

For instance, with the tarrifs becoming non-existent, products and prices have become more competitive for the insurers' survival. Further, the insurers have to look more closely at their costs. The company's manpower requirements need to be optimized to cut expenses. Claim-costs have to be reduced by way of correct assessment of losses, reduction of litigation, structured scales of compensations, effective methods of preserving subrogation rights, getting better value for salvage, etc. Speedy claim-settlements having effective distribution system, better information technology systems, better financial planning and control systems, and effective investment policies—all these areas are expected to get a closer look in the near future. These expectations can be summarized as having a more professional approach in the market. This leads to the creation of a better genre of professionals by way of qualitative changes in recruitment and training.

The regulator will require more alertness in its watchdog role as cut-throat competition in the market can bring in disruptive trade practices, abortive policy wordings, truncated claim settlements as well as expose the industry to unfamiliar civil and criminal offences. The regulator may have to locate early warning symptoms in the market and monitor aberrations to their source.

The modern insurance market calls for better interaction with many external agencies as there are many common areas of interest. Central Building Research Institute (CBRI) sets standards/designs for the construction of buildings. The insurers should understand the import of these guidelines for the buildings that they are insuring. The National Fire Protection Association (FPA) sets standards for fire protection, which are again important for the insurers in granting discounts for risks with better protection. There is scope for interaction with the Road Transport Authorities and the Traffic Police for tracking uninsured vehicles. Similarly, interaction with Automobile Manufacturers' Associations, and Automobile Owners' Associations can help in understanding the motor insurance industry better.

The international market will have to be watched with care. For instance, the Sarbanes Oxley Act (2002) of the USA made it mandatory for the senior management and business process owners to establish and maintain adequate internal control structures for their business ventures. In India, the Securities and Exchange Board of India (SEBI) came up with a corresponding regulation 49 in India. Experts predict a spurt in the demand for directors and officers (D&O) policies in the Indian market shortly.

Two modern innovative technologies that are making global rounds, viz. Parametric Insurance and trans-human insurance are yet to enter the Indian general insurance market. Parametric insurance is a type of insurance that does not indemnify the pure loss, but agrees in advance to make a payment upon the occurrence of a triggering event. The triggering event is often a catastrophic natural event that may ordinarily precipitate a loss or a series of losses. The attraction of parametric insurance that supplements traditional insurance recoveries lies in its commitment to pay for collateral damages that are not covered. The pay-out is a percentage of the recovery from a traditional insurance policy, the proceeds of which can be used as the policyholder sees fit. Both the Indian regulators and the general insurance companies have to realize the importance of such new technologies coming up in the international market.

Insurance industry in India is lagging behind its counterparts in the developed countries in fields such as risk management, loss prevention technique, non-life actuarial studies and arbitration.

Apart from the National Insurance Academy (NIA) situated at Pune, which provides short-term 'on-the-job' training in almost any insurance-related areas, there is no professional institution in India that specialists in risk management, teaches risk improvement techniques and promotes loss prevention as a science. NIA which is running an AICTE approved MBA programme with insurance as an area of specialization, has developed its own academic talent pool supported by industry experts who constitute its guest faculty. NIA has practically become the only specialized academic forum for holistic solutions for the insurance industry's academic needs. The academy has contributed to information technology and actuarial education apart from the traditional risk management and insurance areas.

In the 1980s and the 1990s, the Loss Prevention Association of India (LPAI), an origination totally owned by the public sector companies, had made some attempts in creating public awareness on the subject. The Indian Institute of Risk Management (IIRM) floated by a few corporate houses in the 1980s could not make any significant achievement in the field. The IIRM, Hyderabad is yet to make its mark in insurance academics. The institute of Actuaries of India (IAI) conducts actuarial courses for the industry leading to Associateship and Fellowship qualification. The Indian Insurance institute of India, one of the oldest institutions in the country for insurance academics, awards the licentiate associate and fellowship qualification in insurance. The Institute is headquartered in Mumbai and has local institutes in many states. The College of Insurance, Mumbai, a wing of the Insurance Institute of India concentrates mainly on conventional areas of insurance training designed for junior staff and officers. The process of liberalization in the insurance sector has created a substantial requirement of training for brokers and agents. A few private institutes have been established to cater to this need.

SUMMARY

After going through this chapter, the readers should be able to understand how the insurance market has developed into what it is today. Also, they should be able to recognize the importance of the insurance sector in the country's economy. This chapter would have also enabled them to appreciate the modern day developments in insurance market and familiarized them with the different constituents of the insurance market.

(1) The Malhotra Committee report recommended private participation and entry to foreign companies through joint ventures with Indian partners in both life and non-life insurance sectors. It prescribed a minimum paid-up capital for new insurers as not less than Rs. 100 crore. It recommended the establishment of a strong and effective Insurance Regulatory Authority (IRA). It recommended retention of all major tariffs, for some period of time, and progressive liberalization.

(2) The recommendations of Malhotra Committee were discussed across the country at different forums including the managements of the Life Insurance Corporation, the commerce world, industrialists and various consumer interest-groups. The Consultative Committee of the Parliament and the Ministry of Fianance also held discussions on the report of the Committee on reforms in insurance sector with various stakeholders in the market. After prolonged deliberations, the Government accepted the Committee's recommendation to set-up an autonomous interim insurance regulatory authority (IRA).

(3) Mr. N. Rangachari was appointed the Chairman of the interim IRA.

(4) As per the preamble, the IRDA act was created to provide for the establishment of an authority to protect the interest of holders of insurance policies, to regulate, promote and ensure orderly growth of the insurance industry, and for matters connected therewith.

(5) As per the Act, some of IRDA's functions are:
  (a) Issuing certificate of registration to the insurance companies,
  (b) Protection of the interests of the policyholders,
  (c) Specifying qualifications and code of conduct for insurance intermediaries and agents,
  (d) Specifying the code of conduct for surveyors and the loss assessors, and
  (e) Promoting and regulating professional organizations connected with the insurance and re-insurance business.

(6) The Authority is a body corporate having perpetual succession and common seal. It consists of a Chairperson and other members, not exceeding nine in number, of whom not more than five would serve full-time and no more than four would serve part-time, to be appointed by the Central Government from amongst persons of ability, integrity and standing who have knowledge or experience of life insurance, general insurance, actuarial science, finance, economics, law, accountancy, administration or any other discipline which, in the opinion of the Central Government, shall be useful to the Authority. As per the Act, the Chairperson would hold office for a term of five years or until the age of 65 years. The whole-time members would hold office for a term of five years or until the age of 62 years. A part-time member would hold office for a term not exceeding five years.

(7) IRDA has issued various regulations covering areas such as registration of companies, protection of policyholders, obligations of insurers to rural and social sectors, etc.

(8) The laws relating to the insurance market are spread beyond the Insurance Act and its amendments, over various Acts, Regulations, Circulars and Court judgments. As such, in response to the market request for review, the Government initiative involves removing incongruities and inconsistencies in the present framework and putting in place an integrated set of rules for the country.

(9) The Law Commission of the Government of India initiated the review process.

(10) The Law Commission's Report suggested that the following five specialized domain areas of the Insurance Act be deliberated upon by experts:
- (a) Provisions relating to investments,
- (b) Shareholders' funds and Policyholders' funds,
- (c) Sufficiency of Assets,
- (d) Insurance Surveyors, and
- (e) Tariff Advisory Committee (TAC).

(11) Some of the indicators of growth are:
- (a) Gross Domestic Product (GDP),
- (b) Performance of core intrastate industries such as crude petrol, petroleum refining, electricity, finished steel, cement and coal,
- (c) Index of industrial production, and
- (d) Performance of industry, manufacturing, mining, electricity and tele-communication sectors.

(12) The responsibility of providing insurance coverage for the nation's assets, trade and people is entrusted to the insurance companies which have to assess and accept the risks for insurers and reinsurers which apportion the risk that is beyond their retention capacity, in the international market. Rapid growth in these sectors demands corresponding growth in the insurance sector as well.

(13) GDP denotes Gross Domestic Product for the economy and Gross Direct Premium for the insurance market, currently Rs. 24, 993 crores.

(14) Health, motor owner damage, motor third party damage and personal accident are some areas that are poised for growth.

(15) The National Insurance Company Ltd., The New India Assurance Company Ltd., The Oriental Insurance Company Ltd., The United India Insurance Company Ltd. , The Reliance General Insurance Company Ltd., the IFFCO Tokyo General Insurance Company Ltd., The Tata AIG General Insurance Company Ltd. and the ICICI Lombard General Insurance Ltd. are a few of the companies operating in the Indian market.

(16) Regulators internationally use controls such as Prior Approval, Modified Prior Approval, Flex Rating, File and Use, Use and File, No File/Record Maintenance, State Prescribed, etc. to control insurance products.

(17) India uses a variant of 'File and Use' system with a specified waiting period as in the case of 'Prior Approval' category of products, where the products are deemed approved automatically if the regulator does not take any specific action during the waiting period. Usually, rate revisions under 'File and Use' are based solely on a change in loss experience, while in 'Modified Prior Approval' terms, the rate revision is based on a change in expense relationship and rate classification. Although guidelines on 'File and Use' norms have been set by the IRDA in India yet the system is still in an early stage and yet to develop as full-fledged regulation. The philosophy is that the players will be able to set their own rates and justify them.

(18) For scientific rating to be possibility, the market would need a substantial amount of transitional data of reasonable quality and accuracy. Both historical and contemporary data requires to be analyzed for making business decisions, product innovations, pricing, and effective claims management. Statistical databases for various classes of business detailing various segments based on nature of risk, type of insurance cover, and probable risk exposure would be needed for proper product pricing. This would be possible only with a robust IT back-bone and a centralized national data repository.

(19) Beyond the realms of product pricing and reserving, information technology and a data repository can be used for many purposes, such as claims management, risk management, fraud detection and for finding areas in the market where new products would be required. For instance, if there is a large gap between amounts claimed and paid for eye surgeries, the insurers can probably devise a product for the purpose with higher limits.

(20) In developed nations like the US and the UK, the insurers have been dissuaded from compiling similar data-banks owing to issues regarding the insurers' propriety rights. The insurers are guarded on issues of confidentially whether company specific information will get into the hands of competitors, whether their standards of service would get exposed, whether the insured's right to confidentiality of personal data get compromised, whether the data will expose the insurers' errors to regulatory scrutiny, etc.

(21) Two modern innovations in insurance are 'Parametric Insurance' and 'Trans-insurance' that are yet to enter the Indian general insurance market. Parametric insurance is a type of insurance that does not indemnify the pure loss, but agrees in advance to make a payment upon the occurrence of a triggering event. The triggering event is often a catastrophic natural event, which may ordinarily precipitate a loss or a series of losses. The attraction of parametric insurance for the insurers is the expected reduction in transition costs involved in loss assessment for payment of claims. Trans-human insurance is yet new form of insurance that supplements traditional insurance recoveries to pay for collateral damages. that are not covered. The pay-out is a percentage of the recovery from a traditional insurance policy, the proceeds of which can be used as the policyholder sees fit.

(22) The Sarbanes Oxley Act (2002) of the USA made it mandatory for the senior management and business process owners to establish and maintain adequate internal control structures for their business ventures. In India, the Securities and Exchange Board of India (SEBI) came up with a corresponding Regulation 49. As consequence thereof. The experts predict a spurt in the demand for Directors and Officers (D&O) policies in the Indian market any time.

(23) National Insurance Academy (NIA), situated at Pune provides short-term 'on-the-job' training in almost

any insurance related area; teaches risk management, risk improvement techniques and loss prevention. NIA is running an AICTE approved MBA programme with insurance as an area of specialization. The IIRM, Hyderabad, Institute of Actuaries of India, the Insurance Institute of India, which award, respectively, the Licentiate, Associate and Fellowship qualifications in Insurance, and a few Institutes established to train agents, approved by IRDA, are the main providers of insurance education in India.

SOME ACTS RELEVANT TO THE GENERAL INSURANCE MARKET

Apart from the Insurance Act, 1938 and the Insurance Rules made thereunder, the Insurance Regulatory and the Development Act, 1999, Regulations framed under the IRDA Act, and the General Insurance Business (Nationalization) Amendment Act, 2002 that directly focus on the conduct of insurance business, there are many miscellaneous pieces of legislation, which historically have influenced court judgments on non-life insurance, some of which are listed below:

(1) The Indian Fatal Accidents Act, 1865 deals with accidents and liability to various parties.

(2) The Carriers Act, 1865 with amendments of 1993 defines the rights and liabilities of common carriers engaged in the business of transporting on hire, property from place to place by land or inland navigation.

(3) The Insurance (Marine and Fire) Assignment Act, 1886 deals with assignment of insurance policies.

(4) The Indian Contract Act, 1872 sets the rules on validity and enforceability of insurance contracts.

(5) The Transfer of Property Act, 1882 and its Amendment Act, 1944 set rules on assignment of Insurance policies.

(6) The Marine Insurance Act, 1906 defines concepts of insurance such as description of subject-matter and extent of interest.

(7) The Indian Ports Act, 1908 and the Major Port Trusts Act, 1963 spell out the laws relating to port charges, safety in shipping, safety in Indian ports, etc. The Act contains several provisions for conservation of ports and prescribes penalties for infringements.

(8) The Marine Insurance (Gambling Policies) Act, 1909 differentiates between bona-fide insurance contracts and wager arrangements.

(9) The Indian Companies Act, 1913 contains the rules relating to formation of companies.

(10) The Workmen's Compensation Act, 1923 speaks about employers' liability, compensation to workmen and insurance protection.

(11) The Carriage of Goods by Sea Act, 1925 covers carriage of goods by sea between any port in India and any other port in India or abroad, establishes the responsibility, liabilities, rights and immunities attaching to carriers, and is largely aligned to the recommendations of the international conferences on Maritime Law.

(12) The Law of Property Act, 1925 speaks about exercising subrogation rights over contract breakers/ tort flab. The Indian Sales of Goods Act, 1930 specifies details on transfer of ownership, contracts of sale, etc.

(13) The Law Reforms (Miscellaneous Provision) Act, 1934 sets the rules on rights of legal heirs of accident victims.

(14) The Motor Vehicles Act, 1939 (amending Indian Companies Act, 1862) deals with formation and ownership of companies.

(15) The Companies Act, 1956 (amending Indian Companies Act, 1882) deals with formation and ownership of companies.

(16) The Merchant Shipping Act, 1958 and its amendments from time to time keep Indian shipping (and related insurance) in line with international conventions in matters such as liabilities of ships and ship owners, collisions, limitation of liability for maritime claims, and make insurance mandatory for certain types of ships.

(17) The Emergency Risks (Goods) Insurance Act, 1962 which was framed in the wake of the Chinese aggression, provides for compulsory insurance against emergency risks to person carrying on business in India as a seller or suppliers of goods, if the insurable value of such goods lying in the same residency town or district exceeds Rs. 30, 000. The Act was intended to provide indemnity against loss or damage due to enemy action.

(18) The Emergency Risks (Factories) Insurance Act, 1962, which was also framed in the wake of the Chinese aggression, provides for compulsory insurance against emergency risks of all factories falling within the purview of the Factories Act, 1948. For standing tea crops, inland vessels, plant, machinery and equipment of mines and oil companies, distribution system of fast supply undertakings, and the whole of the generation, distribution and transmission systems of hydroelectric and electric systems, this Act, like its twin, was intended for providing indemnity against or damage due to enemy action.

(19) The Marine Insurance Act, 1963, based substantially on the similar English Act of 1906, governs transactions of marine insurance in India. It defines marine insurance and includes perils incidental to local or inland transit also within its scope. The Act defines many insurance concepts such as insurable interest, insurable value, and disclosure by the assured, valued policy, unvalued policy, flatting policy, double insurance, warranties and assignment of policy, actual total loss, constructive total loss, general average loss, general average contributions, salvage charges, liability to third parties, etc., and prohibits wagering contracts.

(20) The Carriage by Air Act, 1972, applies to international carriage of goods and passengers. It fixes the liability of the carrier for injury or death of passengers and loss of or damage to goods.

(21) The Consumer Protection Act, 1986 deals with consumer rights, product supplers' liability and the insured persons' rights as consumers.

(22) The Railways Act, 1989, holds railway administration responsible for the loss, destruction, damage, deterioration or non-delivery in transit, to the consignee.

(23) The Multi-modal Transportation of Goods Act, 1993 regulates the business of multi modal transportation of goods from any place in India to a place outside India on the basis of a multi-modal transport contract. As per the Act, a multi-modal transport operator is liable for loss of or damage to the consignment.

(24) The Environment Protection Act, 1986 makes entrepreneurs duty bound to protect the environment and responsible for liabilities attaching in case of degradation of the environment due to negligence and/or hazardous activities.

(25) The Arbitration and Conciliation Act, 1996 (in amendment of the Indian arbitration Act, 1940) specifies the arbitration provisions in insurance contracts.

(26) The redressal of Public Grievance Act and Rules, 1998 requires general and life insurance companies to resolve complaints relating to the settlement of claim in a cost-effective, efficient and impartial manner through grievance redressal machinery. The Act is the basis of the Ombudsman system.

(27) The Right to Information Act, 2005 requires public authorities to maintain the records, duly catalogued, and make information on maters that affect the public accessible to the affected persons.

Insurance Forms

INTRODUCTION

This chapter introduces the importance of the forms used in the insurance industry. It also familiarizes you with the purpose and contents of the forms. For better clarity, the forms have been grouped into two categories: (a) those connected with the insurance contract, and (b) those relating to the insurers and intermediaries establishments, and include other documents.

Importance of Forms in Insurance

The insurance contract is said to be a matter of solicitation. This conventionally means that the buyer of insurance asks for the cover and the insurer gives it to him. The agent is seen as an insurance advisor, advising the insured on the right type of insurance he requires for his protection. In the Chinese market, 'insurance solicitor' is the term used for employees who procure business for the insurers, implying that the insurer is soliciting the business. In actual practice, solicitation covers the communication process before the insurance contract is entered into; this implies the accountability of the insured and the insurer to the contract that comes into effect. This process can be broken up as follows:

(1) The insured and the insurer (or his representative) have been introduced to each other,
(2) The need of the insured for risk management has been conveyed to the insurer,
(3) The insurer has explained the insurance product and its benefits to the insured, and
(4) Before entering into the contract, both the parties have (especially the insured has) arrived at a reasonable clarity on the scope and reach of the contract, making them accountable to whatever they are doing.

Often, this process involves a dialogue or a series of dialogues and reading of literature about the insurance product to enable the insured to understand the product. Till this time, the communication is mostly verbal. Once the insured decides to purchase the insurance, he has to formally offer his risk to the insurer for insurance cover. From this point onwards, there are a number of forms that are used by the insurance industry with some variations as regards the contents and composition, depending on the market traditions and the regulatory requirements.

Forms Relating to the Contract of Insurance—Purpose and Constituents

Forms are important for reducing ambiguity in the complex and different kinds of insurance covers within each type, different terms and conditions relating to the covers, and policy-to-policy differences make insurance contracts complex. Insurance contracts touch people from all walks of life; the same type of cover is given to meet the needs of different industries. The contracts sometimes need to be honoured across different countries. From a policyholder's protection point of view, many of the insured may not be able to understand the terms and conditions of the documents completely. When a claim is not paid, he would feel that he was given a raw deal as he did not understand the fine print in the policy. It is also possible that some insurers resort to abortive policy wordings to deprive the insured of some types of claims. Unless the contents are standardized, there would be total chaos and everyone would feel that the insurers, who have drafted the forms, have cheated the insured. It is, therefore, important for the insurers that the forms are transparent and trusted as clean documents.

Transparency and clarity can be achieved only when the people who deal with the terminologies used in the forms, contextual meaning of the constituents of the forms, and the purpose that a form serves first themselves understand and then explain in the simplest possible language, known to the insured. Standardization of forms and terms is to ensure that in the insurance market and in all insurance transactions, all speak the same language and all understand the same meaning that is conveyed. The purposes, contents and importance of some of the forms are discussed below

PROPOSAL FORM

As we saw above, once the solicitation and the process of understanding of the terms of the insurance product *vis-a-vis* the risk are over and the insured decides to purchase the insurance, he has to formally offer the risk to the insurer for insurance cover. This is done using a standardized printed form called the proposal form, filled in by the proposer. The insurer indicates his willingness to accept the proposal and quotes a premium for the cover. Once the negotiations between the insurer and the proposer are completed and the insurer accepted the proposal, and accordingly the premium is paid or an agreement is effected to pay the premium, the contract is completed and becomes effective. All further documentation is only the evidence of the contract and not the contract itself.

The proposal form is the basic document that include the risk to be insured. It is a printed document with a set of questions designed to elicit all information about the particular risk proposed for insurance. Proposal forms are used in most of he branches of insurance. Yet, they are traditionally not used in some branches of insurance. However, traditions differ from market to market. In marine cargo insurance, it is normal to get a questionnaire form filled in, instead. In fire insurance, proposal forms are generally not used for very large industrial risks where risk inspection is carried out before acceptance of risk.

The contents of a proposal form for a particular type of insurance would have certain common features but would vary from market to market or from company to company. The common features of different proposal forms are discussed below:

(1) *Name and address of the proposer*: This would be a basic necessity for identification of the proposer.
(2) *Age, gender and occupation of the proposer*: In personal lives, these may have a bearing on the risk.
(3) *Details of previous insurances*: The insurance history of the proposer and details of situations where insurance was denied to him in the past or special conditions in terms of cover and premium imposed on him are important for the insurer.
(4) *Details of present insurance*: In insurance where a contribution clause is applicable, details of other policies that exist at the same time are important to the insurer.
(5) *Loss experience*: Information on past losses helps the insurer to evaluate the risk better.
(6) *Period of Insurance*: This is vital for the commencement and expiry of the contract.
(7) *Sum Insured*: In most policies, this is the maximum liability of the insurer and the basis on which the premium is calculated. In case of medical reimbursement policies, it would be the maximum amount payable in case of a claim.
(8) *Comments and Recommendations of the counsellor/agent*: In some cases, comments/recommendations of the agent are to be indicated in the proposal form.
(9) *Declaration*: Proposal forms contain a declaration whereby the proposer informs that the information contained in the form is true to the best of his knowledge and belief.
(10) *Warning or Important Note*: This is printed in the format by the insurer, informing the proposer that all facts have to be disclosed and inviting his attention to some of the most relevant facts. The proposer is prompted to reveal facts even if he is not sure whether they are material or not. The note cautions the proposer of the dangers of non-disclosure.

Rebate: Rebates refer to the part of the premium or the commission that is paid back to the insured as an incentive or inducement to buy the policy. Section 41 of the Insurance Act, 1938 prohibits payment of rebates and requires that this prohibition on offering, paying or accepting rebates be incorporated in the proposal forms itself.

(11) *Proposer's Signature and Date*: These are basic requirements for all written contracts.

Commercial or Business Lines of Insurance

For commercial lines of business, the proposal form would have questions specific to the particular line of business in addition to the general information applicable to personal lives. The major differences are discussed below:

(1) The name and address of the proposer becomes those of the corporate entity.
(2) The description of the trade or business would be asked for.
(3) The type of activity carried out in the property proposed for fire insurance is important for estimating the probability of risk.
(4) The type of construction and details of fire protection appliances in a factory are collected.
(5) The basis on which the premium is calculated is asked for. In case of property insurance, the sum insured will be the value of the building and its contents. In marine hull, the sum insured would be the value of the hull and machinery, freight and disbursements.
(6) In motor insurance, details such as the age of the vehicles, its cubic capacity, accident history, driver's data, and geographical area of usage are asked for.
(7) The marine cargo questionnaire asks for details of the shipper or client, description of the goods and the packing. Mode of voyage or transit name of steamer, and sum insured.
(8) In hull insurance, the period of insurance can be the voyage period or a specific period. Details of the age and the tonnage of the vessel, details of other vessels in the fleet, etc. are asked for.

The thumb rule followed in the market is to collect maximum information on the risk that would help the insurer in understanding and rating it properly, while keeping the questions simple enough so that the proposer is able to understand and answer all of them with reasonable accuracy and conviction.

The Cover Note

As we have seen while discussing the proposal form, once the decision to insure is taken by insured, the insurer accepts the proposal and accordingly the premium is paid or an agreement is effected to pay the premium, the contract becomes complete and effective. Further documentation is only the evidence of the contract and not the contract itself.

The insurer, by the policy Document, conveys the evidence of the cover coming into force. Pending the preparation of the policy or in some cases, where traditionally an interim proof is required, an interim form called cover note is required. A letter confirming the cover can substitute the cover note.

In other words, a Cover Note is a document issued by the insurer in advance of the policy as evidence that the cover is in force. In some cases, even after assumption of risk, it may be to finalize some finer points of the cover. In some contexts, after assuming cover, the negotiations would still be on. There are situations where elaborate schedules have to be prepared along with the policy documents. Also, the insured may have to prove to different parties that the insurance is in force. In motor insurance, the existence of the cover has to be proven to the authorities, in marine cargo to the consignees, and in various cases to the banks. The cover note comes in handy for tiding over all such situations and in some cases, the insurer issues documents, which get superseded once the policy is issued.

In the context of life insurance also, the insurer issues a similar letter. This letter of acceptance, which the insurer issues after receiving the proposal form, is actually an offer to the proposer, and the risk is assumed only after the payment of premium is made accordingly. In non-life, in covers such as motor, the cover is in force once the cover note has been issued and the premium may yet have to be paid.

The cover note would have the following components:

(1) Identity of the insurer issuing the cover note.
(2) Serial number of the cover note.
(3) Date of issue.
(4) Name and address of the insured.
(5) Sum insured.
(6) Period of insurance—dates of commencement and expiry.
(7) Risk covered would be stated.
(8) Rate and premium applicable to the risk: In cases where the rates have not been finalized, the provisional rate would be mentioned.
(9) Details of the risk covered: Such as particulars of the building, its construction and occupancy will be mentioned.
(10) The prohibition of rebates wording as per Section 41 of the Insurance Act, 1938, has to be incorporated in the cover note.
(11) In the case of motor, the cover note would contain details such as the registration number, description of the vehicle, cubic capacity, carrying capacity, make and year of manufacture, person or class of persons entitled to drive, and limitation of usage, in addition to the above will be mentioned.
(12) In motor, the cover note is issued for a period of 15 days, extendable by further 15 days period; in all not exceeding two months.
(13) The motor cover note would incorporate a certificate that it is issued in accordance with the provisions of the Motor Vehicles Act, 1988 (Chapters X and XI).
(14) In marine cargo, cover notes are usually required for insuring imports, where details such as the name of the vessel, number and exact value of packages sent, are not known. In exports, too, there can be situations where and the exact value of the consignments that would go by a particular vessel may not be available. Marine cover notes would hence incorporate: (1) the Marine Cover Note number, (2) the date of issue, (3) name of the insured, (4) validity period with start and

end dates, (5) sum insured, (6) clauses attaching, and (7) conditions applicable.

(15) Operative clauses are incorporated in the cover note for clarity. Some examples are given below:

(a) *Fire*: "In consideration of the proposer named in the schedule hereto having proposed to effect an insurance against Fire for the period mentioned therein, on the usual terms and conditions of this company's policies and having paid/made a deposit against/furnished bank guarantee in respect of the premium stated in the schedule, the property as described in the schedule is hereby insured to the extent of the sum insured mentioned therein".

(b) *Marine*: "As requested, you are hereby held covered subject to usual conditions of the company's policy to the extent of Rs. ______ clauses applicable (quoted) and Conditions as applicable (quoted)".

(c) *Motor*: "The insured described in the form referred to below, having proposed for insurance in respect of the motor vehicles(s) described therein and having paid the sum of Rs. ______ as premium, the risk is hereby held covered under the term of the company's usual form of ______ policy applicable thereto (subject to any special conditions mentioned below) unless the cover be terminated by the company by notice in writing in which case, the insurance will thereupon cease and a proportionate part of the premium otherwise payable for such insurance will be charged for the time the company had been on risk".

(d) Additional safety clause is used in some cases by some companies. The cover note is issued pending preparation and issue of a duly stamped policy of insurance, and should the terms and conditions of this company's policy be unknown to the proposer, it shall be incumbent upon him to request the company for a copy of such terms and conditions. Failure to comply with the policy terms and conditions due to the insured being unacquainted with them shall not excuse his failure to act in accordance herewith. By the acceptance of this cover note, the proposer binds himself by the terms and conditions of this company's policy.

(16) A cover Note does not require to be stamped. Nevertheless, it is acted as valid and representing the policy document. Where the insurance is subject to any special clause or condition, the same is mentioned in the cover note.

FORM OF COVER NOTE

Motor Vehicle Insurance
Cover Note No. __________

The insured described in form '52' referred to below, having proposed for insurance in respect of Motor Vehicle(s) described therein and having paid the sum of Rs. _______ as premium, the risk is hereby held covered under the terms of the company's usual form of ____ policy applicable thereto (subject to any special condition mentioned below) unless the cover is terminated by the company by notice in writing; in which case, the insurance will thereupon cease and a proportionate part of the premium otherwise payable for such insurance shall be charged for the time the company had been at risk.

Make and Reg. No. of the Vehicle	*Year of Manufacture*	*Cubic capacity*	*Gross Vehicle weight (GVW) (Goods Carrying Vehicle)*	*Licensed Carrying Capacity (LCC) (Passenger Carrying Vehicle)*	*Insured's Declared Value (DV)*	
					For Vehicle Rs.	For Accessories not included in Manufacturer's Listed Selling Price.

Engine No. ______ Chassis No. ____________

Additional Risks, if any ___________

Special Conditions ______________

Form 52
(See Rule 142(1) of Motor Vehicle Rules, 1989)

(1) Registration mark and number of description of the vehicle insured ____

(2) Name and address of insured __________

(3) Effective date and time of commencement
Time _______

of insurance for the purpose of this Act
Date _______

(4) Date of expiry of insurance ______________

(5) Persons or classes of persons entitled to drive _______________

(6) Any limitation as to use of motor vehicle _______

(7) The period of validity of this cover note will expire on ________

I/we hereby certify that this Cover Note is issued in accordance with the provisions of Chapter XI of the Motor Vehicles Act, 1988.

Certificate of Insurance

In the case of compulsory insurance, such as motor, third party's or employer's liability, the law makes it mandatory for the insurers to issue a Certificate of Insurance. The content of such certificates are usually spelt out in the applicable law itself. The certificate needs to be produced or displayed as prescribed by the law applicable.

Specimen copy of the Certificate of Insurance prescribed for passenger carrying vehicles is given below:

Passenger Carrying Vehicle

CERTIFICATE OF INSURANCE

Policy No. __________ Certificate No. __________

Particulars of Vehicle insured:

Reg. Mark, No. and Place of Regis-tration	Engine No. and Chassis No.	Make	Year of Manu-facture	Type of Body	C.c.	Max. licensed Carrying Capacity incl. Driver Cleaner	Premium (Rs)

GEOGRAPHICAL AREA, INDIA

Name and Address of Insured:

Effective date of commencement of insurance for the purpose of the Act.

From __________ O' Clock on __________

Date of expiry of the insurance, Midnight on ________

Persons or Classes of Persons entitled to Drive

Any person including insured is entitled to drive:

Provided that a person driving the vehicle holds an effective driving licence at the time of the accident and is not disqualified from holding or obtaining such a licence. Provided also that the person holding an effective learner's license may also drive the vehicle when not used for the transport of passengers at the time of the accident and that such a person satisfies the requirements of Rule 3 of the Central Motor Vehicles Rules, 1989.

Limitation as to Use

The Policy covers use only under a permit within the meaning of the Motor Vehicle Act, 1988 or such a carriage falling under sub-section (3) of Section 66 of the Motor Vehicle Act, 1988.

The Policy does not cover use for:

(1) Organized racing.
(2) Pace-making.
(3) Reliability Trials.
(4) Speed Testing.
(5) Use whilst drawing a trailer except the towing (other than for reward) of any one disabled mechanically propelled vehicle.

I/We hereby certify that the Policy to which the certificate relates as well as this Certificate of Insurance, are issued in accordance with the provision of Chapter X and Chapter XI of M.V. Act, 1988.

Date of Issue:

Address of issuing Office:

(Duly Constituted Attorney(s))

FORM OF POLICY DOCUMENT

While discussing the proposal form and cover note, we have seen that the policy document is the formal document that provides the evidence of the contract of insurance. This document needs to be stamped as per provisions of the Indian Stamp Act, 1899. Wherever a tariff is applicable, the policy wordings prescribed by the tariff setting body are to be used. In case of 'File and Use' regulation, the policy format filed as part of the contract and prescribed by the regulator has to be adopted/adhered to. In some classes of insurance, the policy schedule is used along with the policy form. The schedules are specific to the particular contract while the rest of the contract would be general in nature and applicable to all insurances under the particular branch.

The components of the policy form are listed below:

(1) **Heading:** The identity of the insurer and address of his registered office.

(2) **Preamble or Recital Clause:** Essentially, the preamble normally covers four aspects:
   (a) Parties to the contract—the insured and the insurer are introduced.
   (b) Basis of the contract—the proposal/proposal form with the declaration is brought into the picture.
   (c) Consideration for the contract—the payment of the premium is acknowledged.
   (d) Reference to the insurance sought—the fact that the contract relates to a particular type of insurance cover is mentioned.

(3) **Operative Clause:** This is the most important part of the policy, conveying the promise that the insurer is giving to the insured. Some policies use direct wordings, such as "The Company will indemnify ....., for conveying the promise. The clause specifies the perils insured under the policy, the sum insured or other limits of liability, and the circumstances under which the loss would be payable. If the insurance is subject to specific terms, conditions or exclusions, a reference is drawn to the same in the operative clause. The operative clause spells out exactly what the company promises to do. Hence, in some policies, it requires to be divided into various sections.

(4) **Exception:** The set of exceptions to the cover granted by the policy is clearly spelt out under this clause. The exclusions specify the circumstances under which the claim will not be payable. Exceptions can be general in nature, applicable to the type of insurance or applicable to the whole policy. Where the operative clause is divided into various sections, the exceptions may also be section specific.

(5) **Policy Schedule:** In classes of insurance such as fire and accident insurance, the policy schedule is used

along with the policy form. The schedule is a part of the policy that is specific to the particular contract, while the rest of it would be pre-printed and applicable to all insurances under the particular branch. It refers to the personal part or the risk-specific part of the particular insurance contract. The schedule would normally carry information on the following:

(a) Insured's name.
(b) Insured's address.
(c) Policy number.
(d) Date of issue.
(e) Agency identity.
(f) Period of insurance.
(g) Property insured/risk covered.
(h) Sum insured/limit of liability.
(i) Amount of premium (the rate of premium).
(j) Reference to specific conditions, exclusions or aspects of the cover.

(6) *Definition of Terms*: All the terms/jargons (words having special meanings in the context of the insurance) are listed out in a separate section of the policy form.

(7) *Conditions*: Policies contain a list of conditions that are printed on the policy. These are called express conditions found in some or other part of the policy, insurance principles—some to market practices, some to legal principles—while some would be clarifying or modifying these principles. Conditions are usually grouped into three types, viz.,

(a) Conditions precedent meaning disclosure of all material facts before concluding the contract. A breach of this condition allows the insurance company to avoid the policy from its commencement itself (ab initio).
(b) Conditions subsequent—meaning changes/alterations to the risk during the currency of the policy. A breach of this condition allows the insurer to avoid the policy after the breach has come into force.

(c) Conditions precedent to liability—procedure to be followed and time limit. Breaches in this area may prevent the insured from recovering a particular loss from the insurer, even if the policy continues to be in operation for subsequent claims.

Some of the common conditions in use are intended to convey the following ideas using appropriate wordings:

(a) The insured will comply with all terms of the policy.

(b) The insured will notify the insurer of any changes to the risk.

(c) The insured is aware of the implications of fraud.

(d) The insured will notify claims within a particular time and certain prescribed procedures would be followed.

(e) The insured will take due care of the insured risk and take all reasonable efforts to minimize the loss in the event of a loss. (In such situations, the insured should act as if he were not insured).

(f) Disputes on the amount of claim are open to arbitration (if the insurer accepts that the claim is payable).

(g) How the condition of contribution will apply if there are other policies in force covering the same loss.

(h) Situations when the policy can be cancelled.

(i) In declaration type of policies, the premium has to be adjusted at the end of the year based on declarations on the actual sum insured. Procedures for making such declarations and adjustment of the premium are spelt out in the conditions.

(8) **Implied Condition:** Apart from the express conditions mentioned above, there are certain implied conditions that are not spelt out on the policy form. These implied conditions are based on the principles of utmost good faith and insurable interest that we

have seen in the previous chapters:

(a) The subject matter of insurance actually exists.
(b) The subject matter of insurance can be identified.
(c) The insured has insurable interest in the subject-matter of insurance.
(d) The contract and the negotiations leading to it have been based on the principle of utmost good faith.

(9) **Co-insurance Clause:** When there are different insurers to co-insuring the risk, the policy has to be suitably worded a per accepted market practices. A leading insurer or the insurer with the largest share could do the entire documents and record the share of the others on the policy form. One model uses a co-insurance clause. In a collective policy model, one policy could be issued and all the co-insurers would sign the document for their respective shares. In the collective insurance clause model, only the leading insurer would sign the policy with the necessary internal documentation. In any of the models, there has to be an appropriate wording in the policy document.

(10) **Interpretation:** The policy document has to be constructed in such a way that the intention of the policy is clear from the policy itself. The policy is drafted by the insurers, and in case of any ambiguity, courts would naturally tend to favour the insured. Hence, care is taken in clarifying matters related to the policy, in the document itself. The general logic that is followed in such cases is:

(a) As far as possible, printed and written/typed portions of the policy are to be construed together unless there is a contradiction; in case of contradiction, the written/typed portion (understood as written later to clarify the position) overrides the printed portion,
(b) The policy is to be interpreted as a whole, giving effect to every part of the policy, to the extent possible,
(c) Wordings in the policy will have their plain, ordinary and popular meanings; technical words will have their strict technical meaning, and
(d) The ordinary rules of grammar will apply.

(11) **Renewal Notice:** The policies usually incorporate a clause on the renewal of the policy, emphasizing that payment of the premium by the insured and acceptance thereof by the insurer are required for the cover to continue beyond the dates stipulated in the policy. In some cases, the preamble of the policy states that the indemnity under the policy applies.
"During the period of insurance named in the schedule or any subsequent period, in respect of which the insured shall have paid and the insurers shall have accepted the premium required for renewal of the policy".

(12) **Attestations or Signature Clause:** The policy document has to be duly signed by an officer of the company who is authorized by the competent authority to enter into a contract on behalf of the insurance company.

(13) **Endorsements:** Changes to the standard form of the policy at the commencement or alterations to the policy are recorded as annexure to the policy document. Recordings of such alterations are called endorsements. Tinkering of the policy document for accommodating such alterations can cause confusions in drafting and legal complications. Hence, the insurers use standard wordings for the changes that they can normally expect. Tariffs usually prescribe endorsement wordings as well. Endorsements normally relate to the following situations:

(a) Variations of sum insured.
(b) Change of insurable interest by way of sale, mortgage, etc.
(c) Inclusions/Exclusions or additional perils.
(d) Change in the risk itself (physical modifications to a building, different processes inside a factory, change in mode of shipment, etc.).
(e) Transfer of property to another location.
(f) Changes in name or address of the insured.
(g) Cancellation of insurance.

To enable the students to understand how the different aspects that are discussed above are actually woven into a policy form, a copy of the standard form of two-wheeler package policy used in the Indian market is given as Appendix I.

FORMS RELATING TO THE PROVIDERS' ESTABLISHMENT

The importance of insurance to the society and the inherent nature of insurance business were reflected in the various formats prescribed by regulators relating to registration of insurance companies, licensing of agents and brokers, approval of products, filing, accounting, statistical returns and other statements/documents. Some of the forms prescribed by the IRDA for use in the Indian market are discussed below.

Forms Relating to the Insurers' Licensing

As per IRDA—Registration of Indian Insurance Companies Regulations, 2000—an applicant desiring to carry on insurance business in India shall make a "Requisition for Registration Application" in form IRDA/R-I. The contents of the form are listed in Annexure.

Other Intermediaries: The IRDA has prescribed forms for other classes of intermediaries, such as surveyors and loss assessors' and agents' training institutes, on similar lines. Details of these are available in the relevant IRDA Regulations. They are not discussed here.

Forms Relating to Product Approval

As per the guidelines for 'Filing and Use' approvals, the IRDA has prescribed formats for submitting insurance products for approval.

The format seeks the information on the following heads from the insurers:

(1) Product to be identified.
(2) Product features.
(3) Marketing plans.
(4) Underwriting philosophy and claims arrangements.
(5) Actuarial support.
(6) Details of rates and terms.

(7) Details of sales literature and other documents.
(8) Certificate of authorized compliance officer as to the product being in line with the corporate underwriting and rating philosophy.
(9) Certificate of actuary regarding the policy design, rates and projections.
(10) Certificate of lawyer regarding the wordings used and regulatory compliances.

Forms Relating to Statistical Data Submission

As per IRDA's Circular of November 2006 on Data Collection by TAC post de-tariffing of the general insurance products, the IRDA has emphasized the need for data for both the insurer and the regulator. Efforts for collecting authentic and error-free data at the Tariff Advisory Committee's national data repository have been strengthened by invoking provisions of Section 64UE of the Insurance Act, 1938, which *inter-alia* authorize the TAC to require and collect information, etc. The data repository-work at the TAC focused initially on the motor and health insurance segments, and the TAC has prescribed 15 formats for data collection covering different areas of insurance. Non-submission of data could attract penalties according to the IRDA Circular under reference.

These formats with the detailed data dictionaries defining each granule of insurance data at the transaction level are too voluminous to be discussed here. These formats are available at the TAC's website http://www.tac.org.in

Other Forms/Documents

Different formats have been prescribed by IRDA for submission of accounts and disclosure of financial information as per the relevant regulations. These have been appropriately discussed in detail in the book "Financial Management and Insurance Accounting". Similarly, the formats relating to different actuarial reports are discussed in the book "Elements of Actuarial Science". Claims-related documents are discussed in the Chapter on claims: Practices and Procedure. There are a few other documents in the realm of insurance, which though important, may not follow standardized contents or wordings; these cover notices of renewal of policies, surrender/ termination/cancellation of the insurance contract, etc.

SUMMARY

This Chapter has hopefully familiarized readers with various forms used in the insurance industry. The readers have learnt the importance of using standardized forms in the insurance market. They should be able to recognize some of the commonly used forms such as Proposal Forms, Cover Notes and Policy Forms, understand the purpose served by them, and identify the major constituents of these forms.

(1) Once the solicitation and the process of understanding of the terms of the insurance product *vis-à-vis* the risk are over and the insured decides to purchase the insurance, he has to formally offer the risk to the insurer for issuance cover. Although till this stage, communication can be verbal yet the formal offer is done using a standardized printed form called the proposal form filled in by the proposer.

(2) Standardization of forms is important for reducing ambiguity in the complex insurance market. Standardization of forms and terms are to ensure that in the insurance market and in all insurance transactions, all speak the same language and all understand the same meaning that is conveyed.

(3) Different types of insurances, different kinds of covers within each type, different terms and conditions relating to the covers, and policy to policy differences make insurance contract complex. Insurance contracts touch people from all walks of life; the same type of cover is given to cover the needs of different industries, and contract sometimes needs to be honoured across different countries. Unless the contents are standardized, there would be total chaos and everyone would feel that the insurer, who has drafted the forms, has cheated the insured. Transparency and clarity can be achieved only when the people who deal with the insurers, everyone in the insurance industry and the courts are clear regarding the terminologies used in the forms,

contextual meaning of the constituents of the forms, and the purpose that forms serve. Hence, all need to speak the same language and understand the same meaning that is conveyed.

(4) The proposal form is filled in by the proposer to formally offer the risk to the insurer for insurance cover. The proposal form is the basic document that introduces the risk to the insurer. It is a printed document with a set of questions designed to elicit all information about the particular risk proposed for insurance. Proposal forms are used in most of the branches of insurance, though it is not mandatory in all insurances.

(5) (a) Name and address of the proposer.
 (b) Age, gender and occupation of the proposer.
 (c) Details of previous insurance.
 (d) Details of present insurance.
 (e) Loss experience.
 (f) Period of insurance.
 (g) Sum insured.

(6) Proposal forms are used in most of the branches of insurance like motor, houses, liability, etc. Proposal forms are traditionally not used in marine cargo insurance, proposal forms are generally not used for very large industrial risk where risk inspection by the insurer is carried out before acceptance of a risk.

(7) **Declaration:** Proposal forms contain a declaration whereby the proposer confirms that the information contained in the form is true to the best of his knowledge and belief.

(8) **Warning or important note:** This is printed in the format by the insurer informing the proposer that all facts have to be disclosed and inviting his attention to some of the most relevant facts. The proposer is prompted to reveal facts. Even if he is not sure whether they are material or not, the note cautions the proposer of the dangers of non-disclosure.

(9) **Rebate:** Rebate refers to the part of the premium or the commission that is paid back to the insured as an incentive or inducement to buy the policy. Section 41

of Insurance Act 1938, prohibits payment of rebates and requires that this prohibition on offering, paying or accepting rebates be incorporated in the proposal form itself.

(10) Pending the preparation of the policy or in some cases, where traditionally an interim proof is required, an interim form called 'cover note' is issued. A letter confirming the cover can substitute the cover note. In some cases, the insured may have to prove to different parties that the insurance is in force. The cover note comes in handy for tiding over all such situations.

(11) A cover note is a document issued by the insurer in advance of the policy as evidence that the cover is in force. In some cases, even after assuming cover, the terms of the deal may not have been fully concluded as an inspection may be due to finalize some finer points of the cover. Also, after assuming cover, the negotiations could still be on. There are situations where elaborate schedules have to be prepared along with the policy document. Also, the insured may have to prove to different parties that the insurance is in force. In motor, the existence of the cover has to be proven to the authorities—in marine cargo, to the consignees and in various cases to the banks. The cover note comes in handy for tiding over all such situations and in some cases, the insurer issues a letter confirming the cover, instead.

(12) (a) Identity of the insurer issuing the cover note.
(b) Serial Number of the cover note.
(c) Date of issue.
(d) Name and address of the insured.
(e) Sum insured.
(f) Period of insurance, dates of commencement and expiry.
(g) Rate of premium applicable to the risk.

(13) Marine cover notes would incorporate:
(a) Marine cover note number.
(b) Date of issue.
(c) Name of the insured.
(d) Validity period with start and end dates.

(e) Sum insured.
(f) Clauses attaching.
(g) Conditions applicable.

(14) (a) Registration mark/number/description of the vehicle insured.
(b) Name and address of the insured.
(c) Effective date and item of commencement of issuance.
(d) Date of expiry of insurance.
(e) Persons or classes of persons entitled to drive.
(f) Any limitation as to the use of the motor vehicle.

(15) Operative clauses are incorporated in the cover note for clarity. The clauses state the scope of insurance in a nutshell.

(16) In the case of compulsory insurances such as motor third-party, employer's liability, etc., the law makes it mandatory for the insurers to issue a certificate of insurance. The contents of the certificates are usually spelt out in the applicable law itself. The certificate needs to be produced or displayed, as prescribed by the law applicable.

(17) (a) Policy No.
(b) Certificate No.
(c) Particulars of vehicle insured,
(d) Geographical Area.
(e) Name and address of the insured.
(f) Effective date of commencement of insurance.
(g) Limitation to use.

(18) (a) Heading.
(b) Preamble or Recital clause.
(c) Operative clause.
(d) Exceptions.
(e) Policy schedule.
(f) Insured's name and address.
(g) Policy number.
(h) Date of issue.

(19) The operative clause is the most important part of the policy, conveying the promise that the insurer is giving to the insured. The clause specifies the perils insured under the policy, the sum insured or other

limits of liability, and the circumstances under which the loss would be payable. The operative clause spells out clearly what the company promises to do.

(20) Policies contain a list of conditions, which are printed on the policy. These are called express conditions found in some or other part of the policy and need not be available in one cluster. Some of the conditions refer to basic insurance principles, some to the market practices, some to the legal principles, while some more would be clarifying or modifying these principles.

(21) Apart from the express conditions, there are certain implied conditions that are not spelt out on the policy form. These implied conditions are based on the principles of utmost good faith and insurable interest. For instance, it is implied that the subject-matter of insurance actually exists, the subject-matter of insurance can be identified, the insured has insurable interest in the subject-matter of insurance, and the contract and the negotiations leading to its finality/conclusion have been based on the principle of utmost good faith.

(22) One model used is the co-insurers for the proportion insured by them. They issue separate policies with a co-insurance clause. In a collective policy model, one policy could be issued and all the co-insurers would sign the document for their respective shares. In the collective insurance clause model, only the leading insurer would sign the policy with the necessary internal documentation.

(23) Endorsements are normally related to the following situations:
   (a) Variation of sum insured.
   (b) Change of insurable interest by way of sale, mortgage, etc.
   (c) Inclusion/Exclusion of additional perils.
   (d) Change in the risk itself, such as transfer of property to another location.
   (e) Change in name or address of the insured.
   (f) Cancellation of insurance.

(24) (a) An applicant desiring to carry on insurance business in India shall make a requisition for Registration application in form IRDA/R-1.

(b) The form for applying for registration prescribed under the IRDA Regulation, 2000 is Form IRDA/R-2—Application for Registration.

(c) For the purpose of issuing a duplicate copy of the certificate of registration, IRDA has prescribed form IRDA/R-4.

(d) For applying for renewal of the certificate of registration, IRDA has prescribed form IRDA/R-5.

(25) (a) Date of incorporation as a company.

(b) Registration number (issued by the Registrar of the Companies).

(c) Classes of insurance business for which registration is sought.

(d) Amount of paid-up capital and number of equity shares issued and subscribed.

(e) Classification of shares.

(f) Voting rights of each class of shareholders.

(g) Details of shareholders.

(h) Key aspects and key persons of the applicant company.

(26) Form IRDA Agents V-A has been prescribed for individuals applying for/renewing a licence to work as an insurance agent/counsellor.

(27) Form TPA-I under the IRDA (TPA-Health Services) Regulations, 2001 has been prescribed for applying for a licence to work as a Third Party Administrator.

(28) (a) Product identity.

(b) Product features.

(c) Marketing plans.

(d) Underwriting philosophy and claims arrangements.

(e) Actuarial support.

(f) Details of rates and terms.

(g) Details of sales literature and other documents.

(29) (a) Certificate of authorized Compliance Officer as to the product being in line with the corporate underwriting and rating philosophy.

(b) Certificate of actuary regarding the policy design, rates and projections.

(c) Certificate of lawyer regarding the wording used and regulatory compliances.

(30) As per the provision of Section 64UE of the Insurance Act, 1938 and vide the IRDA Circular to this effect, the Tariff Advisory Committee manages the national data repository for the industry.

(31) The TAC gets its powers to collect data from the provisions under Section 64UE of the Insurance Act, 1938 which *inter-alia* authorizes the TAC to require and collect information, etc.

STANDARD FORM FOR TWO-WHEELER PACKAGE POLICY

Whereas the insured by a proposal and declaration dated, as stated in the schedule that shall be the basis of this contract and is deemed to be incorporated herein, has applied to the company for insurance hereinafter contained, and paid the premium mentioned in the schedule as consideration for such insurance in respect of accident loss or damage occurring during the period of insurance.

(The term two wheeler referred to in this Tariff will include motor cycle/scooter/auto-cycle or any other motorized two-wheeled vehicle mentioned in the schedule).

Now this Policy Witnesseth

That subject to the terms, exceptions and conditions contained herein or endorsed or otherwise expressed hereon—

Section I: Loss of or Damage to the Vehicle Insured

The company will indemnify the insured against loss or damage to the vehicle insured hereunder and/or its accessories whilst thereon.

(1) By fire-explosion, self-ignition or lightning.

(2) By burglary, house-breaking or theft.

(3) By riot and/or strike.
(4) By earthquake (fire and shock damage).
(5) By flood, typhoon, hurricane, storm, tempest, inundation, cyclone, hail-storm or frost.
(6) By accidental external means.
(7) By malicious act.
(8) By terrorist activity.
(9) Whilst in transit by road, rail, inland waterway, lift, elevator or air.
(10) By landslide or rockslide.

Subject to a deduction for deprecation; the rates mentioned below in respect of parts replaced:

(1) For all rubber/nylon/plastic parts, tyres, tubes and batteries—50%.
(2) For fibre glass components—30%.
(3) For all parts made of glass—nil.
(4) Rate of depreciation for all other parts including wooden parts will be as per the following schedule:

Age of Vehicle	*% of Depreciation*
Not exceeding 6 months	nil
Exceeding 6 months but not exceeding 1 year	5%
Exceeding 1 year but not exceeding 2 years	10%
Exceeding 2 years but not exceeding 3 years	15%
Exceeding 3 years but not exceeding 4 years	25%
Exceeding 4 years but not exceeding 5 years	35%
Exceeding 5 years but not exceeding 10 years	40%
Exceeding 10 years	50%

The company shall not be liable to make any payment in respect of:

(1) Consequential losses, depreciation, wear and tear, mechanical or electrical breakdown, failures or breakages.
(2) Damage to tyres and tubes unless the vehicle insured is damaged at the same time in which case, the

liability of the company shall be limited to 50 per cent of the cost of replacement.

(3) Loss of or damage to accessories by burglary, house-breaking or theft unless the vehicle is stolen at the same time.

(4) Any accidental loss or damage suffered whilst the insured or any person driving the vehicle with the knowledge and consent of the insured is under the influence of intoxicating liquor or drugs.

In the event of the vehicle being disabled by reason of loss or damage covered under this policy, the company will bear the reasonable cost of protection and removal to the nearest repairer and for redelivery to the insured but not exceeding in all Rs. 300 in respect of any one accident.

The insured may authorize the repair of the vehicle necessitated by damage for which the company may be liable under this policy provided that:

(1) The estimated cost of such repair including replacements, if any, does not exceed Rs. 150.

(2) The company is furnished forthwith a detailed estimate of the cost of repairs.

(3) The insured shall give the company every assistance to see that such repair is necessary and the charges are reasonable.

SUM INSURED DECLARED VALUE (IDV)

The insured's declared value (IDV) of the vehicle will be deemed to be the Sum Insured for the purpose of this policy, which is fixed at the commencement of each policy period for the insured vehicle.

The IDV of the vehicle (and side car/accessories, if any, fitted to the vehicle) is to be fixed on the basis of the manufacturer's listed selling price of the brand and model as the insured vehicle at the commencement of insurance/renewal and adjusted for depreciation (as per schedule below).

The schedule of age-wise depreciation as shown below is applicable for the purpose of Total Loss/Constructive Total Loss (TL/CTL) claims only.

The Schedule of Depreciation for fixing IDV of the Vehicle—

Age of the Vehicle	*% of Depreciation for Fixing IDV*
Not exceeding 6 months	5%
Exceeding 6 months but not exceeding 1 year	15%
Exceeding 1 year but not exceeding 2 years	20%
Exceeding 2 years but not exceeding 3 years	30%
Exceeding 3 years but not exceeding 4 years	40%
Exceeding 4 years but not exceeding 5 years	50%

IDV of vehicles beyond 5 years of age and of obsolete models of the vehicle (i.e. models which the manufacturers have discontinued to manufacture) is to be determined on the basis of an understanding between the insurer and the insured.

IDV shall be treated as the Market Value throughout the policy period without any further depreciation for the purpose of Total Loss (TL)/Constructive Total Loss (CTL) claims.

The insured vehicle shall be treated as CTL if the aggregate cost of retrieval and/or repair of the vehicle, subject to terms and condition of the policy, exceeds 75 per cent of the IDV of the vehicle.

Section II: Liability to Third Parties

(1) Subject to the limits of liability as laid down in the Schedule hereto, the company will indemnify the insured in the event of an accident caused by or arising out of the use of the insured vehicle against all sums which the insured shall become legally liable to pay in respect of:

(a) Death of or bodily injury to any person including occupants carried in the insured vehicle (provided such occupants are not carried for hire or reward) but except so far as it is necessary to meet the requirements of Motor Vehicles Act, the Company shall not be liable where such death or injury arises out of and in the course of the employment of such person by the insured, and

(b) Damage to property other than property belonging to the insured or held in trust or in the custody or control of the insured.

Provided always that the company shall not be liable in respect of death, injury or damage caused or arising beyond the limits of any carriageway or through fare in connection with the bringing of the load to the vehicle for loading thereon or the taking away of the load from the vehicle after unloading therefrom.

(2) The company will pay all costs and expenses incurred with its written consent.

(3) In terms of and subject to the limitations of the indemnity granted by this section to the insured, the company will indemnify the driver who is driving the vehicle on the insured's order or with insured's permission provided that such driver shall as though he/she was the insured, observes, fulfils and be subject to the terms, exceptions and conditions of this policy in so far as they apply.

(4) In the event of the death of any person entitled to indemnify under this policy, the company will, in respect of the liability incurred by such person, indemnify him/her personal representative in terms of and subject to the limitations of this policy provided that such personal representative shall, as though such representative was the insured, observes, fulfils and be subject to the terms, exceptions and conditions of this policy in so far as they apply.

(5) The company may at its own option -

(a) Arrange for representation at any inquest or fatal inquiry in respect of any death which may be the subject of indemnity under this policy, and

(b) Undertake the defense of proceedings in any court of Law in respect of any act or alleged offence causing or relating to any event, which may be the subject of indemnity under this policy.

Avoidance of Certain Terms and Right of Recovery

Nothing in this policy or any endorsement hereon shall affect the right of any person indemnified by this policy or any other person to recover an amount under or by virtue of the provisions of the Motor Vehicles Act.

But the insured shall repay to the company all sums paid by the company which the company would not have been liable to pay but for the said provision.

APPLICATION OF LIMITS OF INDEMNITY

In the event of any accident involving indemnity to more than one person, any limitation by the terms of this policy, and/or of any endorsement thereon of the amount of any indemnity, shall apply to the aggregate amount of indemnity to all persons indemnified and such indemnity shall apply in priority to the insured.

Section III: Personal Accident Cover for Owner-Driver

Subject otherwise to the terms, exceptions, condition and limitations of this policy, the company undertakes to pay compensation as per the following scale for bodily injury/death sustained by the owner-driver of the vehicle in direct connection with the vehicle insured whilst mounting into/dismounting from or traveling in the insured vehicle as co-driver, caused by violent accidental external and visible means which, independent of any other cause, shall within six calendar months of such injury result in:

Nature of injury	*Scale of compensation*
(1) Death	100%
(2) Loss of two limbs or sight of two eyes or one limb and sight of one eye	100%
(3) Loss of one limb or sight of one eye	50%
(4) Permanent total disablement from injuries other than named above	100%

Provided always that:

(1) The compensation shall be payable under only one of

the items (i) to (iv) above in respect of the owner-driver arising out of any open occurrence and the total liability of the insurer shall not in the aggregate exceed the sum of Rs. 1 lakh during any one period of insurance.

(2) No compensation shall be payable in respect of death or bodily injury, directly or indirectly, wholly or in part, arising or resulting from or traceable to (a) intentional self-injury, suicide or attempted suicide, physical defect or infirmity, or (b) an accident happening whilst such person is under the influence of intoxicating liquor or drugs.

(3) Such compensation shall be payable directly to the insured or to his/her legal representative whose receipt shall be the full discharge in respect of the injuries to the insured.

This cover is subject to—

(1) The owner-driver is the registered owner of the vehicle insured herein,

(2) The owner-drier is the insured named in this policy, and

(3) The owner-driver holds an effective driving license, in accordance with the provision of rule 3 of the Central Motor Vehicles Rules, 1989 at the time of the accident.

General Exceptions (Applicable to all Sections of the Policy)

The company shall not be liable in respect of:

(1) Any accidental loss, damage and/or liability caused, sustained or incurred outside the geographical area.

(2) Any claim arising out of any contractual liability.

(3) Any accidental loss, damage and/or liability caused, sustained or incurred whilst the vehicle insured herein is:

(a) Being used otherwise than in accordance with the limitations as to use, or

(b) Being driven by or is, for the purpose of being

driven by him/her, in the charge of any person other than a driver, as stated in the driver's clause.

(4) (a) Any accident, loss or damage to any property whatsoever or any loss or expense whatsoever resulting or arising therefrom or any consequential loss.

(b) Any liability of whatsoever nature, directly or indirectly caused by or contributed to by or arising from ionizing, radiations or contamination by radioactivity from any nuclear fuel or from any nuclear waste or from the combustion of nuclear fuel. For the purposes of this exception, combustion shall include any self-sustaining process of nuclear fission.

(5) Any accidental loss or damage or liability directly or indiscreetly caused by or contributed to by or arising from nuclear weapons material.

(6) Any accidental loss, damage and/or liability directly or indirectly or proximately or remotely occasioned by or contributed to by or traceable to or arising out of or in connection with war, invasion, the act of foreign enemies, hostilities or warlike operations (whether before or after declaration of war), civil war, mutiny, rebellion, military or usurped power or by any direct or indirect consequences of any of the said occurrences and in the event of any claim hereunder, the insured shall prove that the accidental loss, damage and/or liability arose independently of and was in no way connected with or occasioned by or contributed to by or traceable to any of the said occurrences or any consequence thereof and, in default of such proof, the company shall not be liable to make any payment in respect of such a claim.

DEDUCTIBLES

The company shall not be liable for each and every claim under Section-I (loss of or damage to the vehicle insured) of the policy in respect of the deductibles stated in the schedule.

CONDITIONS

This Policy and the Schedule shall be read together and any word or expression to which a specific meaning has been attached in any part of this Policy or of the Schedule shall bear the same meaning wherever it may appear.

(1) Notice shall be given in writing to the company immediately upon the occurrence of any accidental loss or damage and in the event of any claim, and thereafter, the insured shall give all such information and assistance as the company shall require. Every letter claim, writ, summons and/or process or copy thereof shall be forwarded to the company immediately on receipt by the insured. Notice shall also be given in writing to the company immediately. The insured shall have knowledge of any impending prosecution, inquest or fatal injury in respect of any occurrence which may give rise to a claim under this policy. In case of theft or other criminal act which may be the subject of a claim under this policy, the insured shall give immediate notice to the police and co-operative with the Company in securing the condition of the offender.

(2) No admission, offer, promise, payment or indemnity shall be made or given by or on behalf of the insured without the written consent of the company which shall be entitled, if it so desires, to take over and conduct in the name of the insured the defense or settlement of any claim or to prosecute in the name of the insured for its own benefit any claim for indemnity or damages or otherwise and shall have full description in the conduct of any proceedings or in the settlement of any claim and the insured shall give all such information and assistance as the company may require.

(3) The Company may, at its own option, repair, reinstate or replace the vehicle or part thereof and/or its accessories or may pay in cash the amount of the loss or damage and the liability of the company shall not exceed.

(a) For total loss/constructive total loss of the vehicle, the insured declared value (IDV) of the vehicle (including accessories thereon) as specified in the Schedule less the value of the wreck, or

(b) For partial losses, i.e. losses other than total loss/ constructive total loss of the vehicle, actual and reasonable costs of repair and/or replacement of parts lost/damaged subject to depreciation as per limits specified.

(4) The insured shall take all reasonable steps to safeguard the vehicle from loss or damage and to maintain it in efficient condition and the Company shall have at all times free and full access to examine the vehicle or any part thereof or any driver or employee of the insured. In the event of any accident or breakdown, the vehicle shall not be left unattended without proper precautions being taken to prevent further damage or loss and if the vehicle be driven before the necessary repairs are effected any extension of the damage or any further damage to the vehicle shall be entirely at the insured's own risk.

(5) The Company may cancel the policy by sending seven days' notice by recorded delivery to the insured at insured's last known address and in such event, will return to the insured the premium paid less the pro rata portion thereof for the period the policy has been in force or the policy may be cancelled at any time by the insured on seven days' notice by recorded delivery and provide no claim has arisen during the currency of the policy. The insured shall be entitled to a return of premium less premium at the company's short period rates for the period the policy has been in force. Return of the premium by the company will be subject to retention of the minimum premium of Rs. 100 (or Rs. 25 in respect of vehicles specifically designed/modified for use by the blind, handicapped/mentally challenged person). Where the ownership of the vehicle is transferred, the policy cannot be cancelled unless evidence that the vehicle is insured elsewhere is produced.

(6) If at the time of occurrence of an event that gives rise to any claim under this policy, there is in existence any other insurance covering the same liability, the company shall not be liable to pay or contribute more than its ratable proportion of any compensation, cost or expense.

(7) If any dispute or difference shall arise as to the quantum to be paid under this policy (liability being otherwise admitted), such difference shall, independent of all other questions, be referred to the decision of a sole arbitrator to be appointed in writing by the parties to the dispute or if they cannot agree upon a single arbitrator within 30 days of any party invoking arbitration, the same shall be referred to a panel of three arbitrators comprising two arbitrator—one to be appointed by each of the parties to the dispute/difference and a third arbitrator to be appointed by such two arbitrators who shall act as the presiding arbitrator and arbitration shall be conducted under and in accordance with the provisions of the Arbitration and Conciliation Act, 1996.

It is clearly agreed and understood that no difference or dispute shall be referable to arbitration as hereinbefore provided, if the company has disputed or not accepted liability under or in respect of this policy.

It is hereby expressly stipulated and declared that it shall be condition precedent to any right of action or suit upon this policy that the award by such arbitration/arbitrators of the amount of the loss or damage shall be first obtained.

It is also hereby further expressly agreed and declared if the company shall disclaim liability to the insured for any claim hereunder and such claim shall not, within twelve calendar months from the date of such disclaimer, have been made, the subject-matter of a suit in a court of law, then the claim shall, for all purposes, be deemed to have been abandoned and shall not thereafter be recoverable hereunder.

(8) The due observance and fulfilment of the terms, conditions and endorsements of this policy in so far as they relate to anything to be done or complied with by the insured and the truth of the statements and answers in the said proposal shall be conditions precedent to any liability of the company to make any payment under this policy.

(9) In the event of the death of the sole insured, this policy will not immediately lapse but will remain valid for a period of three months from the date of the death of insured or until the expiry of this policy (whichever is earlier). During the said period, legal heir(s) of the insured to whom the custody and use of the Motor Vehicle passes may apply to have this policy transferred to the name(s) of the heir(s) or obtain a new insurance policy for the Motor Vehicle.

Where such legal heir(s) desire(s) to apply for transfer of this policy or obtain a new policy for the vehicle such heir(s) should make an application to the company accordingly within the aforesaid period. All such applications should be accompanied by:

(1) Death Certificate in respect of the insured.
(2) Proof of the title to the vehicle.
(3) Original policy.

SCHEDULE

Policy No. :
The Company
The Insured : Name
Address
Business or Profession:
Period of Insurance:
From ________ o'clock on ___________ to midnight on ___________
Geographical Area: India
The vehicle : Any of the following
(Two-wheeler shall be deemed to include a side car attached to it)

Registration mark and place of registration	Engine No. and Chassis No.	Make	Type of Body	Cubic capacity	Year of Manufacture	Seating Capacity of side Car (if any)	IDV (insurer 's Declared Value)	
							For Vehicle (Rs.)	For Accessories not included in manufacturer's listed selling price (Rs.)

Policy No.	INSURED'S DECLARED VALUE					
	For the vehicle	For side car	Non-electrical accessories	Electrical/ electronic accessories	Value of CNG/ LPG kit	Total value
	Rs.	Rs.	Rs.	Rs.	Rs.	Rs.

LIMITATIONS AS TO USE

The policy covers use of the vehicle for any purpose other than:

(1) Hire or Reward.
(2) Carriage of goods (other than samples or personal luggage).
(3) Organized racing.
(4) Pace-making.
(5) Speed testing.
(6) Reliability Trials.
(7) Any purpose in connection with Motor Trade.

Driver

Any person including insured:

(1) Provided that a person driving holds an effective driving license at the time of the accident and is not disqualified from holding or obtaining such a license.
(2) Provided also that the person holding an effective learner's license may also drive the vehicle and that such a person satisfies the requirements of rule 3 of the Central Motor Vehicles Rules, 1989.

LIMITS OF LIABILITY

Under Section II-1(i) of the policy, death of or bodily injury such amount as is necessary to meet the requirements of the Motor Vehicles Act, 1988.

Under Section II-1(ii) of the policy, damage to Third Party Property Rs. __________"

"Insert Rs. 6000/Rs. 1 lakh as the case may be.

P.A. Cover for Owner-driver under section III (CSI) Rs. __________

Deductible under Section 1: Rs. __________

No Claim Bonus

The insured is entitled for a No claim Bonus (NCB) on the Own Damage section of the policy, if no claim is made or is pending during the preceding year(s), as per the following table:

Period of Insurance	*% of NCB on OD Premium*
The preceding year	20%
Preceding two consecutive years	25%
Preceding three consecutive years	35%
Preceding four consecutive years	45%
Preceding five consecutive years	50%

No claim bonus will only be allowed provided the policy is renewed within 90 days of the expiry date of the previous policy.

PREMIUM COMPUTATION TABLE

(Insurers to give here details of computation of the premium. A specimen premium computation table is given at the end of this section).

Subject to I.M.T. Endt. Nos. and Memorandum ________ printed/herein/attached hereto

Under Hire Purchase Agreement with________________

Hypothecated with ________________

Lease agreement with ________________

Date and signature of proposal ________________

In witness whereof this policy has been signed at __________ this _________ day of __________ in lieu of cover Note No. __________ dated ___________ receipt No. _____________ dated __________________________

Address of the Issuing Office:
(Duly Constituted Attorney(s))

IMPORTANT NOTICE

The insured is not indemnified if the vehicle is used or driven otherwise than in accordance with this Schedule. Any payment made by the Company by reason of wider terms appearing in the Certificate in order to comply with the Motor Vehicles Act, 1988 is recoverable from the insured. See the clause headed "AVOIDANCE OF CERTAIN TERMS AND RIGHT OF RECOVERY".

5

Types of Insurance

INTRODUCTION

This Chapter introduces the different types of losses covered under general insurance. It also discusses in detail the different types of insurances available in the market. The insurance policies are grouped and explained the way they are used both in the Indian and international contexts. In view of the rapid changes expected in the market as a result of de-tariffing and the introduction of 'File and Use' approval systems, product innovations are expected sooner than later. It is possible that products of a different composition replace many of the insurance products existing in the market today. This possibility has been taken into account while discussing the types of insurance in this Chapter. Readers/students are provided with the necessary conceptual clarity to understand the products despite the changes.

TYPES OF LOSSES COVERED UNDER INSURANCE

We have seen that insurance contract aims at mitigation of financial hardships due to losses. Losses can be of various types, based on the risk insured and its exposure to various perils. As insurance contracts are designed to indemnify losses, different risks with different kinds of exposure have to be distinguished and given appropriate covers, terms, etc. Contracts are, therefore, worded suitably. Understanding losses and classifying insurance products into different loss types helps the insurers in dealing more professionally with the varied requirements of the insurance market.

Losses are broadly grouped as losses from damage or destruction of property, losses due to liabilities, losses of income and personal losses. The first type erodes the insured assets, the second increases his liabilities, the third chokes up his sources of income, and the fourth hurts him by way of physical hardship or death.

Property Losses: Property losses can be direct or real losses, as used in real estate. These include loss or damage sustained by land, buildings, structures, appurtenant attachments, machinery, equipments, stock-in-process and the like. This property is considered more prone to perils, such as fire, earthquake, lightning, flood, storm, tempest, inundation, landslide, accidents in the processing phase, etc. Personal property is not attached to land. It is movable and can be stolen, accidentally dropped or damaged by fire. Property losses can be indirect as well. These are also losses to property but not direct losses. Damage to a refrigerator can cause loss of medicines kept within. Seepage of rain water through the wall can cause an electrical short circuit leading to a fire loss in the factory. A person falling on the road and fracturing himself can lose his watch in the process.

Liability Losses: These are the losses that arise from a legal obligation cast on the insured to pay. Liabilities can arise when one's vehicle accidentally hits someone or something on the road. If one's tree falls on the neighbourer's house, a liability can arise. If one's sewerage drips and falls while at work, liability can arise. An injury or a disease contracted by a worker due to certain conditions in a factory can cause a liability to the factory owner. Liability can arise out of deficiency of services rendered, defects of products sold, by negligence or by oversight. In the Indian social set-up, liabilities are not normally enforced as the victims are generally tolerant. In the western markets and the USA, however, as people are more aware of their rights and less tolerant of others' faults, liability is perceived a major risk. Consequently, there is a large demand for liability insurances.

Income Losses: Net income losses are those that are caused by increased expenses or reduced income. Losses can be caused as a consequence of one's sources of income getting dried up. A daily wage worker who can not go to work due to ill-health is one such example. Retrenchment is another cause of loss of personal income. When one's house is damaged by flood, one may have to vacate it and stay in a rented house.

Suppose a factory is gutted by fire. It may not be able to complete pending orders or realize sales proceeds from its customers, while it would continue to pay interest on borrowed capital, and pay fixed costs on rent and electricity for the building and salary to its employees. It may have to pay demurrages to third parties, pay its suppliers, and repay loans and advances already availed of. Losses due to business interruption or consequential loss fall under this category.

Personal Losses: Personal losses are those faced by a person, such as death, sickness, accident, unemployment and superannuating. In the organizational context, losses to the business entity relating to performance of key persons, business discontinuation, losses due to death or disablement of a customer, all these are collectively grouped as personal losses. Some authors call these losses as personnel losses.

However, these categorizations are not water-tight. There are many areas where the loss types so overlap and policies are issued covering different types of losses, depending on the market demand. Innovative products and products that are tailor-made for corporate requirements may be of a dumpsite type (all inclusive) or hybrid types (chopped and put together from different groups). However, all these are for the consumption of the insured. For the insurer who bears the risk, each and ever component of the contract is appropriately researched and accurately priced. The insurer is in business and has to run his business productively and professionally. Like the clothes-seller who gifts a silk tie to a customer who buys a designer shirt, knows his costing well enough not to gift a designer shirt to a customer who buys a silk tie. An insurer is expected to know his costing well enough to make his product appear attractive as a bundle but not to sell his product at a loss.

Types of Property Insurances

Property insurances deal with the 'real' risks that include exposure to perils such as fire, earthquake, lightning, flood, storm, tempest, inundation, landslide, or personal property that can be stolen, accidentally dropped, damaged by fire, etc. These insurances are designed to cover loss or damage sustained by buildings, factories, shops, multiplexes, roads, buildings under construction, bridges, goods stored at site, etc. The cost of covering the risk would depend on various physical attributes of the risk such as the geographical location, strength of the building, hazardous nature of the processes carried out in the premises, fire protection systems, burglar alarms, electrical installations, nature of material stored, etc.

Fire Insurance (Static Property)

Fire insurance design is based on the All India Fire Tariff effective from 31-3-2001 issued by the Tariff Advisory Committee (TAC), a Statutory Body. The product has been de-tariffed from January 1, 2007 in respect of rates, but the cover is expected to continue for some time. The product composition is expected to change once the cover is also allowed to be insurer-designed.

In any market situation, a basic fire policy would exist the way it is today and operate as a commercial policy covering buildings, offices, machinery, contents and personal belongings in the office. The fire policy mitigates the risk of losses of the insured arising from fire breakout.

Salient features of the Standard Fire and Special Perils policy are given below:

Cover

Losses due to the following causes are covered:

(1) Fire, lightning, explosion and implosion.
(2) Aircraft damage, riot, strike, malicious damage and terrorism.
(3) Storm, tempest, flood and inundation.
(4) Impact damage and subsidence.
(5) Landslide/rockslide.
(6) Bursting and/or overflowing of water tanks, apparatus and pipes.

(7) Missile testing, leakage from automatic sprinkler instillations and bush fire.

Sum insured

The value of the property is considered while fixing the sum insured. The property can be insured on depreciated cost (market value) or replacement cost basis. Some insurers recommend reinstatement (replacement) basis for full protection.

Basis of Premium

Premium rate will depend on construction of building and occupancy. Discounts/loadings on premium are given based on past claims experience for risks exceeding Rs. 50 corers sum insured at any location and installation of fire extinguisher appliances. The amount of premium depends on a number of actors based on the underwriting policies of different insurers.

Condition of Excess

5 per cent of every claim resulting from lightning, storm, tempest, flood and inundation, subsidence, and landslide is treated as excess. The insurance policy doesn't cover the first Rs. 10, 000 (or as applicable) of each and every claim.

Significant Exclusions

Losses arising out of perils of war and allied perils, theft, wilful act or gross negligence, loss of earnings, loss of bullion, documents, currency, etc. for an amount exceeding Rs. 10, 000 unless expressly stated.

Main Extensions

(1) Earthquake (fire and shock).
(2) Spontaneous combustion.
(3) Deterioration of stocks in cold storage.
(4) Impact damage due to own vehicle(s).
(5) Omission to insure additions.
(6) Architect's/surveyor's/consulting engineer's fees in excess of 3 per cent of claim amount.
(7) Debris removal, in excess of 1 per cent of claim amount.

General Conditions

The insured should take all possible steps to minimize the loss.

HOME INSURANCE

Salient features of a Home Insurance Policy are given below:

Policy Coverage

Coverage damages to the structure and contents of one's home from natural and man-made calamities. Choice is allowed to buy insurance for only the building (structure), or only the contents (belongings), or both.

Calamities Covered

(1) Fire, earthquake and lightning,
(2) Riot, strike and malicious damage,
(3) Explosion and implosion,
(4) Storm, cyclone, tempest, tornado, hurricane, flood and inundation,
(5) Damage due to impact by vehicles,
(6) Missile testing operation,
(7) Subsidence, landslides and rockslides,
(8) Leakage from automatic sprinkler installations,
(9) Aircraft damage, and
(10) Bursting and/or overflowing of water tanks, apparatus and pipes.

Burglary Cover (only for contents)

The contents of one's home are also covered against loss due to burglary or an attempted burglary. It also covers loss of jewellery, silver articles and precious stones kept under lock and key, up to 25 per cent of the total content sum insured or Rs. 1 lac, whichever is lower.

Optional Covers

(1) Terrorism cover—covers any damages and losses to the structure and/or contents of your home due to acts of terrorism.

(2) Additional expenses of rent for alternative accommodation—if you are forced to shift into an alternative accommodation because your home is destroyed or damaged by any insured peril, the policy will cover you against the additional rent. The maximum coverage is upto Rs. 1, 00, 000 for upto 6 months. The cover is available only if you are insuring the structure of your home.

Policy Exclusion

(1) Wilful destruction of property,
(2) Loss, damage and destruction caused by war, wear and tear, atmospheric conditions, etc.,
(3) Losses if the home has been unoccupied for more than 30 days,
(4) Cash, bullion, painting, works of art and antiques,
(5) Loss to the structure and/or contents of your home due to acts of terrorism.

How to Calculate the Sum Insured for

(1) Home Structure: The home insurance policy insurers the structure of the home for its reconstruction value (and not for market value). Reconstruction value is defined as the cost incurred to reconstruct the home if it is damaged. On the other hand, market value is a combination of cost of land, demand and supply scenario, etc.

Sum insured is calculated by multiplying the built-up area of the home with the construction rate per sq. foot (e.g. if the built up area of your home is 1000 sq. foot and the constitution rate is Rs. 800 per sq. foot, the sum insured for the home structure works out to Rs. 8, 00, 000). However, this value can be revised appropriately if expensive material such as marble flooring, etc. has been used in construction. If the home has lawn/garden surrounded by a perimeter wall, the construction rate can be revised to include the cost of construction of this wall in home structure sum insured.

(2) **Home Contents:** The contents of the home are furniture, durables, clothes, utensils, jewellry, etc. These are to be valued on market value basis, i.e. the current market value of similar items after deprecation. Depreciation does not apply to jewellry.

Examples of Benefit Offered by Some Insurers

For comprehensive cover for both structure and contents of the home, 15 per cent discount on a 3-year home insurance policy and 25 per cent discount on 5-year policy is given.

Engineering Insurance (works in progress)

Engineering insurance basically covers property risks while work is in progress. Insurance can cover completed sites for operations as in the case of Machinery breakdown, Boiler and pressure Vessel, Plant or Electronic equipment insurance. Engineering insurance covers works that are under construction process, such as contactors' all risks, eruption all right, etc.

Salient features of a **Machinery Breakdown Policy (Engineering)** are given below:

Scope of Cover

The insurance policy broadly covers loss due to all kinds of accidental, electrical and mechanical breakdowns due to internal and external causes. Cover is granted during the time the machinery is in operation or at rest, or in the process of dismantling, overhauls or during subsequent re-erection at the same premises.

Sum Insured

Value proposed for insurance should be equal to new replacement cost including freight, erection costs, and custom duty, if any.

Premium

Rate of premium depends upon the type of machinery. Discounts are offered in respect of stand-by facility, availability of spares, and favourable claims experience, and subject to rules laid down in the tariff.

Significant Exclusion

The insurance policy does not cover loss and/or damage from:

(1) Fire and allied perils.
(2) Theft.
(3) Overloading experiments.
(4) Wilful acts or gross negligence.
(5) Gradually developing flaws.
(6) Deterioration from normal use.

Excess

Policy is subject to a compulsory excess, which depends upon the value of the machinery.

Main Extensions

(1) Air freight.
(2) Express freight (excluding air freight), overtime and holiday wages.
(3) Insured's own surrounding property.
(4) Third party liability.

Salient features of a Boiler and Pressure Vessels Policy are as below:

Scope of Cover

The policy broadly covers boilers and other pressure vessels, both fired and non-fired against losses due to explosion or collapse.

Sum Insured

Sum insured should be reinstatement cost of the boiler.

Premium

The premium chargeable depends on the type of boiler, type of fuel used and the age of equipment. Discount is allowed for seasonal factories and stand-by facilities.

Significant Exclusions

The policy does not cover loss and/or damage arising from:

(1) Fire and allied perils.
(2) War and nuclear perils.
(3) Losses arising out of overload experiments.
(4) Gradual wear and tear of parts.
(5) Failure of individual tubes, loss due to chemical reactions.
(6) Wilful acts or gross negligence.
(7) Loss which is manufacturer's or repairer's responsibility.
(8) Consequential loss from explosion or collapse.

Main Extension

(1) Surrounding property of the insured (including the property held in trust or on commission).
(2) Legal liability for third party bodily injury and property damage.
(3) Express freight.
(4) Air freight.
(5) Additional customs duty can also be covered by payment of additional premium.

Salient features of an Electronic Equipment Insurance Policy:

(1) Material damage to electronic equipment (which can include systems software) due to sudden and unforeseen events, under Section I.
(2) Cost of external data media, including cost of reconstruction of data under Section II.
(3) As also increased cost of working under Section III. While Section I is compulsory, Section II and Section III are optional.

Sum Insured

(1) **Section I:** New replacement cost of the insured

property including freight, erection cost, and customs duty, if any.

(2) **Section II:** Cost of restoring the external data media by replacing lost or damaged data media by new material and lost information.

(3) **Section III:** Sum insured should represent the hiring charges per hour for substitute equipment for ensuring continued data processing for the period of indemnity specified, including personnel and transportation charges.

Premium

Rate of premium is 1 per cent for equipment valued more than Rs. 1, 00, 000, and a valid maintenance agreement is required to be in force, failing which 100 per cent loading is attracted.

Significant Exclusion

The Policy does not cover losses/damages due to:

(1) Wear and tear,
(2) War, wilful act or wilful negligence, and
(3) Aesthetic defects and consequential loss.

Excess

The policy is subject to compulsory excess. Excess depends upon value of equipment. Separate excess applies to Winchester Drive. Higher voluntary excess qualifies for reduction in premium level.

There are policies such as contractors' All Risks Insurance, Contraltos Plant and Machinery insurance, Civil Engineering construction risks Insurance, Erection All risks Insurance, Deterioration of stocks Insurance, etc., which are similar in nature. These are not being discussed in detail.

TRANSIT INSURANCE

Losses of property and merchandise while in transit are historically important for insurance transactions. Goods in transit include those sent by airplanes, ships, railways, roadways and waterways. Goods can be sent by own vehicles, containers, ships or airplanes, or by chartered vessels. Very often, goods shift between multiple modes of transits with multiple trans-shipments and storages at various stages of the transit. Between the consignor and consignee of goods, there are various parties involved, such as port authorities, forwarding agents, cargo handlers, for lift operators and others.

Goods in transit are exposed to perils of the sea, loss of the ship, water damages, contamination from other cargo, pilferage, theft, breakage of roads/bridges, road accidents, overturning/ derailment of land conveyance, etc., the mode of sending the cargo. Such as break bulk, full container load, packed in cartons, shrink wrapped, fully pressed bales, etc. are also relevant for the insurance.

MARINE CARGO POLICIES

Internationally, marine cargo policies are generally issued based on institute Cargo clauses framed by the Institute of London Underwriters (ILU). The inland transit policies also are largely guided by the ILU framework.

Salient features of a marine Cargo (import-export) insurance policies are as under:

Introduction

The coverage is generally defined by reference to clauses known as institute clauses. The ICC (C), ICC (B) and ICC (A) clauses define different levels of coverage against marine risk and the cargo may be covered subject to any one of these clauses. The type of policy available is the specific policy to cover single consignment or an open policy.

Scope of Cover

There are three types of covers:

(1) Institute Cargo Clause (C) named peril basis.
(2) Institute Cargo Clause (B) named peril basis.
(3) Institute Cargo Clause (A) offers the widest form of cover under Marine Cargo Insurance in so far as it relates to the perils covered.

ICC (A) is unnamed perils clause.

Sum Insured

This is an agreed value policy. Normally insurance is taken for CIF +10%.

Premium

Rate depends on factors such as:

(1) Nature of cargo.
(2) Scope of cover.
(3) Packing.
(4) Mode of conveyance.
(5) Distance.
(6) Past claim experience.

Significant Exclusions

(1) Wilful misconduct.
(2) Ordinary leakage.
(3) Improper packing.
(4) Delay.
(5) Inherent vice.
(6) War, strike, riot and civil commotion.

Main Extensions

On payment of additional premium, the insured can opt for certain extensions to the cover provided under the policy.

Extensions available include war, strike, riot and civil commotion, and delay insurance cover.

INLAND TRANSIT POLICIES

Inland transit policies by and large follow the framework of the marine cargo policies with due changes to cover rail, road and associated risks.

Salient features of a marine cargo (inland transit) insurance policies are as under:

Introduction

This policy broadly covers the risk of physical loss or damage to the insured's goods (machinery, raw materials, finished goods, etc.) during transit under a contract of affreightment.

Scope of Cover

There are two types of covers available from the insurers:

(1) **Basic Risk Policy**: It covers loss or damage to specified goods caused by fire, lightning, breakage of bridges, overturning of vehicles, and collision with or by carrying vehicle, subject to specified exclusions.

(2) **All Risks Policy**: It covers all risks of loss or damage to specified goods subject to exclusions.

Sum Insured

This is an agreed value policy. Normally insurance is taken for CIF + 10%.

Premium

Rate depends on factors such as nature of cargo, scope of cover, packing, mode of conveyance, distance and past claims experience.

Significant Exclusion

This policy does not cover loss or damage due to:

(1) Wilful misconduct.

(2) Ordinary leakage.

(3) Improper packing.

(4) Delay.

(5) Inherent vice.

(6) War, strike, riot and civil commotion.

Main Extension

Extensions available include strike, riot and civil commotion.

There are other segments of inland transit insurance covering inland waterways, storage cover incidental to transit-goods sent by hand cart, bullock cart and camel cart, postal insurance, etc. These are relatively small segments used only in a very limited manner and hence are not being discussed in this chapter.

Accident Insurance

Accident insurance is a large area of insurance covering a large number of small value policies such as scooters and auto-rickshaw, and medium value such as cars, vans, buses and commercial vehicles. At the other end of the spectrum, airplanes, helicopters, ships, yachts and customized limousines are there with very high claims. While the high value segment cases are infrequent, involving high value claims, these cases hence are treated differently by the insurers.

Motor Vehicle Insurance

Vehicle insurance in India was de-tariffed with effect from January 1, 2007. The policy terms are still frozen to those fixed by the Tariff Advisory Committee. The insurers are allowed to fix rates for the Own Damage part themselves. As third party liability insurance is mandatory under the Motor Vehicles Act, IRDA has fixed rates for the third party cover so that the policy is kept affordable to the users of motor vehicles.

The insurances available are mainly (1) policy covers only limited liability to third parties (TP) as per the Motor Vehicles Act, 1988, (2) policy covers own damage (OD) or damage to the vehicles, (3) personal accident cover for owner-driver, and (4) under a comprehensive package policy, increased cover for third party liability for bodily injury and/or death, damage to property of third parties and loss or damage to the vehicle insured (Own Damage or OD)

Salient features of a comprehensive motor vehicle (Private Car) insurance policy are as follows:

Policy Coverage

Motor insurance policy wordings are governed by the Indian motor tariff. It covers you against any loss or damage caused to your vehicle or its accessories due to the following natural and man-made calamities:

(1) **Natural Calamities:** Fire, explosion, self-ignition or lightning, earthquake, flood, typhoon, hurricane, storm, tempest, inundation, cyclone, hailstorm, frost, landslide, rockslide.

(2) **Man-made Calamities:** Burglary, theft, riot, strike,

malicious act, accident by external means, terrorist activity, and any damage in transit by road, rail, inland waterway, lift, elevator or air.

Rates

(1) **Personal Accident Cover:** The motor insurance provides compulsory personal accident cover of Rs. 2 lakh for individual owners of the vehicle while driving. You can also opt for a personal accident cover for passengers.

(2) **Third party legal liability:** This protects you against legal liability arising due to accidental damages, such as any permanent injury/death of a person, and any damage caused to the property.

Policy Exclusion

Under this policy, you are covered against:

(1) Normal wear and tear and general aging of the vehicle.

(2) Depreciation or any consequential loss.

(3) Mechanical/electrical break-down.

(4) Wear and tear of consumables such as tyres and tubes.

(5) Vehicles being used otherwise than in accordance with limitations as to use.

(6) Damage to/by a person driving the vehicle without a valid license.

(7) Damage to/by a person driving the vehicle under the influence of drugs or liquor.

(8) Loss/damage due to war, mutiny or nuclear risk.

Key Benefits

(1) You can claim towing charges up to Rs. 1, 500.

(2) Cashless claim settlement is available across India. Refer all India cashless Charge List.

Avail of the following Bonuses and Discounts

(1) No Claim Bonus: If you do not make a claim during the policy period, a No Claim Bonus (NCB) up to 50 per cent is offered on renewals. This discount can go as high as 90 days of the expiry date of the previous policy.

(2) **Transfer your NCB:** You can transfer full benefits of No Claim Bonus when you shift your motor insurance policy from one company to another. The discount rate remains the same provided you show evidence that you are entitled to No Claim Bonus from your previous motor insurance company.

Evidence

It can be in the form of a renewal notice or a letter confirming the NCB entitlement from the previous insurer or a written declaration.

No Claim Bonus (NCB) Declaration

I/We declare that the rate of NCB claimed by me/us is correct and that no claim has arisen in the expiring policy period. I/we further undertake that if this declaration is found to be incorrect, all benefits under the policy will stand forfeited.

Voluntary Excess Discount

A further discount on the premium is available if you opt for a voluntary excess in addition to the compulsory excess. (Compulsory excess is the amount of loss that the insured has to bear in each and every claim).

Additional Discount

You can also avail of additional discounts if you are a member of a recognized Automobile Association in India.

ARAI Device

(1) **Cover yourself and your family:** You can also opt for personal accident cover of Rs. 2 lakh for other unnamed passenger in your car, for example, your family, friends, relatives, etc.

(2) **Customise your insurance with additional cover:** Electrical and/or non-electrical items fitted to the vehicle can be insured separately; for example, fog lights, music system, seat covers, etc.

Bio-Fuel Kit

In case of vehicles fitted with bio-fuel systems such as petrol/diesel and CNG/LPG, permitted by the concerned RTO, the CNG/LPG kit fitted to the vehicle is to be insured separately at an additional premium of 4 per cent on the value of such kit. You need to specifically declare this in the proposal form.

Sum Insured

The vehicles are insured at a fixed value called the insured's declared value (IDV), which is the sum insured for motor OD. IDV is calculated on the basis of the manufacture's listed selling price of the vehicle (plus the listed price of any accessories) after deducting the depreciation for every year as per the schedule provided by the Indian motor tariff. If the price of any electronic and/or electrical item installed in the vehicle is not included in the manufacturer's listed selling price, then the actual value (after depreciation) of this item can be added to the sum insured over and above the IDV.

The Schedule of Depreciation for Fixing IDV of the Vehicles

Age of the Vehicle	*% of Depreciation*
Not exceeding 6 months	5%
Exceeding 6 months but not exceedings 1 year	15%
Exceeding 1 year but not exceeding 2 years	20%
Exceeding 2 years but not exceeding 3 years	30%
Exceeding 3 year but not exceeding 4 years	40%
Exceeding 4 year but not exceeding 5 years	50%

Salient features of a Motor (Goods Carrying Commercial Vehicle) third Party Liability Insurance Policy are as follows:

Policy Coverage

This cover is applicable to Public and Private Carriers including Motorized three-wheelers and Motorized Pedal Cycles.

The Indian Motor Tariff defines goods carrying commercial vehicle as:

(1) Public carriers (other than three-wheelers).
(2) Private carriers (other than three-wheelers).
(3) Goods Carrying Motorized Three-wheelers and motorized Pedal Cycles (Public Carriers).
(4) Goods Carrying Motorized Three-wheelers and Motorized Pedal Cycles (Private Carriers).

Cover

The policy covers the following:

(1) Personal injury
(2) Property damage

Third Party Insurance Cover for Personal Injury

Liability for death or injury to third parties means that you are insured against death or injury (caused by your vehicle) to pedestrians, occupant(s) of other vehicles, and outsiders other than passengers.

Factors Determining the Premium

The premium for Commercial Vehicles Insurance is calculated on:

(1) Carrying capacity or gross vehicle weight, and
(2) Value of the vehicles.

Accessories will be charged extra, as specified. If you do not make a claim during the policy period, a No Claim Bonus (NCB) is offered on renewals.

Sum Insured

The vehicles are insured at a fixed value called the Insured's Decelerated Value (IDV). IDV is calculated on the basis of the manufacturer's listed selling price of the vehicle (plus the listed price of any accessories) after deducting the depreciation for every year as per the schedule provided by the Indian Motor Tariff.

If the price of any electrical and/or electronic item installed in the vehicle is not included in the manufacturer's listed selling price, the actual value (after depreciation) of this item can be added to the sum insured over and above the IDV.

Exclusions

Under this policy, you are not covered against:

(1) Own damage losses.
(2) Any claim arising out of personal accident.
(3) Third party legal liability covers for commercial vehicles other than goods carrying commercial vehicles.
(4) Any accidental loss, damage and/or liability caused, sustained or incurred outside the geographical area.
(5) Any claim arising out of any contractual liability.
(6) Any accidental loss, damage or liability due to war, mutiny or nuclear risk.
(7) Any employee(s) of the insured other than the owner-driver of the goods carrying vehicle.
(8) Damage to any bridge and/or way-bridge and/or via duct and/or to any road and/or any thing beneath by vibration or by the weight of the insured vehicle and/or load carried by the insured vehicle.

Marine Hull Insurance

Ships involve heavy capital and a loss can be crippling even to big steamer companies. A ship is insured according to the value of the ship's hull or body, its machinery and other integral attachments, freight, and disbursements against marine perils. Ocean going vessels, sailing vessels, trawlers, barges, fishing vessels, etc. are conventionally covered under hull. Vessels are generally classified as mechanically self-propelled vessels of steel construction, which are further classified into various groups, and smaller crafts built of steel, wood, etc. not subject to any classification.

Ships are insured as per the Institute Voyage Clauses for a particular voyage or for the Institute Time Clause for a specific period. There are specific clauses designed for different types of vessels such as sailing vessels, barges or tugs, and for different specific covers including ship-building, ship-breaking and ship-repairing. Oil drilling rigs and off-shore oil platforms, fixed off-shore pipelines and jetties are also covered under hull insurance.

Salient features of a marine hull insurance policy are the following:

Scope of Cover

The purpose of hull insurance is to cover ship owners' various insurable interests and these include:

(1) Hull and Machinery Insurance.
(2) Insurance of Freight.
(3) Loss of Hire Insurance.
(4) Loss of Profit Insurance.

The Institute Time Clauses form the basis for most policies used for insurance of vessels and their machinery.

Sum Insured

It is an agreed clause policy.

Premium

The premium will depend on the following factors:

(1) Type of vessel, trading limits, age, tonnage and technical aspects of machinery.
(2) Management and ownership considerations.
(3) Past claims experience.
(4) Valuation of vessel.
(5) Type of cover required.
(6) Size of the deductible.

Significant Exclusion

The exclusions will depend upon the type of cover availed and would be governed by the Institute Time Clauses and the Institute Voyage Clauses.

Excess

The policy will be subject to deductibles, which will depend on the type of cover availed.

Aviation Hull Insurance

Insurance of Aviation hull covers different types of customized products based on international wordings. The aviation portfolio encompasses the following types of covers:

(1) **Hull All Risk Insurance Policy:** This policy is suitable for small aircraft operators belonging to flying clubs, companies engaged in agricultural spraying operations, aircraft especially designed for VIPs and business executives, and for those engaged in industrial aids. The policy's scope includes all physical loss or damage sustained by the insured aircraft including total loss and disappearance. All losses are paid subject to deductibles.

(2) **Spares All Risk Insurance Policy:** Covers loss or damage to spares, tools, equipments and supplies owned by the insured or the property for which the insured is responsible whilst on ground or in transit by land, sea, air, including in own aircraft or whilst on the premises of other party for storage only.

(3) **Hull/Spares War Risk Insurance:** Indemnity is provided to the aircraft as well as spares for damage caused by war, invasion, acts of foreign enemies, hostilities, civil war, rebellion, revolution, resurrection, martial law, strikes, riots, civil commotion, malicious acts and sabotage.

(4) **Aviation Personal Accident (Crew Member) Insurance:** This policy is designed to cover the insured person against injury, disablement or death, arising as a result of an accident that is generally granted on annual basis. The cover operates while mounting or dismounting from and whilst travelling an aircraft, while the aircraft is being used within the geographical scope as per its permitted usage. This cover can also be on 24-hour basis. The capital sum insured varies according to the status of the insured or his/her earning capacity as fixed by the insurers.

(5) **Loss of License Insurance:** Operating crews of the aircraft are required to have valid license. License is liable to be suspended either temporarily or

permanently on medical grounds. Consequential financial loss is covered by the loss of license policy. The cover provided is in respect to incapacity causing permanent total disablement or temporary total disablement due to bodily injury or illness.

Besides the aforesaid general aviation policies, various other tailor-made insurance policies as per specific requriemetns of the insured also exist.

Some of the basic aviation insurance models are discussed below:

Salient features of Aircraft Hull and Spares/All Risks/ Aviation Liability Insurance are as under:

Covered Risks

(1) Accidental physical loss or damage to the aircraft/ aircraft spares.
(2) Legal liability to third parties towards bodily injury/ death and property damages, passengers' bodily injury/death, baggage, cargo and mail, premises, hangar-keepers.
(3) Catering and vehicle liability on airports can also be covered.

Major Exclusions

(1) Wear and tear.
(2) War risk.
(3) Radioactive contamination.
(4) Illegal use.
(5) Noise pollution.
(6) Insured's own property, etc.

Salient features of Aircraft Hull/Liability Insurance Policy are as under:

Brief Description

This policy is meant for the owners/operators of smaller aircraft being used for the purpose of private pleasure, training, industrial aid, business, commercial, off-shore operations, etc.

Covered Risks

(1) Accidental Physical loss or damage to the aircraft.
(2) Bodily injury/death of the passenger(s).
(3) Loss of passengers' baggage.
(4) Bodily injury/death and property damage to the third parties.

Major Exclusions

(1) Wear and tear.
(2) War risk.
(3) Radioactive contamination.
(4) Illegal use.
(5) Noise pollution.
(6) Insured's own property, etc.

INCOME INSURANCE

While the regular property insurance covers material losses, there are other losses that an insured would suffer due to the interruption in business. We have seen that a fire and special perils policy compensates only for material damage to the insured property. It specially excludes any consequential loss. In case of major loss caused by fire, there could be an interruption in business operation leading to reduction in turnover, finally resulting in possible loss of profits. However, standing or fixed charges continue to accrue regardless of whether there is any production or not. Such loss cannot be covered under the policy. Losses of this type would include the following:

(1) Net profit of the business venture.
(2) Standing or fixed charges (overhead expense) such as salaries, wages, taxes and interest, which have to be paid despite the loss.
(3) Increased costs of working or the abnormal expenses incurred post-loss to keep the venture afloat.
(4) Losses due to failure of electricity, gas and water supply.
(5) Interruption of business at other locations, such as suppliers' and customers' premises.

Insurance of this loss of income is called by different names as consequential loss, business interruption, loss of profits, etc. A consequential loss policy compensates for the revenue loss suffered by the enterprise. Hence, for complete protection to the business enterprise and its profitability consequential loss policy is very essential in addition to fire insurance policy.

Business Interruption/Loss of Profits Insurance

This type of policy offers a solution by covering profit loss due to reduction in turnover arising from interruption of business following damage to the property insured. This policy can be taken only in conjunction with the fire policy or the machinery break-down policy. This policy is also known by various names such as consequential loss policy or business interruption policy or loss of profit policy.

Salient features of a consequential loss (fire) insurance policy are as under:

Scope of Cover

The policy broadly covers loss of net profit on account of interruption of business consequential upon natural damage to property due to fire or any other insured peril under the standard fire and special perils policy.

It also covers standing charges that continue to be incurred during the period of interruption and the increase in cost of working, necessarily and reasonably incurred to maintain the business as far as possible at its normal level, so that loss under net profit and standing charges are avoided or at least minimized.

Sum Insured

Sum to be insured under this policy is the estimated gross profit of the indemnity period. The maximum period is from the beginning with the occurrence to the damage, for which cover of loss of gross profit is required, and should reflect the maximum period anticipated for reinstatement of the damaged property. The maximum indemnity period permissible under the policy is 3 years.

Premium

Basic rate depends on fire and special perils rate. Final rate is influenced by the indemnity period chosen. At inception, gross profit is taken on an estimated basis and is subject to declaration of the actual figures after expiry of policy, based on final audited account.

Excess

Claims are payable in full without any deduction.

Significant Exclusions

The insurance policy does not cover the following risks:

(1) Loss of gross profits, which is not consequent upon property damage or due to an insured peril.
(2) Loss due to material damage to property.
(3) Difference between value of stock at the time of fire and the value at the time of subsequent replacement, deterioration of undamaged stock after fire.
(4) Cost of preparing fire and/or loss of profits claim.
(5) Third party claims and loss of goodwill.

Main Extensions

Policy can be extended to cover suppliers' and customers' premises or public utilities, on which the business is dependent and cost by way of auditors' fees for making the claim on the insurers.

Advance Loss of Profits Insurance

The Advance Loss of Profit (ALOP) policy is taken by the principal of an erection all risks policy or a contractor All Risks Policy as he stands to lose in case of any delay in the commissioning of the project. A marine-*cum*-erection/storage-*cum*-erection or contractor's All Risk Policy covers only physical damage to property, which at best, covers the expenses incurred for repairing for replacing the damaged property.

Salient features of an Advance loss of profits insurance policies are.

Scope of Cover

The advance loss of profit policy is designed to cover:

Loss of Gross Profit = Net Profit + Standing Charges

Or

Loss of Gross Earnings = Turnover – Specified Working Expenses

Or

Fixed Operation and management Costs (Debt Service Charges, increased Cost of Working, and Special Expense such as Penalties).

The policy pays for the actual loss of gross profit incurred during the period of delay, commencing from the scheduled date of commencement of commercial operation till the actual date of commencement of commercial operation, subject to a time excess and indemnity period selected. The delay however should have occurred due to a claim payable under marine cum erection policy, storage cum erection policy or contractor's all risks policy.

Special Exclusion

The policy does not cover delay due to:

(1) Inventory Losses.
(2) Delay in shipment of supplies.
(3) Normal project schedule slippages.
(4) Non-availability of funds for repairs/replacement to damaged items.
(5) Cancellation of licenses or government restriction, etc.

Sum Insured

The sum insured should represent the anticipated gross profit (i.e. Net Profit + Standing Charges) for the indemnity period selected.

Net Profit is taken to mean the business profit before taxation.

Standing Charges are the fixed charges/expenses incurred even in the absence of business activity (e.g. interest charges, salary and wages, director's fees, O&M costs, liquidated damages, etc.).

Indemnity period should be selected keeping in mind the maximum period required for re-importing, re-erecting and/or re-testing any part of the project.

Credit Guarantee Insurance

Credit Guarantee Insurance provides a business with protection against failure of its customers to pay their debts. Like any form of insurance, credit insurance is purchased to protect a business from a large loss that could impair its performance.

Despite company's best efforts, large or catastrophic losses occur due to:

(1) On large long-term buyers unexpectedly failing (bankruptcy).
(2) A significant change in the market (or economy) where a number of buyers become distressed and are unable to meet their obligations in time.
(3) A sudden shift in the political or economic conditions of a buyer's country (in the case of exports as it happened in Iraq).

It is also a risk management tool that can provide concrete solutions for the trade expansion issues being considered. The credit insurance policy is an insurance product rather it sets in motion an ongoing process of partnership between you and the insurer. The insurer vets a debtor's creditworthiness and monitors his financial position to identify possible problems if a debt goes bad and cannot be collected (or collected only partially), a claim is paid.

Salient features of a credit guarantee insurance policy are given hereunder:

Coverage

(1) Declared insolvency of the buyer, i.e. the buyer is declared bankrupt.
(2) He has made a valid assignment/compositions/ arrangement for the benefit of his creators.
(3) A receiver has been appointed.
(4) Order has been made for compulsory winding-up.

(5) An effective resolution has been passed for voluntary winding-up.
(6) An arrangement binding on all creditors has been sanctioned by the court or equivalent authority.

Protracted Default

Protracted default is the non-payment for specified number of days after the expiry of the due date for payment of any undisputed invoice submitted by the insured (suppliers) to his buyer.

Political Risks (for exports only)

Political risk is the risk undertaken on non-payment by the buyer caused by a political act such as war or civil war, sabotage, embargo, cancellation of import/export contract, and imposition of import/export restrictions by a state.

Major Exclusions

(1) Disputed debts.
(2) Default of agents/employees.
(3) The insured accepting an arrangement with the buyer, without prior approval of the insurer.
(4) If the rights under the policy are assigned by the insured without prior approval of the insurer.
(5) Interest, taxes, consequential losses, etc.
(6) Dishonesty and fraud.
(7) Disregard of agreed credit management procedures.
(8) Sales made to subsidiaries/associates/public/government bodies.
(9) Claims in excess of discretionary/sanctioned credit limits.

Basis of Indemnity

(1) The basis of indemnity will be the invoice value excluding interest and taxes.
(2) Up to 85 per cent of the insured loss.
(3) Payment will be the insured percentage of the insured loss, for sales made during the policy period, net of excess and subject to the overall indemnity limit under the policy.

Risk Monitoring

(1) The insurer assesses the creditworthiness of buyers for fixing credit limits.
(2) An extensive information database and constant monitoring provides an early warning to the insured that the buyer is in financial difficulty.
(3) It enables the insured to withdraw from the relationship on a structured basis.

Procedure for Obtaining Cover

(1) Completion of proposal form.
(2) Submission of proposal form along with payment of processing fee.
(3) Issue of quotation by the insurer.
(4) Payment of premium by the client.
(5) Issue of policy document.
(6) Working out credit limit, application for new buyers.

Premium Payable

(1) Premium rate is the amount obtained by applying a rate per cent on the annual insured credit sales turnover.
(2) Provisional premium to be paid in advance, on estimated turnover, subject to adjustment on actual turnover.

Fidelity Guarantee Insurance

The term fidelity guarantee insurance embraces policies indemnifying employers against financial loss on account of forgery, deflection, embezzlement and fraudulent conversion by employees. The object is to provide protection in respect of the default of an individual acting in capacity, such as cashier, accountant, store keeper, etc. The cover may be required in respect of a single employee or a number of employees. There are three types of policies normally issued for this class of business, viz. individual policy, collective policy and floating policy. The insures find it necessary to obtain the private reference and/or former employer's report forms in addition to the completed employer's and employees' application form, as appropriate.

Scope of Cover

The commercial fidelity guarantee policy provides indemnity against loss of money or goods as a result of acts of fraud or dishonesty on the part of the employee(s).

Covered Risks

The policy covers direct pecuniary loss caused by an act of fraud or dishonesty committed by any salaried person employed by the insured. This loss should have occurred in connection with the employee's duties during the period of his emplacement, and should be discovered within six months of his/her death, dismissal or retirement, or six months after the policy ceases to exist, whichever is earlier.

Individual Policy

The policy covers one individual only for a stated amount.

Collective Policy

A schedule is included in the policy document. The insured decides the amount of guarantee required for each individual according to his/her responsibilities and position.

Floater Policy

A single amount is shown in the policy, which represents the company's liability in respect of any one individual and its total liability in respect of all the employees guaranteed who are individually named in the schedule. Such policies can be granted where the number of persons to be guaranteed is not less than five.

Blanket Policy

It is possible to issue in certain selected cases blanket policies without the names of the guaranteed persons being shown but in respect of all employees who are grouped according to categories such as employees handling cash, other clerical staff, etc. They are issued only to large well-established business houses conducted on sound lines.

Premium Rating

Rates vary from 0.50 per cent to 1.50 per cent per annum on the amount of guarantee, depending upon the merits of each case.

Liability Insurances

Liabilities can arise from a legal obligation on the insured to pay. Liability can occur from many day-to-day activities. There are many examples of liability ranging from workmen's compensation, third party liability on road accidents, professional liability, product liability, and many other liabilities. There is a large demand for liability insurances in the developed markets.

Motor TP Insurance

As per the Motor Vehicles Act, 1988, it is mandatory for every owner of a vehicle plying on public roads to take an insurance policy to cover the amount that the owner becomes legally liable to pay as damages to third parties as a result of accidental death, bodily injury or damage to property. A certificate of insurance must be carried in the vehicle as a proof of such insurance.

Cover Available

The policy covers the vehicle owner's legal liability to pay compensation for the following conditions:

(1) Death or bodily injury to a third party/person.
(2) Damage to third party property.

Personal Accident Cover for Owner-driver is also included

Liability is covered in respect of death or injury and damage to third party property for Rs. 7.5 lakh for a commercial and private vehicle, and Rs. 1 lakh for scooter/motor cycle.

Additional Cover

(1) Legal liability to employees.
(2) Legal liability to non-fare paying passengers in commercial vehicles.

Public Liability Insurance

Legal liability under the law of tort can arise under several circumstances in the insured's premises, such as collapse of building structure, accidental falling of fixtures, bad maintenance or poor house-keeping resulting in accident to visitors on the premises, and accidental leakage of toxic substance that pollutes the atmosphere and injures or kills people.

The terms liability means responsibility and legal liability means responsibilities that can be enforced by law. Legal liability may be classified into Criminal Liability and Civil Liability. Only civil liability claims are payable. Civil liability claims will arise if there is *prima facie* evidence of negligence by the insured resulting in injury or death to any third party or resulting in damage to property belonging to a person other than the insured, or that in the insured person's custody.

Negligence will be proved only when the following conditions are satisfied:

(1) Existence of duty of care.
(2) Breach of this duty.
(3) Injury suffered by a person, or property damaged as a result of that breach.

Salient features of a Public Liability Insurance Policy are as under:

Highlights

This policy covers the amount that the insured becomes legally liable to pay as damages to third parties as a result of accidental death, bodily injury, and loss or damage to the property belonging to a third party. The legal cost and expense incurred in defending the case with prior consent of the insurance company are also payable subject to certain terms and conditions.

One can insure more than one unit situated in different locations under a single policy.

The policies offer a benefit of retroactive period on continuous renewal of policy, whereby claims reported in subsequent renewal, but pertaining to earlier period after first inception of the policy, also become payable.

Scope

Three types of public liability policies are issued:

(1) **Public Liability Non-Industrial Risk:** For offices, hotels, cinema houses, hospitals, schools, etc.
(2) **Public Liability Industrial Risk:** For godowns, warehouses and factories.
(3) **Public Liability Insurance Act, 1991:** This is a mandatory policy to be taken by the owners, users or transporters of hazardous substances as defined under the Environment (Protection) Act, 1986 in excess of the minimum quantity specified under the Public Liability Insurance Act, 1991.

Add on Covers

The Public Liability Policy can be extended to cover the following risks on payment of an additional premium:

(1) Natural calamities such as flood, earthquake, etc.
(2) Pollution risk subject to NOC from Pollution Control Board (PCB).
(3) Transportation risk.

Sum Insured

In Public Liability Policy, the sum insured is referred to as limit of indemnity. This limit is fixed according to per accident and per policy period, which is called Any One Accident (AOA) limit and Any One Year (AOY) limit, respectively. The ratio of AOA limit to AOY limit can be on the basis of (a) 1:1, (b) 1:2, (c) 1:3 or (d) 1:4.

The AOA limit, which is the maximum amount payable for each accident, should be fixed taking into account the nature of activity of the insured, the maximum number of people who could be affected and the maximum property damage that could occur in the worst possible accident in the insured's premises.

In terms of the Public Liability Insurance Act, 1991, the AOA limit should represent the paid-up capital of the company subject to maximum of Rs. 5 crore. The AOY limit is fixed at 3 times the AOA limit (max. Rs. 15 crore).

With reference to the Public Liability Insurance Act, 1991,

any award that exceeds the AOA limit will be paid by the government through Environment Relief Fund to which the insured has to contribute an amount equivalent to the premium paid under the Public Liability Insurance Act Policy.

Exemptions

The policy will not pay for claims arising out of the following situations:

(1) Contractual liability.
(2) Intentional non-compliance of any statutory provisions.
(3) Loss of goodwill.
(4) Slander.
(5) Fines and penalties.
(6) Libel.
(7) False arrest.
(8) Defamation.
(9) Mental injury, etc.

Product Liability Insurance

Policy indemnifies the insured against legal liability to third parties in consequence of death/bodily injury arising from the use of product sold to them.

Salient features of a Product Liability Insurance Policy are given below:

Scope of Cover

Policy indemnifies the insured for all sums that the insured shall become legally liable to pay as damages in consequence of accidental death/bodily injury or disease to third party or damage to their property arising out of any defect in the products manufactured and covered under the policy after such products have left the premises of the insured.

Excess

The policy is subject to compulsory excess, i.e. in the event of a claim, the insured must bear 0.50 per cent to 1 per cent of the limit of indemnity.

Premium

The premium will depend on the kind of product produced by the insured, i.e. the insured's classification as per the risk group, turnover, ratio of any one accident limit to any one year limit, etc.

Exports

The export of products to the USA, Canada, Europe and other countries can also be insured under the policy.

Vendors' Legal Liability

The policy can be extended to include the liability of vendors.

Technical Collaborator Liability

The liability arising out of any agreement of technical collaboration can be covered as an extension.

Main Exclusions Permissible

(1) Product recall.
(2) Deliberate, wilful or international non-compliance of any statutory provision.
(3) Loss of goodwill, and loss of market.
(4) Fines, penalties, and punitive/exemplary damages.
(5) War and war like situations.
(6) Any loss occurring prior to the retroactive date mentioned in the policy.

Professional Liability Insurance

The cover granted under the Professional Liability Insurance Policy provides indemnity for legal liability to third parties, arising out of errors and omissions or negligence in professional service rendered by the insured.

Policies will be issued for a period of 12 months (one year). These policies are usually issued for Doctors, Medical Establishments, Engineers, Architects, Chartered Accountants, Lawyers and other professionals.

Salient Features of a Professional Liability (Medical Practitioners) Insurance Policy are the following:

Salient Features

This insurance covers legal liability arising from errors and omissions on the part of Registered Medical Practitioners while rendering professional service.

Scope of Cover

The policy indemnifies any act committed by the insured, who shall be a Registered Medical Practitioner, giving rise to any legal liability to third parties. The insured includes the policyholder and his qualified assistant or employees, as named in the proposal form.

It applies to claims arising out of bodily injury and/or death of any patient caused by or alleged to have been caused by error, omission or negligence in professional service rendered, or which should have been rendered by the insured or qualified assistants named in the schedule or any nurse or technician employed by the insured.

(1) Legal liability as fixed by courts in India to pay compensation.

(2) Defence costs and expense. This means all costs, fees and expenses incurred with the prior consent of the insurer in the investigation, defense or settlement of any claim made against the insured, provided the claim falls within the ambit of the policy.

The amount of payment under (a) and (b) will not exceed the amount insured for in the policy under the limit of 'Any One Accident' (AOA) in respect of any or all claims made against the insured arising out of any one accident.

Special Benefit

(1) Retroactive Benefit: This means that the insured will be covered for any professional act or omission occurring during the period of insurance, starting from the first date of the first policy, provided that the policy is renewed without interruption and is in force when the claim arising out of the act or omission is made in writing against the insured during the policy period. Policy period means the period incepting from the date and hour mentioned in the policy schedule and terminating at midnight on the expiry date indicated in the policy schedule.

(2) **Notification Extension clause:** If the insured notifies during the policy period any special event or circumstance that the insurer accepts may give rise to a claim, the acceptance of such notification means that the insurer will deal with the claim as if it has been made during the policy period.

(3) **Extended claim Reporting Clause:** In the event of non-renewal or cancellation of the policy, the insurer will allow a time limit of up to 90 days, provided another policy does not exist, for notification of claims for accidents that had taken place during the period of insurance.

Meaning of AOA and AOY

AOA means Any One Accident, which may include one or more or a series of claims arising out of the same cause or error or omission relating to professional service. AOY means Any One Year. The insured can choose an indemnity limit that can be in the ratio of 1:1, 1:2, !:3, or 1:4 of AOA or AOY, and the premium will be charged on AOY limit.

Main Exclusions Specified

(1) Liability arising from any criminal act or act in violation of any law or ordinance.
(2) Service rendered under the influence of intoxicants or narcotics.
(3) Dental treatment under general anesthesia, except in a hospital.
(4) Use of drugs for weight reduction.
(5) Plastic surgery, except for repair of scar being the result of previous surgery, or in connection with burns or other traumatic injury.
(6) AIDS-related conditions.
(7) Liability arising due to intentional non-compliance of statutory provisions.

(8) Personal injuries caused by x-ray and radio-active substances.
(9) Liability caused by intentional disregard of technical or administrative management of the need to take all care to prevent claims.
(10) Liability to employees/apprentices/contractors/ third party, general public.
(11) Fines, penalties, punitive or exemplary damages.
(12) Any loss of goodwill, loss of market, etc.

Important Conditions laid down

(1) Early written notice of any claim to the insurer. Sending of any claim, writ, summons or process and all documents to the insurer.
(2) No admission, offer, promise or payment to be made without the consent of the insurer.
(3) The insurer has the right to take over and conduct, in the name of the insured, the defense/settlement of the claim.
(4) The insured shall give all such information and assistance to the company as it may reasonably require.
(5) No short period policy is permitted, i.e. all policies will be for 12 months.

Indicative Premium Rate

Varies between 0.30 to 0.50 per cent or per thousand rupees depending upon:

(1) Category of Doctor, and
(2) AOA : AOY ratio chosen.

Workmen's Compensation Insurance

This liability policy covers employer's liability towards his workmen. An employer, as a principal or contractor, engaging workmen as defined in Workmen's Compensation Act, 1923, would need to cover his liability to them under statute and at common law. The workers' compensation policy covers the employer's liability towards his employees who come within the definition coverage for employment related injury (including death). The employer can cover employees who do not qualify as workmen, under a separate table.

Salient features of a workmen's Compensation Insurance Policy are as under:

Scope of Cover

The policy provides for two forms of insurance viz.,

(1) **Table A:** Indemnity against legal liability to all employees (whether or not coming within the definition of the term workmen) under the Workmen's Compensation Act, 1923 and subsequent amendment to the said act prior to the date of issue of the policy, the Fatal Accidents Act, 1855 and the Common Law.

(2) **Table B:** Indemnity against legal liability under the Fatal Accidents Act, 1855 and the Common Law. (Table B policies may not be issued to cover employees who fall within the definition of workmen under the Workmen's Compensation Act, 1923 as amended) (Code Misc.10)

Sum Insured

The policy does not mention the sum insured. The estimated earnings of the workmen for the policy period are mentioned on the policy.

Premium

The premium rate depends on the occupation of the workmen and their annual earnings.

Significant Exclusion

The insurance policy does not cover losses arising out of war and allied perils, nuclear activities, and contractual liabilities.

Main Extensions Permitted

(1) **Medical Expenses:** On payment of extra premium, medical, surgical and hospital expenses, including

the cost of transport to hospital for accidental employment injuries.

(2) **Occupational Disease:** Liability in respect of diseases mentioned in Part C of Schedule III of the Workmen's Compensation Act, on additional premium; the diseases should arise out of and in the course of employment.

Apart from the above, there are other types of liability policies—Director and Officers' Liability Policy, Lift (Third Party) Insurance, Employer's Liability Policy, Carrier's Liability Insurance, Golfer's Indemnity Insurance, etc. The above five types of liabilities are indicative of the different types of liabilities that can arise and can be covered by insurance.

Personal Insurances

Personal lines of insurance relate to losses faced by a person, such as death, sickness, accident, unemployment and superannuation.

Health Insurance

Health care costs are high and getting higher. Payment of hospital bills relating to a serious accident or major illness is scary for many. Health or Medical policies protect a person and his/her family in case they need expensive medical care. Some health insurances offer cashless benefit at hospitals, meaning that the insurer will make the payment directly to the hospital. Some policies are of medical reimbursement types. Variations of health insurance policies offer lump sum payment on a per day/ per event basis, instead of paying the hospital bills in lieu of reimbursing hospitalization expenses.

Salient Features of a Health Insurance Policy are mentioned below:

Scope

Expenses incurred by the insured for hospitalization for illness/diseases or injury sustained (domiciliary hospitalization also payable as per policy) which include hospital charges (room, boarding and operation theatre), fees for surgeon, anesthesia, nursing, specialist's fees, etc. and cost of diagnostic tests, medicines, blood, oxygen, etc. as well as cost of appliances such as pacemaker, artificial limbs, etc.

Cover

Illness/disease, accidental injury sustained leading to one or more class(es) of expenses listed above are covered.

The Insured Covered

(1) Any person in the age group of 5 to 75 years.
(2) Children between 3 months to 5 years can be covered only along with parents.
(3) Institutions (Government or Private) for their employees.
(4) Clubs/associations for their members in the said age group.
(5) Group schemes for homogeneous groups of more than 50 persons.

Other Benefits

(1) Domiciliary hospitalization benefits can be included under group medi-claim policy and a premium discount can be availed.
(2) A discount of 10 per cent of total premium for coverage of family under a single policy.

Policy Will Pay

(1) Actual hospitalization expense of various types listed above, subject to a maximum of Rs. 15, 000 to Rs. 5, 00, 000 depending upon the sum insured/ chosen at the inception of the policy (sum insured is maximum liability under the policy).
(2) Actual domiciliary hospitalization expenses limited to Rs. 30, 000 to Rs. 50, 000, depending on the sum insured/chosen at inception.
(3) Cost of health check-up reimbursable at the end of four continuously claim-free underwriting years limited to 1 per cent of average sum insured of four claim-free years.

(4) The sum insured will be increased by 5 per cent, cumulative bonus, for every claim-free year. If there is a claim in a policy with cumulative bonus of 10 per cent, the sum insured will be reduced by the earned bonus.

(5) Maternity expenses incurred in hospital/nursing home as in-patient, subject to limit of sum insured or Rs. 50, 000, whichever is lower, on payment of extra premium and the policy being extended to cover maternity benefits. This benefit is only available in group policies.

(6) All terms, benefits and conditions of the cover are subject to the definitions of various terms under the policy.

Exclusions

Broadly, there would be no claim under the policy under the following circumstances; these are excluded from its scope/ purview:

(1) Domiciliary hospitalization.

(2) Pre and post-hospitalization treatment.

(3) Treatment of Asthma, Chronic Nephritis and Nephritis Syndrome, Gastroenteritis, Diabetes Mellitus and Insipidus, Epilepsy, Hypertension, Influenza, Cough and Cold, all Psychiatric or Psychosomatic Disorder, Pyrexia of Unknown Origin for less than 10 days. Tonsillitis and URT(I) Arthritis, Rheumatism, etc. (the list is illustrative, not exhaustive).

(4) Any treatment relating to any illness/disease already in existence at the time of proposal.

(5) Any disease/injury during first 30 days of commencement of policy (accidental injury is not an exclusion).

(6) During first year of cover, Cataract, Benign Prostatic Hypertrophy, Hysterectomy for Hemorrhagic on Fibromyoma, Hernia, Hydrocele, Congenital Internal Disease, Fistula in Anus, Sinusitis and related disorder.

(7) Any pre-existing disease/illness is not covered during renewal also.

(8) Vaccination, inoculation, circumcision or change of life or cosmetic or aesthetic treatment, and plastic surgery and dental treatment unless requiring hospitalization, necessitated due to accident or as part of any illness.

(9) Cost of spectacles, contact lenses, and hearing aids.

(10) Convalescence, general debility, rundown conditions, sterility, venereal disease, intentional self-injury and use of intoxicants.

(11) Any variation of deficiency syndrome or AIDS.

(12) Hospital/nursing home charges not consistent with or include the diagnosis and treatment.

(13) Vitamins and tonics not forming part of any treatment.

(14) Any treatment related to pregnancy, childbirth and voluntary medical termination of pregnancy during the first 12 weeks of pregnancy.

(15) Nuclear perils and war group of perils.

(16) Naturopathy treatment.

Personal Accident Insurance

Personal accident insurance policy covers a person against accidental death, permanent total disablement (PTD) and permanent partial disablement (PPD). There are many Personal Accident Plan options (Accidental Death and Permanent Total Disablement Cover) with different sum insured.

Salient features of a Personal Accident Insurance Policy are mentioned below:

Policy Coverage

A comprehensive personal accident plan would usually cover the insured for an agreed amount of cover, say Rs. 20, 00, 000.

(1) Death of the Insured (Personal): In case of death of the insured due to an accident (including on account of terrorism or acts of terrorism) within the policy period, the nominee (mentioned in the policy) is compensated with the sum insured.

(2) **Permanent Total Disablement (PTD):** Personal accident plan pays compensation against the permanent and total loss of limbs, sight, etc. (including due to terrorism or acts of terrorism causing an accident).
Note: If any such injury as mentioned above shall result in the inability to remain gainfully employed then the capital sum insured payable will be 100 per cent.

(3) **Permanent Partial Disablement (PPD):** Personal accident covers total and/or partial loss of use of the defiled body parts or loss by actual physical separation (including on account of terrorism or acts of terrorism).

(4) **Carriage of Dead Body:** Reimbursement of expenses incurred for transportation of the insured person's dead body to the place of residence subject to a maximum of 2 per cent of capital sum insured or Rs. 2500 whichever is less.

Key Benefits

(1) Covers accidental death or permanent total disablement (PTD) on account of an accident, with option to cover permanent partial disablement (PPD).
(2) Flexible plan options, with sum insured of Rs. 3, 5, 10 and Rs. 20 lakh.
(3) Covers claims arising out of terrorism or acts of terrorism.
(4) Choice of cover 3, 4, or 5 years.
(5) No health check-up required.
(6) Renewable till the age of 70 years.

Eligibility

(1) Age criteria at entry is minimum 18 years, maximum 70 years.
(2) The applicant can buy the policy for his spouse aged between 18-70 years.
(3) The policy cover is renewable till the age of 70 years.

Policy Exclusions

The company shall not be liable under this policy for the following matters:

(1) Compensation/claim under more than one of the categories specified in the.policy coverage in respect of the same period of disablement of the insured person.

(2) Claims arising from sickness/illness.

(3) Death, injury or disablement of the insured person.

- (a) From intentional self-injury, suicide or attempted suicide;
- (b) Whilst under the influence of intoxicating liquor or drugs;
- (c) Whilst engaging in aviation or ballooning, or whilst mounting into or dismounting from or traveling in any balloon or aircraft other than as a passenger (fare paying or otherwise) in any duly licensed standard type of aircraft anywhere in the world;
- (d) Directly or indirectly caused by venereal disease or insanity;
- (e) Arising or resulting from the insured committing any breach of the law with criminal intent;
- (f) War, invasion, act of foreign enemy, hostilities (whether war be declared or not) civil war, rebellion, revolution, insurrection, mutiny, military or usurped power, seizure, capture, arrest, restraints and detainment of all kinds;
- (g) Nuclear weapon induced treatment; and
- (h) Childbirth or pregnancy, or in consequent thereof.

Life Insurance

Life insurance is a personal insurance, may be the most personal of them all. Life insurance covers one's own life and the lives of one's close relatives, premature death, disability and dependency during old age are some of the greatest risks people are willing to cover. This is one of the most common types of insurance covers and is designed to pay-out to the loved ones in the event when a person dies. There are certain restrictions in place with this types of cover, for instance, suicide is not covered. The subject being so vast, it is the topic of a separate book and hence not dealt with in this chapter. The author has brought into publication a separate book on Life Insurance.

SPECIALISED INSURANCES

Readers must have by now seen that the categorizations of various insurances are broad and indicative of certain basic characteristics. Many of the areas are overlapping, as over-segmentation and mutual exclusiveness are difficult to achieve when loss and related hardship is the subject-matter.

There are many policies that may not exactly fall in a specific category or where such categorization may be practically meaningless. Some of such insurances are discussed below.

Agriculture-related Insurance

Indian agriculture is heavily dependent on natural factors, particularly rainfall. Rainfall variations cause variability in crop yields. Again, rainfall is increasingly unpredictable and uncertain. Indian agriculture is a gamble in the monsoons. Although there are no ways of controlling weather factors, agriculture insurers strive to mitigate the adverse financial effects that rainfall can have on the rural economy, particularly farm incomes. While going through the salient features, the readers will realize how the products are different from the other insurances and the points of comparison as well are different, some of them interesting too.

Salient features of Varsha Bima (an Agriculture Insurance Policy) are as under:

Scope

Varsha Bima covers anticipated shortfall in crop yield on account of deficit rainfall. It is voluntary for all classes of cultivators who stand to lose financially upon adverse incidence of rainfall and can take insurance under the scheme. Initially, Varsha Vima was meant for cultivators for whom National Agricultural Insurance Scheme (NAIS) was voluntary.

Period of Insurance

The insurance operates during June to September for short duration crops, June to October for medium duration crops, and June to November for longer duration crops. Further, these subjects (periods) are state-specific, mentioned in List 'B' in the Constitution. In case of the sowing failure option, the period covered is from June 15 to August 15.

Insurance Buying Period

A cultivator can buy Varsha Bima only upto June 15 for the sowing failure option and June 30 for other options.

Coverage Options

(1) Option-I: Seasonal Rainfall Insurance

Coverage is against negative deviation of 20 per cent and beyond in actual rainfall (in mm) from normal rainfall (in mm) for the entire season. Actual rainfall is the monthly cumulative rainfall from June to November (with June to September or October for short and medium duration crops). The pay out structure is designed in such a way that the yield is correlated to various ranges of adverse deviation in rainfall.

The sum insured per hectare is the maximum pay out corresponding to the maximum potential loss. The claim pay out shall be on a graded scale (in slabs), corresponding to different degrees of adverse deviation in actual rainfall.

(2) Option-II: Rainfall Distribution Index

Coverage is against adverse deviation of 20 per cent and beyond in actual rainfall index from normal rainfall index for the entire season. The index is constructed to maximize the correlation for weekly rainfall within the season. The indices vary from India Meteorological Department (IMD) station-to-station and crop-to-crop. The sum insured per hectare is the maximum pay out corresponding to the maximum potential loss. The claim pay out shall be on a graded scale (in slabs), corresponding to different degrees of adverse deviation in actual rainfall index.

(3) Option-III: Sowing Failure

Coverage is against adverse deviation in actual rainfall (in mm) from normal rainfall (in mm) beyond 40 per cent between June 15 and August 15. The sum insured per hectare is the maximum input cost incurred by the cultivator till the end of the sowing period and is pre-specified. The claim pay out shall be on a graded scale, corresponding to different degrees of rainfall deviation. The maximum payout of 100 per cent of sum insured is available at deviations of 80 per cent and above.

(4) Option-IV: Vegetative Phase

Coverage is against adverse deviation in actual rainfall (in mm) from normal rainfall (in mm) beyond 20 per cent between August 1/August 16 and September 30/October 31 to November 30. The sum insured per hectare is the maximum payout corresponding to the maximum potential loss. The claim pay out will be on a graded scale, corresponding to different degrees of rainfall deviation. The maximum pay out of 100 per cent of sum insured is available at deviation of 80 per cent and above.

Sum Insured

The sum insured is pre-specified and is normally between cost of production and value of production. In case of the sowing failure option, it is the maximum input cost incurred by the cultivator till the end of the sowing period, which again is pre-specified.

Premium

The premium may vary from option to option and crop to crop. The premium rates have been optimized *vis-a-vis* benefits, and starts from 1 per cent.

Time Schedule and Procedure of Claim Payment

The procedure for working out claims is automated, i.e. there shall be no necessity for submission of loss information or claims intimation by the insured cultivator. Normally, claims are paid on the basis of actual rainfall data within a month from the end of the indemnity period.

Salient features of a Horticulture (Agriculture Insurance) Policy are given below:

Cover

Trees/plants/shoot/vegetative part only for crop duration or 12 months, whichever is shorter.

The Insured

Farm owners/lessees cultivating the plantations/horticulture.

Risks Covered

Coverage and indemnity to the insured to the extent of loss or damage to the crop by operation of any one of the following perils:

(1) Fire including forest fire and bush fire.
(2) Lightning.
(3) Riot, strike, and acts of terrorism.
(4) Storm, hailstorm, cyclone, hurricane, flood and inundation.

Benefits

The input costs or recurring expenses incurred for raising the crop (establishment and maintenance) till the date of the loss are paid. Limits of indemnity on input cost basis are fixed at each stage of the crop. Claims are subject to franchise and excess deductibles.

Exclusions

The policy excludes to pay for loss or damage to crop arising due to:

(1) Theft, malicious damage, and negligence,
(2) Natural mortality,
(3) War and nuclear perils,
(4) Insects, pests and diseases,
(5) Drought, earthquake, climatic variations,
(6) Water-logging,
(7) Inconsequential losses, and
(8) Damage to structures, capital items, irrigation systems, agricultural implements, and harvested produce.

Salient features of Weather Insurance (an agriculture-related insurance) Policy are as under:

Scope of Cover

Weather insurance is an indemnity for losses that may arise due to abnormal weather conditions. These abnormal weather conditions can be events such as excess of rainfall, shortfall in rainfall or variations in temperature, wind velosity and humidity.

Product Structure

(1) **Peril Identification:** Peril identification involves appreciation of agronomic properties of the crops or nature of the economic activity. Detailed correlation analysis is carried out to ascertain the manner in which the weather impacts yields of the crops (output) of other economic activities.

(2) Index Setting: In weather insurance, the claim is settled on the basis of a transparent index. The index is created by assigning weights to critical time periods of crop growth. The past weather data is mapped on to this index to arrive at a normal threshold index. The actual weather data is then mapped to the index to arrive at the actual index level. In case there is a material deviation between the normal index and the actual index, compensation is paid out to the insured on the basis of a pre-agreed formula.

(3) **Back testing for Payouts:** In order to ensure the robustness of the structure, the normal index is extensively tested based on historical data, to ascertain if the payouts made on the basis of the chosen indices would have adequately indemnified the loss in the past or not.

(4) **Pricing:** Pricing is determined based on components of expected loss, volatility of historical losses and management expense.

(5) **Monitoring:** This claim-related of weather data is collected during the policy period and concurrent assessment of the ground conditions.

(6) Claims Settlement: The claims settlement is a hassle-free process, as the beneficiary is not required to file a claim for loss to receive a payout. Instead, some companies compensate the beneficiary at the end of the crop season for any deviations from the normal conditions on the basis of the data collected from an independent source accessible to all, such as a local weather station, thus removing thc nccd for carrying out field surveys.

Promotional Low Value Insurance

These are policies intended to provide social support to the underprivileged sectors and those segments of the economy that are not commercially viable due to their low turnover, geographically not easily accessible, and possibly, economically and educationally backward. In essence, these relate to the country's rural and social sectors.

Salient Features of Poultry Insurance Policy are the following:

Brief Description

This provides indemnity to poultry birds, which include layers, broilers and hatchery birds, (breeding stock) which are exotic and cross-bred. Indigenous and non-descriptive birds will not be insured.

The scheme is applicable to poultry forms consisting of a minimum 100 birds under scheme category and 500 birds under non-scheme category, and under General broilers, 100 per batch, layers 500 per batch and hatching 2000 birds per batch. These limits have been revised upwards quite a few times.

Covered Risk

The policy shall provide indemnity against:

(1) Death of birds due to accident (including fire, lightning, flood, cyclone, strike, riot and civil commotion, and terrorism), or
(2) Diseases contracted or occurring during the period of insurance.

Major Exclusions

(1) Wilful injury,
(2) Transit by a mode,
(3) Theft and clandestine sale,
(4) Intentional slaughter,
(5) Avian Leucosis complex disease,
(6) War and nuclear perils,
(7) Improper management,
(8) Undergrowth,
(9) Cannibalism,
(10) Predators' action,
(11) Permanent and partial disablement,
(12) Loss of production, and
(13) Standard exclusions

Salient features of Honey Bee Insurance Policy are as under:

Brief Description

This policy is to cover beehives and/or colonies belonging to individuals, cooperative societies, and those sponsored and subsidized under various projects of respective State and the Central Government. This cover is only for Indian Honeybee and Italian Honey bee.

Covered Risks

Total loss or damage to beehives and/or bee colonies as a result of an accident caused by fire, flood, inundation, storm, tempest, cyclone, hurricane and tornado. Additional covers are theft, specified viral disease, and transit loss during migration.

Major exclusions are partial loss/damage of whatsoever nature, loss of production wax moth and ectoparasitic termites, and loss of bee colony resulting from death of queen bee.

Salient features of Failed Well Insurance Policy are as under:

Brief Description

The scheme is applicable only to those wells financed by banks where re-financing by NABARD is involved. This is applicable to shallow tube well, filter point, dug wells, bore wells and dug-*cum*-bore wells.

Covered Risks

Risk of failure of well due to failure of guaranteed yield and the expenditure actually incurred by farmers towards boring/digging of the wells.

Major Exclusions

(1) Cessation of work, whether total or partial,
(2) Negligence,
(3) War and allied perils,
(4) Quality of water and structure failure,
(5) Exclusions are as per NABARD scheme,
(6) Flood, earthquake and other convulsions of nature, and
(7) Riot and strike risk.

Salient features of Animal Driven Cart/Tonga Insurance Policy are the following:

Brief Description

This insurance covers all types of animal-driven carts, driven by any animal, such as bullock, male buffalo, castrated bullock, camel, horse, mule, donkey, yak, etc. This policy has four sections. Sections I and II are compulsory. Section III and IV are optional. Section I covers the animal driven cart, Section II covers the animal pulling the cart. Section III covers the third party liability. Section IV indemnifies the driver. The values of the animal and carriage are to be declared separately. The sum insured shall be 100 per cent of the market value of the animal and carriage. If the animal is insured for the purpose of pulling or driving the carriage by a separate policy, the cart/tonga/coach alone can be insured keeping on the record the particulars of the animals insured. In case of normal cover offered by the policy, no veterinary examination is required. However, if full death cover for the animal is required by the proposer, a veterinary surgeon's certificate is to be obtained at the cost of the proposer. The animal should be identified by ear tagging or branding with hot iron or tattooing, as per Cattle Insurance Market Agreement.

Covered Risk

(1) **Section I:** Loss or damage to the cart/tonga/coach by:
   (a) Accidental external means, or
   (b) Fire, explosion, lightning, storm, tempest, flood, inundation, earthquake, burglary or theft.

(2) **Section II:** This section provides indemnity against death or permanent total disablement of the animal used for pulling or driving the carriage.

(3) **Section III:** Third party liability arising out of an accident caused by cart/tonga/coach insured, including passengers' liability up to Rs. 5, 000 per accident and Rs. 10, 000 for all accidents.

(4) **Section IV:** This Section indemnifies the driver against death or disablement due to driving the cart or whilst mounting into or dismounting from the cart.

Comprehensive Insurance

There are many areas where policy types overlap in scope. Similarly, there are products covering different types of losses bunched together depending on the need of a customer. A home insurance policy is a common example of such a policy that covers certain aspects of fire insurance, engineering insurance (break-down of an air-conditioner or refrigerator), personal accident insurance, travel insurance, and liability insurance, all rolled into one. In an industrial scenario, products are tailor-made for corporate requirements as composite types (all inclusive) or hybrid types (chopped and put together from different groups). Examples of a few such products are provided for enabling the readers to understand such products.

Salient Features of Industrial All Risks Insurance Policy are given below:

Brief Description

This policy is a comprehensive package policy that covers almost all risks and perils, which a large industry may face during its operations. This policy covers buildings, machinery, furniture, fixtures, fittings and electrical installations on re-instatement value, while the stock is covered on market value basis. Under-insurance on each item of the schedule will be ignored if it does not exceed 15 per cent of the sum insured. Policy also covers equipments and machinery sent for repairs outside the premises for a period of 60 days. Transit risk inside the compound of an industry is also covered.

Covered Risks

(1) Bursting and overflowing of water tanks, apparatus and pipes;
(2) Deterioration of stocks due to power failure following damage to premises of public power stations and electric service feeders (for cold storages);
(3) Forest fire, leakage and contamination covers;
(4) Spoilage material damage cover,
(5) Sprinkler leakage cover,
(6) Subterranean fire;
(7) Spontaneous and landslide cover;
(8) Burglary (other than larceny);
(9) Machinery breakdown/boiler explosion/electronic equipment, and
(10) Business interruption following fire or machinery breakdown.

Major Exclusions

(1) Damage to the property caused by faulty or defective design materials, or workmanship, inherent vice, wear and tear, etc.
(2) Interruption of water supply, gas, electricity or fuel systems.
(3) Collapse or cracking of the building.
(4) Wilful act or gross negligence.
(5) War, invasion, mutiny, rebellion, revolution, etc.
(6) Damage—direct or indirect—by nuclear weapons material.
(7) Contamination by radioactivity.

Salient features of Office Insurance Policy are the following:

Scope of Cover

Office Insurance Policy is a comprehensive insurance policy for the office. The policy covers:

(1) **Fire (Building and Contents):** Losses to the building and contents against (a) fire, lightning, riot, strike, storm, cyclone, flood, and terrorism. (b) Loss or damage due to terrorism can also be covered as an add-on cover.

(2) **Burglary:** This cover protects the contents of your office against any loss or damage caused by burglary or an attempted burglary.

(3) **All-risk Functional Equipment:** This cover provides for the damage caused to the equipment in the office.

(4) **Cost of Data Re-instatement:** This covers the cost incurred in restoring the data lost because of an insured peril.

(5) **Cash-in-Safe:** This cover provides for losses resulting due to burglary of cash kept in safe.

(6) **Cash in Transit:** This cover covers losses due to burglary of cash while it is being carried from the bank/ATM to your office.

(7) **Glass Breakage:** This covers for loss or damage to any fixed plain glass caused by any accident, external factor and mobile phones.

(8) **All-Risk Non-functional Items:** This cover provides for damage or loss to mobile equipment such as laptops and mobile phones.

(9) **Fidelity:** It covers direct financial losses sustained due to fraud or dishonest acts by salaried employees.

(10) **Cheque Forgery:** This covers for losses caused by forgery or alteration of cheques, drafts or any other negotiable instruments issued by you or in your favour.

(11) **Personal Accident:** Body injuries sustained due to an accident, resulting in death or permanent/total disability; ambulance charges up to Rs. 2000 for carriage of the dead body, in the event of death.

(12) **Mediclaim:** According to the terms and conditions of the Mediclaim section.

(13) **Public Liability:** This cover provides for legal liability on behalf of the proposer for: (a) Accidental Death or bodily injury to a third party, excluding resident employees or domestic staff. (b) Accidental damage to third party property.

(14) **Professional Indemnity:** It provides for legal liability to your employees.

(15) **Employer's Liability:** It provides for legal liability to your employees.

(16) **Tenant's Legal Liability:** This cover provides for legal liability imposed on the proposer, due to unintentional property damage for the loss or damage to the property caused by fire, explosion or water damage to the premises. It could be in the form of a building or contents owned by or belonging to another and used by the insured in the capacity of a tenant or a person holding them in custody for which the proposer is legally responsible.

Exclusions

(1) **Under-Insurance:** In case the actual value of the insured property at the time of loss under the Fire Policy is found to be greater than the sum insured chosen by you then the claim would be proportionately reduced.

(2) **Wilful Destruction:** Loss, damage or destruction of property caused by war perils, wear and tear, and atmospheric conditions, wilful destruction.

(3) **Loss:** If the dwelling is unoccupied for more than 30 days.

(4) **Any item:** Covered under 'Contents for fire and Burglary', value of which is more than Rs. 10, 000, unless specified in the proposal form.

Premium

The premium depends on the construction of the asset, the occupancy and the accident prevention measures implemented in the office. Appropriate discounts/loading are given, based on past claims history.

Specialty Insurance (Examples of Hybrid Cover)

There are various specialty covers for some specific sectors as mentioned below:

Films and Television

Making a film involves heavy investment and consequently involves significant risks. With film production in India getting an industry status, the burning need of the hour for production houses is insurance coverage. This insurance cover is tailor-made for all aspects of the film industry, such as films and documentaries, television serials, advertising films etc.

Sports Tournaments

The policy provides specific coverage for sporting tournaments, such as cricket, hockey, golf, athletics, football, swimming, etc.

Events

With the advent of professional event managers, there is now a more professional approach to the business of event management. Bajaj Allianz offers insurance covers for various events, such as musical events, award ceremonies, product launches, fashion shows, exhibitions, etc.

Scope of Coverage

The insurance coverage is highly customized to suit specific requirements; the basic coverage includes the following:

(1) Event cancellation,
(2) Cast insurance,
(3) Extra expenses,
(4) Film negative,
(5) Fire (allied peril),
(6) Personal accident,
(7) Money (in transit and in safe),
(8) Hospital cash,
(9) Burglary, and
(10) Public Liability.

Although these are suggested yet the insurance covers are practically enhanced or modified to suit specific requirements.

Other Specialty Insurances include:

(1) Oil and Gas Insurance that covers drilling and pipeline risks.
(2) Satellite insurance that covers infrequent events, such as the pre-launch phase, launch phase and in-orbit phase of satellites.
(3) Title insurance is that insures against loss from defects in title to real property and from the invalidity or unenforceability of mortgage liens. It is meant to protect an owner's or lender's financial interest in real property against loss due to title defects, liens or other matters.

SUMMARY

The readers should be able to understand the main types of loss categories covered by insurance and familiarized themselves with the different types of insurances after reading this chapter.

The readers must be able to have a reasonable degree of familiarity about the various policies in use in the insurance industry, and appreciate the basic structure and underlying logic/rationale of the major product types. The insured can deal with confidence in the insurance market. To recapitulate—

(1) Physical losses or damages to real or personal property are property losses.
(2) Loss to building by earthquake, and loss to machinery by fire are examples of property losses.
(3) Legal losses are the ones that arise from a legal obligation on the insured to pay.
(4) Death, sickness and disability are the examples of personal losses.
(5) Fire, lightning, explosion and implosion are some of the perils included in a fire policy.
(6) Theft, wilful act or gross negligence, and loss of earnings are some of the exclusions of a fire policy.
(7) Cover for Terrorism, and for additional expenses on rent for alternative accommodation are two of the

optional covers provided under a Home insurance policy.

(8) Machinery break-down policy broadly covers loss due to all kinds of accidental, electrical and mechanical break-down due to internal and external causes.

(9) The boiler and pressure vessel's policy does not cover loss and/or damage arising from:
   (a) Fire and allied perils,
   (b) War and nuclear perils,
   (c) Losses arising out of overload experiments, and
   (d) Gradual wear and tear of parts.

(10) Electronic Equipment Insurance Policy covers loss or damage in the form of:
   (a) Material damage to electronic equipment (which can include systems software) due to sudden and unforeseen events,
   (b) Cost of external data media, including cost of reconstruction of data, and
   (c) Increased cost of working.

(11) Marine Cargo Export/Import Policy includes—
   (a) Institute Cargo Clause (C): named peril basis.
   (b) Institute Cargo Clause (B): named peril basis.
   (c) Institute Cargo Clause (A): offers the widest form of cover under Marine Cargo Insurance in so far as it relates to the perils covered. ICC (A) is an unnamed perils clause.

(12) An inland Transit Policy includes:
   (a) Basic Risk Policy that covers loss or damage to specified goods caused by fire, lightning, breakage of bridges, overtrumping of vehicles, and collision with or by carrying vehicle, and is subject to specified exclusions.
   (b) All Risks policy that covers all risks of loss or damage to specified goods is subject to exclusion.

(13) Natural Calamities covered under a comprehensive Motor Policy are:
   (a) Fire, explosion, self-ignition or lightning.
   (b) Earthquake, flood, typhoon, hurricane, storm, tempest, inundation, cyclone, hail storm, frost, landslide or rockslide.

(14) A comprehensive Motor Policy does not cover against:
   (a) Normal wear and tear and general ageing of the vehicle;
   (b) Depreciation or any consequential loss;
   (c) Mechanical/electrical breakdown; and
   (d) Wear and tear of consumables such as tyres and tubes.

(15) The vehicles are insured at a fixed value called the insured's declared value (IDV), which is the sum insured for motor OD.

(16) The Motor Liability Policy excludes the following:
   (a) Own damage losses,
   (b) Any claim arising out of personal accident,
   (c) Third party legal liability covers for commercial vehicles other than goods carrying commercial vehicles,
   (d) Any accidental loss or damage and/or liability caused, sustained or incurred outside the geographical area, and
   (e) Any claim arising out of any contractual liability.

(17) Hull insurance covers various interests such as:
   (a) Hull and machinery insurance;
   (b) Insurance of freight; and
   (c) Loss of hire insurance.

(18) The premium will depend on the following factors:
   (1) Type of vessel, trading limits, age, tonnage, and technical aspects of machinery.
   (2) Management and ownership considerations.
   (3) Past claims experience.
   (4) Valuation of vessel.
   (5) Type of cover required.
   (6) Size of the deductible.

(19) Some policies used under Aviation insurance are:
   (a) Hull all risk insurance policy.
   (b) Spares all risk insurance policy.
   (c) Hull/spares all risk insurance.
   (d) Hull deductible insurance.
   (e) Aviation personal accident (crew member) insurance.

(20) The loss of profits insurance policy does not cover—
   (a) Loss of gross profit, which is not consequent upon property damage due to an insured peril,
   (b) Loss due to natural damage to property,
   (c) Third party claims, and
   (d) Loss of goodwill.

(21) The ALOP policy does not cover delay due to:
   (a) Inventory losses,
   (b) Delay in shipment of supplies,
   (c) Normal project schedule slippages,
   (d) Non-availability of funds for repairs/ replacement of damaged items,
   (e) Cancellation of license, or
   (f) Government restrictions, etc.

(22) The Credit Guarantee Policy cover includes:
   (a) Declared insolvency of the buyer, i.e. the buyer is declared bankrupt.
   (b) He has made valid assignments/composition arrangement for the benefit of his creditors.
   (c) A receiver has been appointed.
   (d) Order has been made for compulsory winding-up.
   (e) An effective resolution has been passed for voluntary winding-up.

(23) Some of the exclusions of a credit guarantee policy are:
   (a) Disputed debts,
   (b) Default of insured's agents/employees,
   (c) Interest, taxes, consequential losses, etc.,
   (d) Dishonesty and fraud, and
   (e) Disregard of agreed credit management procedures.

(24) The Commercial Fidelity Guarantee Policy provides indemnity against loss of money or goods as a result of acts of fraud or dishonesty on the part of the employees.

(25) The motor TP Liability Policy covers the vehicle owner's legal liability to pay compensation for:
   (a) Death or bodily injury to a third party (person), and
   (b) Damage to third party's property.

(26) The public liability policy covers the amount that the insured becomes legally liable to pay as damages to third parties as a result of accidental death, bodily injury, and loss or damage to the property belonging to a third party.

(27) In a public liability policy, the sum insured is referred to as limit of indemnity. This limit is fixed per accident and per policy period, which is called Any One Accident (AOA) limit and Any One Year (AOY) limit, respectively.

(28) The public liability policy will not pay for claims arising out of:

   (a) Contractual liability.
   (b) Intentional non-compliance of any statutory provision.
   (c) Loss of goodwill.
   (d) Slander, fines, penalties, and
   (e) Libel, false arrest, defamation, mental injury, etc.

(29) A Product liability policy indemnifies the insured all sums which the insured shall become legally liable to pay as damages in consequences of accidental death/bodily injury or disease to third party, or damage to their property arising out of any defect in the products manufactured and covered under the policy, after such products have left the premises of the insured.

(30) The professional liability policy indemnifies any act committed by the insured, who shall be a registered medical practitioner, giving rise to any legal liability to third parties. The insured includes the policyholder and his qualified assistants or employees, as named in the proposal form,

(31) Retroactive benefit cover means that the insured will be covered for any professional act or omission occurring during the period of insurance which means from the first date of the first policy, provided that the policy is renewed without interruption and is in force when the claim arising out of the act or omission is made in writing against the insured during the policy period.

(32) Some exclusions of a professional liability policy are:
   (a) Liability arising from any criminal act or act in violation of any law or ordinance.
   (b) Services rendered under the influence of intoxicants or narcotizes.
   (c) Use of drugs for weight reduction.
   (d) Due to intentional non-compliance of statutory provisions.

(33) According to a workmen's compensation policy, an employer, as a principal or contractor, engaging workmen, as defined in the Workmen's Compensation Act, would need to cover his liability to them under statue and the common law. The workmen's compensation policy covers the employer's liability towards his employees who come within the definition, covering employment-related injury (including death). Employer can also cover employees who do not qualify as workmen under a separate table.

(34) The Workmen's Compensation Policy does not have a sum insured but the estimated earnings of the workmen for the policy period are mentioned on the policy.

(35) A health insurance policy covers the expense incurred by the insured for hospitalization for illness/diseases or injury sustained (domiciliary hospitalization also payable as per policy). These include:
   (a) Hospital charges (room boarding and operation theatre).
   (b) Fees for surgeon, anesthesia, nursing, specialist, etc.
   (c) Fees for diagnostic tests, cost of medicines, blood, oxygen, etc.
   (d) Cost of appliances such as pacemaker, artificial limbs, etc.

(36) The exclusions under a health insurance policy are:
   (a) Domiciliary hospitalization.
   (b) Pre and post hospitalization treatment
   (c) Any treatment relating to any illness/disease already in existence at the time of proposal.

(d) Any disease/injury during first 30 days of commencement of policy (accidental injury is not excluded),
(e) Any pre existing disease/illness are not covered during renewal also, and
(f) Cost of spectacles, contact lenses, and hearing aids.

(37) The Personal Accident Insurance Policy covers a person against:
(a) Accident death,
(b) Permanent total disablement (PTD), and
(c) Permanent partial disablement (PPD).

There are many personal accident plan options (Accidental Death and Permanent Total Disablement cover) with different sum insured.

(38) The Varsha Bima Policy covers anticipated shortfall in crop yield on account of deficit rainfall. It is voluntary for all classes of cultivators who stand to lose financially upon adverse incidence of rainfall and can, thus, take insurance under the scheme.

(39) The benefits payable under the Horticulture insurance policy include:
(a) The input costs or recurring expenses incurred for raising the crop (establishment and maintenance) till the date of the loss.
(b) Limits of indemnity on input costs basis are fixed at each stage of the crop.

(40) The Horticulture Insurance Policy excludes payment for loss or damage to crop arising due to:
(a) Theft, malicious damage, and negligence,
(b) Natural mortality,
(c) War and nuclear perils,
(d) Insects, pests and diseases,
(e) Drought, earthquake, and climatic variations,
(f) Water logging,
(g) Inconsequential losses, and
(h) Damage to structures, capital items, irrigation systems, agricultural implements, and harvested produce.

(41) Weather Insurance Policy covers losses that may

arise due to abnormal weather conditions. These abnormal weather confusions can be events such as excess of rainfall, shortfall, or variations in temperature, wind speeds and humidity.

(42) The aviary insurance policy provides indemnity against death of birds due to accident (including fire, lightning, flood, cyclone, strike, riot and civil commotion, and terrorism), diseases contracted or occurring during the period of insurance.

(43) The Honey Bee Insurance Policy provides cover for total loss damage to beehives and/or bee colonies as a result of an accident caused by fire, flood, inundation, storm, tempest, cyclone, hurricane and tornado. Additional covers are covered against theft, specified viral disease, and transit loss during migration.

(44) The Animal Driven Cart/Tonga Insurance Policy covers all types of animal driven carts driven by animals such as bullock, male buffalo, castrated bullock, camel, horse/mule, donkey, yak, etc.

(45) The animal should be identified by ear-tagging or branding with hot iron or tattooing as per the Cattle Insurance Market Agreement.

(46) The IAR policy provides cover against:

(a) Bursting and overflowing of water tanks, apparatus and pipes.

(b) Deterioration of stocks due to power failure following damage to premises of public power stations and electric service feeders (for cold storages).

(c) Forest fire.

(d) Leakage and contamination cover.

(e) Spoilage material damage cover.

(f) Sprinkler leakage cover.

(g) Subterranean fire.

(h) Spontaneous and landslide cover.

(i) Burglary (other than larceny).

(j) Machinery break-down/boiler explosion/ electronic equipment.

(k) Business interruption due to fire.

(l) Business interruption due to machinery breakdown.

(47) The IAR Policy does not cover:
- (a) Damage to the property caused by faulty or defective design. materials or workmanship, inherent vice, wear and tear, etc.
- (b) Interruption of water supply, gas, electricity of fuel systems.
- (c) Collapse or cracking of the building.
- (d) Wilful act or gross negligence.
- (e) War, invasion, mutiny, rebellion, revolution, etc.
- (f) Damage, direct or indirect, by nuclear weapons material.
- (g) Contamination by radioactivity.

(48) The Office Insurance Policy covers the following:
- (a) Fire (building and contents).
- (b) Burglary.
- (c) All-risk functional equipment.
- (d) Cost of data reinstatement.
- (e) Cash in safe.
- (f) Cash in transit.
- (g) Glass breakage.
- (h) All-risk non-functional items.
- (i) Fidelity.
- (j) Personal accident.
- (k) Public Liability, etc.

(49) The exclusions under an Office Insurance Policy are:
- (a) Under Insurance.
- (b) Wilful destruction of property.
- (c) Loss, damage or destruction caused by war perils.
- (d) Wear and tear.
- (e) Atmospheric conditions, etc.

6

Underwriting and Rating Practices

INTRODUCTION

In this Chapter, effort has been made to introduce the readers to the concept of underwriting in the general insurance context. The common practices followed in underwriting have been duly elaborated. Rating practices as followed in the general insurance market are also discussed in this chapter hence this chapter gives readers a broad idea of risk management practices as well.

UNDERWRITING PRACTICES

It is observed that Insurance underwriting, for the common man, is the process of issuing insurance policies; he/she cannot viualise beyond this. The formalist theory of contract stipulates that every contract must have six elements—offer, acceptance, consideration, meeting of the minds, capacity to enter into contract, and legality. When we look at insurance as a contract, the offer part is done by the insured through the proposal form. The insurer has to carry out the four of the other five parts and inform the proposer the consideration, which is the amount of premium, payable by him.

Turning to the concept of underwriting, we can say that it involves evaluating the risk, measuring the risk exposure, in totality and market-segment-wise, determining the premium that needs to be charged to insure that risk, and taking the decision whether to accept or reject a risk. Insurance underwriters decide how much coverage the client can be given, how much they should pay for it, or whether to even accept the risk and insure them at all. The function of the underwriter is to acquire or to "write" business that will make money for the insurance company, and to protect the company's book of business from risks that he feels will make a loss. Underwriting also involves checking whether there is a meeting of minds between the insured and the insurer. If the underwriter is satisfied on these counts, using the accepted practice of the company, he finds out the cost at which the risk can be accepted and conveys the same to the insured, which indicates that the insurer is willing to accept the risk at the quoted price. Once the consideration is paid by the proposer and accepted by the insurer, the contract comes into force.

Risk assessment in economic and social context is an ongoing process. The insurer is always engaged in continuously assessing the risk and arriving at specific lines of cumulated exposure. Therefore, before conveying to the insured his acceptance or before the finer details of the contract are finalized, the insurer has to go through various steps. He has to evaluate the risk offered and its exposure. He has to decide how much cover can be given to the risk offered and how much they should receive (premium) for accepting it, or whether to even accept the risk for insurance at all. Any factor that causes a greater likelihood of loss should theoretically be charged a higher rate. This basic principle of insurance must be followed if insurance companies are to remain solvent. Every insurance company sets its own set of underrating guidelines to help the underwriting personnel to determine whether or not the company should accept the risk. Over a period of time, markets evolve a set of guidelines that become standard for all the players in the market. However, each company will have its internal set of guidelines as well.

ACCEPTANCE OF NEW BUSINESS

When we talk of new business in insurance context, it means a complete study of the risk from various angles and in context. The insurers usually prescribe an elaborate state of conditions while accepting new businesses. This is to ensure that the company's finances are not put to risk by aggressive marketing without proper quality checks. If the particular risk offered for insurance has a greater chance of making a loss than other similarly placed risks, it can be called bad business. If, in the case of the particular business, there are reasons to expect that practically the loss will not be an uncertainty but a certainty or almost a certainty, the insurance has to be understood as bad business. In other words, the element of uncertainty that is normally expected in insurance contract would not be the same in a bad risk and the insurer would have to pay for it. Due to competition, the insurers may have to knowingly accept bad business, but the decision to do so would be at the discretion of the underwriter. Such decisions are made by seniors in the company with sufficient safeguards to bring the business as close as possible with other similarly insured.

Internal Guidelines

Internal guidelines are meant for proper and scientific house-keeping. The insurers have to decide up to what sum insured risks can be underwritten at a particular hierarchical level in the company. This means delegation of powers to officials down the line for expediency and to keep all officials responsible to the extent stated; they also learn to decide on the basis of relevant data and information. Further, the standards to be set for bringing the risk or the operation of the insured peril more or less to the level of other risks in the same category have also to be decided by the insurers. So, in respect of each type of insurance, the insurers have to decide upon the following:

(1) Irrespective of the sum insured, at what level should a business be underwritten?
(2) Up to specified levels of sum insured, specify who can underwrite?
(3) Which types of sum insured need approval of the controlling office?
(4) What underwriting safeguards should be specified for each type of risk at different levels of sum insured?

(5) What procedures should be followed to evaluate the risk?
(6) What internal procedures should be followed for collecting premium, after sales services, etc.?

Decisions can not be uniform and stereotype. The decision regarding acceptance would vary depending on the type of insurance, as the exposure can be different in different types hence the guidelines would be in good detail. The Alabama Insurance Association (AIA) defines underwriting guidelines as rules, standards, guidelines, or practices, whether written, oral, or electronic, that is used by an insurance company (or its agent) to decide whether to accept or reject an application for insurance policy, or to determine what rate will apply once the application is accepted.

REJECTION

The readers will experience that there are many occasions when risks offered for insurance are rejected if they are not found good enough to be accepted as per the insurers' internal standards prescribed for accepting businesses. For example, military vehicles are not accepted for comprehensive insurance. People beyond a particular age and those who are seriously sick are not covered for life insurance or health insurance. In short, risks that the underwriter perceives as extra hazardous as per the company's standards are declined. For instance, as per the Alabama Insurance Association's Underwriting Guidelines, underwriters are allowed to accept buildings less than 25 years of age for fire insurance, whereas if the building is more than 25 years of age, insurance can be given only if a wiring documentation is provided, stating that the electrical writing, heating system, plumbing and roof have been renovated within the previous 20 years.

Limits on Sum Insured

Limits have direct relation to the type of policy and the kind of risk. In a tariff market, fairly high limits of acceptance are allowed to lower offices in the case of standard policies. In some cases, such as motor, agents are allowed to accept business and issue cover notes and certificates of insurance. In case of insurances such as all-risks on jewellery, baggage, personal accident special contingency, etc. involve risk with higher sum insured. Many insurers, in such cases, prescribe approval of the controlling office. Private sector insurers in India practically have more centralized systems for acceptance.

Limits by Types of Insurance

Usually, certain classes of business, such as aviation, bankers' indemnity, bloodstock, jewellers' block, public liability, product liability, professional indemnity and certain types of engineering insurances are accepted only at the controlling office level. In India, insurances for satellites, off-shore drilling, etc. are accepted only at the head office level, often after elaborate discussions with the re-insures.

Accommodation Risks

There are certain categories of risks categorized as bad risks, which are fit to be declined and are sometimes called declined risks. However, in many cases, due to market compulsions, the insurers have to cover these risks also. In such cases, the proposal form, risk inspection report, details of other business from the same client, loss experience, special situation justifying acceptance, etc. are submitted to the controlling office. Acceptance of such risks would be usually subject to restrictive conditions, special clauses, warranties and loadings on premium. Examples of risk of this type are marine transit risk of cement in bags, sugar on all-risk basis, perishable goods on all-risks basis, gold and currency above specified values, etc. Fire risks of explosive factories, ammunition works, fire works factories, and celluloid factories, etc. also come under this category. Burglary policies for jewellers, workmen in explosives factories, fidelity guarantee of gold-shop employees, etc. are some other examples. These bad risks once accepted are referred to as accommodation risks.

Control by Inspection

In some cases, the insurers insist on pre-acceptance survey of the risk. Acceptance would, therefore, be necessarily subject to inspection. Post-acceptance inspections are mostly to finalize the rates and impose restrictive wordings. Inspections are done by the insurers' own engineers or by outsourced inspectors. This topic will be elaborated later on when risk management is discussed. Business interruption policies are sometimes issued and those too only if the insured's books of accounts are being regularly audited by reputed audit agencies: reputation and credit in the market speak in their favour.

Restrictive Wordings

Certain clauses and warranties are imposed depending on special features of the risk. The following are the examples of such wordings used in marine insurance:

(1) Breakage excluded—for asbestos sheets and cement pipes.
(2) Denting/scratching excluded for refrigerators.
(3) Denting/scratching excluded for motor vehicles.
(4) Bursting/tearing excluded for cargo in paper bags.
(5) Breakage excluded for transformers and second-hand machinery.
(6) Breakage excluded for sheet-glass and glassware.
(7) Leakage and contamination of oil excluded in second-hand drums.
(8) Buckling excluded for cattle prone to buckling of knees while standing in transit.
(9) Cutting clause damage for end of pipes to be cut and balance used.

Conditions of Excess

Compulsory excess (or co-payment) is imposed for certain risks, such as own damage of old vehicles, health insurance, leakage from transformers in transit, pilferage in fast moving consumer goods, fires in spray painting units, theft losses in a shopping mall, etc. Comprehensive insurance of costly imported cars is often subject to an excess clause.

Other Restrictions

Motor vehicles of older age attract higher rates. Cargo sent by overage vessels, under-tonnage vessels and tramp-vessels attract higher rates as a disincentive for using sub-standard modes of transit. Certain parts of the factory carrying out hazardous operations may require to be separated by brick walls or fire proof doors to make the rest of the factory safer.

Provisional Acceptance

In view of business compulsions, sometimes, the insurers take the decision to accept the risk without having the necessary information about the risk to price it appropriately. In such cases, the insurers may have to wait for the risk to be inspected or wait for a confirmation of the rates and/or conditions from the controlling office. Sometimes, although the details of a high value risk would be known yet matters such as the insurers' capacity to retain the risk, co-insurance terms, and reinsurers' quotations based on international rates and terms may not be clear for some time. In such cases, the insured may not be willing to wait for the procedural informalities. He may be under obligation to his financiers, or his consigner/buyers to show the proof of insurance. Sometimes, he has to prove the existence of the cover to certain government agencies. In cases such as motor third party insurance and public liability insurance, the insured requires a certificate of insurance, which is also required to be issued along with the cover note. Also, there would be market pressures on the insurer, from competitors who would like to snatch away the business. In such a case, inspection of the risk or confirmation of rates, conditions from the controlling office are awaited, the risk is provisionally accepted by the underwriter. The Insurance Act and the respective tariffs allow for this contingency and provide for the insurance cover to be effected subject to collection of a provisional premium. Acceptance of risk conveyed by the insurer is evidenced by issuance of the cover note. Cover notes are serially numbered and strictly accounted for by way of cover note registers.

Policies are Issued

Once the complete details are collected and all the formalities/elements (ingredients) of the contract are finalized, the policy is issued as a composite document covering all information of the risk and the contract. Policies are also serially numbered and entered in a register for effective control. The policy numbers are included or updated in the cover note register and the premium register. The policy document is stamped in accordance with the Indian Stamp Act and delivered to the insured.

RENEWAL OF BUSINESS

Policy numbers and details are entered in an expiry register (renewal register) according to the scheduled date of renewal. This register helps the insurers to track the insured ahead of the expiry date of the policy and try to retain the business. With increased competition, the insurers are increasingly keen on retaining their good businesses. This is advantageous to them in many ways. In some cases, the acquisition costs are saved or reduced on the renewals. The insurer is comfortable in dealing with an existing insured as the risk is a known one, the claims history is readily available, and administrative costs on risk inspection, etc. are saved. Another reason for retaining the insured with him is to improve the brand loyalty factor. That is an insurer can expect a satisfied regular customer to get his other insurance transferred to the company. He may also talk good about his insurance experience to others and eventually bring in more business. Although renewal is a fresh contract of insurance on fresh terms, issuance of a renewal notice may not be mandatory, most insured parties consider it a matter of courtesy and a good gesture.

In case of accident insurance, a fresh proposal form is not asked for at renewal. However, the terms are fresh depending on the current age of the vehicle, revised IDV, etc. In fidelity guarantee policies or personal accident policies, the individual limits may have to be revised or changes in employee cadres given effect to.

Bonus

Bonus is an incentive offered to the existing clients. The insurers offer an incentive on claims-free insurance by granting a bonus on renewal. The bonuses are often linked to the number of claims-free years completed, as well as works as a disincentive for making minor claims. This helps the insurers in retaining good business in certain classes where frequent transfers of business are expected. Motor own-damage and health insurance are such examples. Conversely, loading based on bad claims experience is applied when the insurance is offered for renewal.

When it comes to portability of insurance policies or insurance shifting from one insurer to another, different practices are followed in the market as regards bonus, etc. A view is that the insured has earned it and has a right to keep the discount. Another view is that if the insurer, who has already enjoyed claims-free years, is willing to give a bonus, it can be binding on other insurers, who will be getting only a reduced premium from day one. In tariff markets, generally such bonuses are honoured. Portability of malaises is generally not a matter of dispute as the insured would not shift the business to a new insurer unless he has a good reason for doing so.

RATING PRACTICES

Insurance rate refers to the consideration that is vital to the contract; it is called premium in insurance parlance. The price of the insurance is usually expressed as the cost of a unit of cover, e.g. Rs. 'x' per mille or in some cases as Rs. 'x' per cent. Until December 31, 2006, in the Indian market, rates were fixed for all major lines of business by the Tariff Advisory Committee (TAC), after which a tariff-free regime has come into place. The tariff- free regime follows a 'File and Use' model where the individual insurer has to actuarially justify the rates charged by him. Post-de-tariff, from January 1, 2007, the insurers are by and large allowed to charge their own rates except for motor third party policies where the IRDA has fixed a guideline rate. In other lines also, some minor restrictions exist, which are, however, only transient provisions to prevent a sudden plunge of the rates.

Pricing is a complex process and the job of financial/ actuarial experts. Correct pricing ensures stability in the insurance market, which in turn bolsters the confidence of the insuring public in the system of insurance. In short, in developing markets, policyholders' interests are protected by standardization of products and administered prices. Insurance polices have to be priced correctly to ensure on the one hand that the insured do not end up paying more, and on the other hand, to provide the insurers with sufficient funds to pay the claims to the insured, whenever the need arises.

Rates are fixed/reviewed by adjustment and it is a regular practice among insurers. In the Indian context, Section 64 UC(2) of the Insurance Act, 1938, prescribes that in fixing, amending or modifying any rates, advantages, terms or conditions relating to any risk, the Advisory Committee shall try to ensure that "there is not unfair discrimination between risks of essentially the same hazards".

Rating Concepts

An insurer's pricing objectives depend on the overall objectives of the insurers and the state of the insurance market. These pricing objectives may be expressed in three main ways:

(1) To achieve a specified rate on return of capital;
(2) To maximize profits; and
(3) To maintain or extend market share.

For all economic activities, there are basic principles. The basic principle followed in rating is that insurance companies should remain solvent to satisfy their obligations to the insured and the society. This would include ensuring the survival of the insurance company, achieving optimum strategic positioning, providing quality and value for the service, contributing to the society's well-being, and maximizing the returns on a given type of risk.

As per the guidelines issued by the Motor Accidents Authority (MAA), the regulatory body of the New South Wales state of Australia, for the preparation of rate filing reports, premium is defined as:

> "Premiums must be sufficient to pay all acquisition and policy administration costs, provide a sum of money to meet the best estimate of the cost of claims (including claims management expense), provide a profit margin representing an adequate return on capital invested and compensation for the risk, and provide for other matters a prudent insurer would make provision for".

Insurance pricing methods can be divided into three major categories—

(1) "Manual rate", which refers to a rate designed to apply on a generic basis to similar risks within the

same market, filed with the department by an insurer or rate service organization, and made part of the rating manual used by an insurer or rate service organization.

(2) "Experience rating", which refers to a rating system whereby a manual rate for insurance is adjusted or modified, based on the past loss experience of the insured.

(3) "Modification rating", which refers to a rating procedure that provides a listing of various risk characteristics or conditions and a range of modification factors that may be applied for the characteristics or conditions of the manual rate of a particular insurance risk. The effect of the modification factor is to increase (debit) or decrease (credit) the manual rate (definitions are as per the Utah State insurance rules in the USA).

For rating, the terms of the insurance contract, the conditions under which losses are payable (the insurance cover), and the past experience of losses in the particular type of insurance are taken into reckoning. The rating hinges on the frequency and severity of past losses. The calculation that goes into the rating depends on the accuracy of the statistical data. The data should be of a sizeable quantity, reasonable quality, credibility and relevance. For large property risks, the probable maximum loss (PML) of the risk is also estimated. The PML of a particular risk is the estimate of the maximum loss that would occur as a result of damage caused by the most destructive peril to be insured. With regard to the location, constitution, occupation and protection of the risk, PML is usually expressed as a percentage of the sum insured (Hart, Buchanan and Howe).

PREMIUM OF POLICIES

It is prudent decision that any factor that causes a greater likelihood of loss should theoretically be charged a higher rate. Thus, for rating purposes, the insurers try to see the insured risks as forming part of some class of risks that share similar characteristics. At the same time, for rating purposes, the insurers have to try to distinguish the specific risk from the class of risks to find out the degree of differential treatment the risk would attract depending on its individual characteristics. For instance, for a health insurance cover, the insurers charge older people significantly higher premiums than they charge younger people for term life insurance. Old people are more likely to fall sick than younger people. That is, a particular old man proposing himself for health insurance would be seen as part of the common class of other old men and rated accordingly. But if the insurer finds that the old man enjoys excellent health, has healthy exercising habits, is a non-smoker and non-drinker, and that both his parents had lived into their nineties, the insurers would distinguish him as a specific risk, and would like to reduce his rates substantially from the common rates applicable to other old men.

In the case of a motor insurance, information on the driver's experience and claims-free record are significant. The insurance company uses the information to assess the likelihood that a driver will have an accident, and adjusts premium accordingly. A driver who drives great distances at high speeds, for example, might be charged a different rate than a deriver who drives short distances at low speeds. The rate will be justifiable only if the insurer is sure that a high-speed long distance driver incurs greater risk to an insurance pool than the slow, around town driver. Therefore, in treating the insured differently, the insurers should be able to logically and actuarially justify their reason for doing so, so that the discrimination is not unjust or unlawful.

RATING CONCERNS

We have seen that the rate would depend on various factors, deciding the factors having bearing upon the case of insurance and ascribing appropriate weights to them is the insurer's challenge. Depending on the type of insurance product (line of business), the insurance companies sometimes use automated rating packages by encoding the rating rules, thereby reducing the amount of manual work in working out premiums.

In the case of marine cargo insurance, the rate would depend on factors such as nature of cargo, scope of cover, packing, and mode of conveyance, distance and past claims experience. An example of a Risk-Based Pricing Model (RBPM) in Marine Cargo Insurance is given below:

Sr. No.	*Factor*	*Weightage*
1.	Frequency/periodicity of despatch	5%
2.	Mode of transit	10%
3.	Per bottom value	5%
4.	Nature of goods sent (perishable, hazardous, high value, unstable by design/weight)	20%
5.	Trans-Shipment—single or multiple	20%
6.	Duration of transit	5%
7.	Storage locations—single or multiple	5%
8.	Duration of storage	5%
9.	Consignment in bulk/containerized, packing type and material	5%
10.	Claims history of insured	5%
11.	Claims history of carriers	5%
12.	Geographical location(s) of transit	5%
13.	Season of shipment	3%
14.	Salvage value of consignment	2%
	Total	100%

EXAMPLE

Factors and Weights-I

On a composite matrix, a range of weightage points can be ascribed to multiple rating factors based on the loss propensity of marine cargo consignment, as given below:

The total rate to be charged for a marine cargo policy can be distributed over the 14 factors mentioned above, contributing to 100 per cent of the premium. Such mathematical rating models help companies in fixing rates in a balanced manner, i.e. the underwriter would be more objective in his decisions if there is a rating structure in place.

Factors and Weights-2

In the motor context, weightage points can be ascribed to multiple rating factors to rate a vehicle, as given below. It is possible that many more rating factors could be added or a few removed depending on the conditions of a particular market.

Sr. No.	*Factor*	*Weightage*
1.	Vehicle colour	10%
2.	Vehicle age	20%
3.	Vehicle engine capacity	20%
4.	Vehicle make	05%
5.	Anti-theft protection	05%
6.	Age of driver	05%
7.	Gender of driver	05%
8.	Profession of driver	05%
9.	Lifestyle of driver	05%
10.	Driving experience of driver	05%
11.	Accident history	05%
12.	Average distance commuted daily	05%
13.	Regular place of packing	03%
14.	Type of road mostly used	02%
	Total	100%

We now understand that the total rate to be charged for a motor vehicle can be derived from the above weightage proportionate to their loss-making potential, which can be spread over the above mentioned 14 factors, contributing to 100 per cent of the premium. Such rating factors and weightage become the backbone of a Risk Factors Rating System (RFRS) or Risk Factors-Based Rating system, which is used in countries like Japan.

RISK ASSESSMENT

The readers must have seen that risks are evaluated before acceptance or immediately after acceptance of proposals for finalizing rates through intricate process. Risk evaluation can involve an inspector's visit to check the site and seeing the physical features of the risk. This can include checking the construction of the building, its height, the processes done in it, its proximity to other risks, the geographical location for chances of flood or earthquake or cyclone prone areas, etc. The insurers may suggest risk improvements such as installation of fire-proof doors, burglar-alarms and smoke-detectors, or offer incentives by way of discounts for improving the risk. The insurers do mathematical modelling based on risk perceptions. Methods of identifying hazards, objectively assessing them, and weighing their loss-potential on mathematical scales, and finding out the probability of an operating hazard are studied by risk managers. Again, the perceived frequencies and severities with which hazards can operate on a given risk are studied using certain models called hazards can operate on a given risk are studies using certain models called 'Hazards Identification Study' (HAZID) and Hazard and Operability Studies (HAZOP), which enable the insurers to evaluate risk potential accurately and scientifically. The basic HAZOP model given below indicates how the mathematical weights work in risk evaluation.

Hazard Operation Model

MITIGATION ↑			*IMPROBABLE*	*UNLIKELY*	*POSSIBLE*	*LIKELY*	*PROBABLE*
PREVENTION ←	*SEVERITY*	*LIKELIHOOD*	1	2	3	4	5
LIGHT		-1	-1	-2	-6	-4	-5
SERIOUS		-2	-2	-4	-9	-8	-10
MAJOR		-3	-3	-6	-12	-12	-15
CATASTROPHIC		-4	-4	-8	-16	-16	-20
MULTI CATASTROPHIC		-5	-5	-10	-20	-20	-25

Hazard Operability Model

-25 TO –20	NON-OPERATABLE	EVALUATE AREA / ZONE / COUNTRY
-16 TO –10	INTROLERABLE	DO NOT TAKE THIS RISK
-9 TO –5	UNDESIRABLE	EVALUATE RISK THOROUGHLY BEFORE INSURING
-4 TO -2	ACCEPTABLE	PROCEED CAREFULLY PLAN RISK IMPROVEMENT
-1	NEGLIGIBLE	SAFE TO PROCEED

It is but obvious that as the likelihood increases, the loss becomes more of a certainty than fortuitous event. As the severity goes up, it becomes increasingly difficult for the insurers to absorb the losses. Risk management reduces the likelihood (or probability) of a loss and reduces the severity (or intensity) of a loss. Loss prevention and loss minimization activities are initiated at the instance of the insurers. They form agencies to educate target groups on reducing losses by various methods. Drivers of tanker carrying hazardous goods are trained on fire prevention, cargo handlers at ports are trained to handle cargo with care, pedestrians are taught road discipline, and the general public is advised on precautions to be taken while bursting crackers during festival season. The philosophy is if any loss is averted or any risk preserved, the insurers gain; beyond this, of course, the preservation of the nation's wealth is everyone's responsibility.

CUSTOMER SERVICE

Customer service is crucial in services industry for customer is the king. There is a maxim that customer is always right. Therefore, customer service is an integral part of an insurer's business, just like in any other business enterprise. In insurance, the customer comes in for a long-term relationship and not an across the counter dealing. He looks forward to the insurer as a friend in need who will come to his help when he needs him the most. In a way, having parted with the premium, he would also feel weak and dependent on the insurer for fulfilment of his part of the promise. In this background, retaining the insured's trust and goodwill is very important. In general insurance, conventionally there are mainly two aspects of customer service. The first is the prompt completion of all formalities and issuance of the policy. The second is prompt settlement of claims. However, there are areas such as easy-to-read literature, customer-friendly forms, clarity on the contract trust, courteous behaviour from staff and intermediaries, updating of changes in address, hassle-free endorsement process, sending of information mailers, advertisements that endorse the trust aspects, receiving a timely renewal notice, etc. that keep the customer relations on a happy note.

The acid test of the efficiency and customer-orientation in insurance contract is when the claim occurs and that is where the insured expects the entire customer service that the insurers can provide. This aspect will be discussed in the other chapter.

SUMMARY

After going through this chapter, the readers should develop a basic understanding of underwriting as a professional understand some of the common underwriting practices, and familiarize themselves with general insurance pricing practices. They should also be able to integrate their understanding of risk management in the context of general insurance.

(1) Underwriting involves evaluating the risk, measuring the risk exposure, determining the premium that needs to be charged to insured for that risk, and taking the decision to accept or reject a risk.

(2) Every insurance company sets its own set of underwriting guidelines to help the under-writer determine whether or not the company should accept the risk.

(3) The insurers' internal guidelines are usually the following:

   (a) At which level should a business be underwritten?

   (b) Which types/what sum insured levels need approval of the controlling office?

   (c) What underwriting safeguards should be specified for each type of risk at different levels of sum insured?

   (d) What procedures should be followed to evaluate the risk?

   (e) What internal procedures should be followed for collecting premium, rendering after-sales services, etc.

(4) Risks offered for insurance are rejected if they are not found good enough to be accepted as per the insurers' internal standards prescribed for accepting businesses.

(5) Sometimes, due to market compulsions, the insurers cover certain bad risks, though fit to be declined. This would be usually subject to restrictive conditions, special clauses, warranties and loadings on premium. Once accepted, these risks are called accommodation risks.

(6) Examples of restrictive wordings are:
   (a) Breakage excluded for asbestos sheets and cement pipes.
   (b) Denting/scratching excluded for motor vehicles.
   (c) Bursting/tearing excluded for cargo in paper bags.
   (d) Breakage excluded for sheet glass and glassware.

(7) Although in certain cases, an inception of the risk or a confirmation of rates/conditions from the controlling office is pending, the risk is provisionally accepted by the underwriter.

(8) The insurers are keen on retaining their good businesses. This is advantageous to them as acquisition costs are saved or reduced on the renewals. The insurer is comfortable dealing with an existing insured as the risk is a known one and the claims history is already available. Renewals also improve the brand loyalty factor and most insured entities consider it a matter of courtesy and good gestures.

(9) The insurers offer an incentive on claims-free insurances by granting a bonus on renewal. The bonuses are often linked to the number of claims-free years completed, as well as works as disincentive for making minor claims. This helps the insurers in retaining good business in certain class where frequent transfers of business are expected.

(10) Insurance rates are usually expressed as the cost of a unit of cover, e.g. Rs. 'x' per mile, or in some cases as Rs. 'x' percent.

(11) Section 64 UC(2) of the Insurance Act, 1938 prescribes that in 'fixing, amending or modifying any rates, advantages, terms or conditions relating to any risk, there should be no unfair discrimination between risk of essentially the same hazard".

(12) This basic principle followed in rating is that insurance companies should remain solvent to satisfy their obligations to the insured and the society. This would include ensuring the survival of the insurance company, achieving optimum strategic positioning, providing quality and value for the

service, contributing to the society's well-being, and maximizing the returns on the given type of risk.

(13) Manual rate refers to a rate designed to apply on a generic basis to similar risks within the same market, filed with the department by an insurer or rate service organization and made part of the rating manual used by an insurer or rate service organization.

(14) Experience rating refers to a rating system whereby a manúal rate for insurance is adjusted or modified based on the past loss experience of the insured.

(15) Modification rating refers to a rating procedure that provides a listing of various risk characteristics or conditions and a range of modification factor that may be applied for the characteristics or conditions of the manual rate of a particular insurance risk. The effect of the modification factor is to increase (debit) or decrease (credit) the manual rate.

(16) By PML of a particular risk, the insurer come to estimate the maximum loss that would occur as a result of damage caused by the most destructive peril to be insured, with regard to the location, construction, occupation and protection of the risk.

(17) In contrast to other old men, if the insurer finds that particular old man enjoys excellent health, has healthy exercising habits, is a non-smoker and non-drinker, and that both his parents had lived into their nineties, the insurers would distinguish him as a specific risk and would like to reduce his rates substantially from the common rates applicable to other old men.

(18) Mode of transit, per bottom value, and duration of storage.

(19) Vehicle's age, vehicle's engine capacity, and vehicle make.

(20) A score of '-1' indicates that the possibility of the loss-making event occurring is improvable and if it happens, the loss would be light.

(21) A score of '-25' indicates that the possibility of the loss-making event occurring is probable and if it happens, the loss would be multi-catastrophic.

(22) The first score of '-5' indicates that the possibility of the loss-making event occurring is 'probable', and if it happens the loss would be 'light'. The other score of '-5' indicates that the possibility of the loss-making event occurring is 'improbable', and if it happens, the loss would be multi-catastrophic.

(23) The customer looks forward to the insurer as a friend in need who will come to his help when he needs him the most. He expects prompt completion of all formalities and issuance of the policy. He also expects prompt settlement of claims, courteous behaviour from staff, intermediaries, and timely information such as renewal notice.

Claims: Practices and Procedure

INTRODUCTION

This chapter introduces the concept relating to claims settlement. It familiarizes the readers with the different types of claim-documents, the procedure of claim-settlement, and the practices involved in them. It also discusses the post-settlement issues related to the insurers.

CLAIMS: CONCEPT AND PRACTICE

In the previous chapter, we have discussed about the customer service angle of the insurer's business. In insurance, the customer looks forward to the insurer as the source of solace when the tragedy insured against hits. He expects the insurer to come to his help when he needs him the most, like the proverbial friend in need. The consumer of the insurance product, having fulfilled his part of the obligation of the insurance contracted by paying the premium, waits with expectation, and worrying how the big insurance company will react to his loss and whether it would fulfil its part of the promise. He is weak as an individual or as a corporate, pitted against an insurance company that is financially strong. When he is further weakened by the disaster that has struck him, he would not like to fight a legal battle with the insurer. However, when confronted with a loss, he would be only too quick to be offended by any act of discourteous behaviour/response, or injustice from the side of the insurer.

For judging the efficiency of the insurer, the acid test of the insurance contract is when the claim occurs and the insured expects all the services that the insurer can provide. This is an unexpected happening for the insured. But for the insurer, he should always be on the alert, expecting someone to suffer a loss and lodge a claim. He needs to be in a position to render whatever service is expected of him as per the contract of insurance, to retain the customer's goodwill. He needs to look into the claim professionally enough to ensure that the claim is payable within the framework of the contract, that the quantum of the amount claimed does not exceed the amount stipulated under the contract, and there is no moral or moral hazards involved in the claim.

The insurer has to have a proper system for claims settlement. The insurer primarily fulfils his contractual obligations to the insured in return for the premium that the company has received. By handling the claim professionally, the insurer ensures that his company pays only to the extent that it is bound to pay as per the contract and not for anything beyond its purview. If the insurer settles the claim recklessly, beyond what he has agreed for, he compromises on his company's interest and he sends a negative feedback to the market that he is careless and can be fooled. If he pays less, he loses customers' goodwill, exposes himself to legal quarrels, and in the process tells the market that he does not deliver what he promises and is not trustworthy. In essence, the insurer needs to handle the claim professionally enough to fulfil his promise to the insured, as well as to retain the goodwill of the market and attract more business in the process. Some authors opine that claims settlement is the biggest advertisement of an insurer.

Losses can be identified under different types, based on certain characteristics. Some of them are listed below:

Definite Loss

In this type of loss, the events that caused the loss should have (at least in principle) taken place at a known time, in a known place, and from a known cause. The classic example is death of an insured on a life insurance policy. Fire losses, automobile accidents, and workers' injuries meet this criterion. The types of losses that may be definite only in theory (e.g. occupational disease where prolonged exposure to injurious conditions would be involved, but where no specific time, place or cause is identifiable) do not fall under this type. In definite losses, the time, place and cause of a loss are clear enough that a reasonable person, with sufficient information, can objectively verify all the three elements.

Accidental Loss

In this type, the event that constituted the trigger of a claim would be fortuitous or at least outside the control of the beneficiary of the insurance. The loss would be pure in the sense that it results from an event for which there is the only opportunity for cost. Events that contain speculative elements, such as ordinary business risks do not fall under this category.

Large Loss

Here, the size of the loss is large from the perspective of the insured, where the insurance premiums have covered the expected cost of losses plus the cost of issuing and administering the policy, adjusting losses and supplying the capital needed to reasonably assure that the insurer will be able to pay claims. This is in contrast to small losses where the above incidental costs may be several times the size of the expected cost of losses and where paying such costs are not in the interest of the insured.

Calculable Loss

A calculable loss is one in which there are two estimable elements (even if not formally calculable)—the probability of loss, and the attendant cost. Probability of loss is generally an empirical exercise, while cost has more to do with the ability of a reasonable person in possession of a copy of the insurance policy and a proof of loss associated with a claim presented under that policy to make a reasonably defined and objective evaluation of the amount of the loss recoverable as a result of the claim.

Limited Risk of Catastrophically Large Losses

In this type of risk, the essential risk is often aggregation.

Sometimes, by the factors commonly applicable to all the policyholders exposed (not by factors relating to the individual characteristics of a given policyholder), the same event can cause losses to numerous policyholders of the same insurer. In such cases, the ability of that insurer to issue policies becomes constrained. Typically, the insurers prefer to limit their exposure to a loss from a single event to some small portion of their capital base. Where the losses are aggregated or where an individual policy could produce exceptionally large claims, the capital constraint will restrict an insurer from issuing more policies. The classic example is earthquake insurance, where the ability of an underwriter to issue a new policy depends on the number and size of the policies that it has already underwritten. In extreme cases, the combined capital of the insurers can be small compared to the needs of potential policyholders in areas exposed to aggregation risk. In commercial fire insurance, it is possible to find single property, total exposed value of which is well in excess of any individually insurer's capital constraint. Such properties are generally shared among several insurers, or are insured by a single insurer who syndicates the risk into the reinsurance markets.

Although these differentiations may not mean anything significant to the insured yet the insurer improves his knowledge in the process, and his research team tries to find the patterns in losses and evolve new strategies from the knowledge.

CLAIMS PROCEDURE

A claim is normally a major affair for an insured that happens once in a very long time. For an insurer, claims settlement is a major day-to-day activity where he parts with huge sums of money on a regular basis. We have seen in unit 2 how he needs to maintain the required solvency levels to meet the regular requirements of small and medium claims, and the sporadic requirements of large claims. He should have the required liquid funds for claims settlement. The management of the insurer's finances is not discussed as part of this chapter.

It is observed that an insurer comes across claims from different types of policies, of which many are unique. Claim-settlement is a highly specialized professional activity and the claims professional would require a sound understanding of the policy wording, extensions, endorsement, exclusions, possible interpretations of the wordings, and practices in the industry, plus a reasonable knowledge of the applicable laws, principles and practices of the insurance contracts as a whole. He should be rule-minded but should have the pertinence and flexibility to understand the insured's point of view and appreciate his predicament with sympathy. He should be tactful, courteous and balanced enough not to irritate or antagonize the insured even in situations where claims are reduced substantively or even rejected. He should be able to project a positive image of the company even in difficult situations. Claims processing and settlement is a well laid out process where every step is standardized, recorded and documented. An insurer receives claims everyday, and has to process and settle them on a regular basis. So, the insurers develop internal systems and processes for recording, tracking, checking, processing, surveying, making *ad-hoc* payments, asking final settlements, disposing salvage, disputing claims, arbitrating on settlements, etc.

Although the claims settlement styles and practices may vary from company to company and from portfolio to portfolio, there are certain common procedures that are followed by most of the insurers across different markets. There are basically three groups of activities—preliminary procedure, investigation procedure and settlement procedure.

PRELIMINARY PROCEDURE

(I) Notice of Loss

It is important that the insured informs the insurer of the loss promptly or as early as possible under the circumstances. In some cases, the conditions of limitation make it imperative for the insured to intimate claims within a specific period. The time limits for intimation vary from product to product. Intimation of claims is mostly a written communication, but there are cases where telephonic intimations are accepted for speedy action.

(a) The promptness of intimation is important for the insurer to investigate and assess the loss. The assessment of claims becomes difficult with passage of time.

(b) In some policies such as burglary or road accidents, the insured may have to inform the police also.

(2) Minimizing Losses

Timely intimation of claims is important for minimizing losses.

(a) As per the principle of 'good faith', in the event of a loss, the insured should take all necessary care to protect his property and reduce damages as if no insurance existed. This is a legal/contractual obligation. For instance, an insured cannot just leave a damaged car on the road and walk away because the car is insured.

(b) In some cases, the insured may be able to advise cause within limiting period, taking care meanwhile for minimizing the loss by protecting the salvage and suggesting prompt action. Getting a damaged car towed to garage, or moving damaged cargo to a godown are such examples.

(c) Loss limiting/minimizing expenses are paid by the insurers under the sue and labour or duty of insured clause in marine policies.

(3) Procedural Formalities

The step-by-step process that an insurer follows on claims intimation is as follows:

(a) Ask for the policy number and details to ensure that claim is on a valid policy issued by the company.

(b) Check whether the claim has occurred within the validity period of the policy.

(c) Check whether the loss or damage is by a peril insured under the policy.

(d) Examine whether the subject-matter of the loss is the same as stated in the policy.

(e) Check whether the claim intimation has been received within the stipulated time limit.

(f) Make an entry in the claims register and allot a number to the reported loss.

(g) Open a separate file for the reported loss, cross-linking it with the entry in the claims register.

(h) File the relevant papers relating to the claim, the policy copy or extracts thereof, and the claims intimation.

(i) Issue claims form to the insured. These are structured formats devised to capture maximum information on the loss that happened. The claims form is discussed under the section relating to documentation in this unit.

(j) Receive the duly filled claims form.

INVESTIGATION PROCEDURE

(1) Investigation and Assessment

Investigation and assessment start with filing of the claims form. On receipt of the claims form, the insurer decides on the process of investigating and assessing the claim. For minor losses, the claim is paid on the strength of the claim form. For some losses, an officer of the insurance company does the investigation and assessment, and makes recommendation for the payment accordingly.

(a) In larger claims (Rs. 20, 000 or more) or where the insurers may not be technically qualified to assess the claim, services of an external investigator are used.

(b) Investigations are done by independent surveyors/ loss adjusters who are qualified professionals in the area of the claim. In the Indian market, surveyors are licensed by IRDA.

(c) Sometimes, for the sake of expediency, the surveyor is appointed and the loss investigated even before the claim form is filed in.

(2) Survey Report

The surveyor is provided with the claims form and any other document available with the insurer to enable him to undertake the exercise of conducting survey in a meaningful manner.

(a) The surveyor's job would, *inter-alia,* include "examining, inquiring, investigating, verifying and checking upon the causes and the circumstances, of the loss in question, including extent of loss, nature of ownership and insurable interest", as per chapter IV, Section 13 of the IRDA Regulations of Insurance Surveyors and Loss Assessors, 2000.

(b) The survey report would, *inter-alia,* comment on the admissibility of the claim *vis-a-vis* the policy, estimate the quantum of the loss, and assess the liability under the contract of insurance.

(3) Re-Survey

In case of doubt or dispute, a re-survey can be carried out and if there is variation, sometimes, a third survey can also be done by still another surveyor.

(4) Documentary Proof

The insurer can ask for all relevant documents to find out whether the claim is admissible, and to assess the quantum and circumstances of the loss.

SETTLEMENT PROCEDURE

(1) Establishing Admissibility

The insurer has to be satisfied that the claim is admissible under the contract and the quantum of claim amount payable, based on his internal investigation or the surveyor's report and/ or relevant documentation.

(a) Once the insurer is satisfied about his liability under the contract of insurance, the claim is paid by cheque.

(b) The necessary discharge vouchers are singed by the insured.

(c) A letter of subrogation is issued by the insured, authorizing the insurer to claim all rights and recoveries due from third parties.

(d) The claims file is made complete with the survey report and all supporting documents, along with copies of relevant vouchers.

(e) The details of the payment are entered in the claims register with cheque number, etc.

Disputed Claim

Claims clearance is not a smooth affair at all times. Sometimes, there are disputes over claims. Disputes usually occur when the insurer does not admit liability to settle the claim or the amount of settlement is not acceptable to the insured; such matters end up in courts, ombudsmen or arbitrators, depending on the situation. These are discussed in more detail under a separate topic in this chapter.

The claim-procedures applicable to most insurance types in the Indian market have the following requriemetns:

(1) The loss or damage should be reported to the insurer immediately.
(2) On receipt of claim intimation, the insurer will forward a claim form.
(3) Submit the completed claim form along with an estimate of the loss to the insurer. It is preferable to submit an itemized estimate with separate values.
(4) The insurer will arrange for inspection of the damaged items to assess the loss. In case of major losses, a specialist, licensed surveyor, is deputed.
(5) The insured has to provide the required document to substantiate the extent of loss.
(6) In case the cause of loss is not established, it is for the insured to prove that the loss or damage has occurred due to an insured peril.
(7) On agreement of claim amount between the insured and the insurer, the claim is settled.
(8) Average clause is to be applied as per the terms and conditions of the policy.
(9) Excess, as stated as per the policy terms and conditions, will be deducted from the claim payable.
(10) No claim should be admitted or a compromise arrived at by the insured without the approval of the insurers.
(11) Every accident involving third parties is required to be reported to police.

Now-a-days, step-by-step procedures for preferring claims are posted on the insurers' websites so that the insured are educated on these aspects. A few examples are given below.

Motor Insurance Claim Procedure

There are broadly three types of motor (auto) insurance claims. Auto insurance claims can be in the form of accidental claims, theft claims or third party claims.

(1) The insured should write the number of the other vehicle in case of an accident or third party claim.
(2) Names of witnesses should also be written down.
(3) File an FIR with the nearest police station.
(4) The insured should then contact the insurance company and get a claim number.
(5) The notice of accident should be filed with the insurers.
(6) A surveyor is appointed who calculates and reports the approximate value of loss or damage.
(7) Based on the report of the surveyor, the insurance companies try to send the amount to the insured within one to three weeks.
(8) If damage is a major one, the accident may be reported before the vehicle is removed from the spot so that the insurer can arrange for spot inspection of damage.
(9) The vehicle may then be moved to a workshop, preferably to authorized workshop, for estimation of repair charges.
(10) On receipt of the completed claim form and estimate of repairs, the insurers will arrange for a detailed inspection of damage, and cost of repairs will be ascertained.
(11) Upon the completion of the above procedure, the repairers will be authorized to carry out repairs. The insurers may undertake to settle the repair bills directly with the garage or reimburse the insured.
(12) An individual might have to pay the repair charges himself and later get them reimbursed.
(13) The insurers will ensure that a person duly licensed

to drive, drove the vehicle at the time of accident and that the vehicle is the one insured in their books. For this purpose, they will verify the Registration Certificate and the Driving Licence of the driver who dove at the time of the accident.

(14) The insurers would like to collect the damaged parts for which replacements have been allowed, as salvage. This ensures that replacements with new parts have actually been effected.

(15) In case of theft of the car or its accessories, it has to be reported to the police and the final report of the police should be submitted.

Industrial Insurance Claim Process

(1) The insured should inform the insurer's office by phone, letter or fax.

(2) The necessary steps should be taken to minimize the loss.

(3) The estimate of repair should be obtained from the repairers of choice of the insured.

(4) The claim process takes anywhere between one to three weeks.

(5) The repair estimate and claim form should be submitted to the surveyor deputed by the insurance company.

(6) After getting clearance from the surveyor, proceed for repairing machine or ordering for replacement, as the case may be.

(7) Submit actual bills of repair/replacement with proof of payment to the surveyor of the claim process.

Fire Insurance Claim Procedure

(1) Individuals/corporates must inform the insurer as early as possible, in no case later than 24 hours.

(2) Provide relevant information to the surveyor/claim representative appointed by the insurers.

(3) The surveyor then analyzes the extent/value of loss or damage.

(4) The claim process takes anywhere between one to three weeks.

Agriculture Insurance Claim Procedure

Farmers, under the agriculture insurance claims, can claim from the banks by submitting a claim form. The claim representative will analyze the extent of damage caused to the crops. Based on the report of the surveyor, the claim is paid to the farmers within a month.

Travel Insurance Claim Procedure

The insured must submit the duly filled claim forms along with the original ticket or boarding pass or copy of the passport showing the travel dates and original bills/vouchers. The companies take 7-21 days for processing the claims.

Claim-procedures would have slight variances from company to company but the general pattern usually practised can be understood through the above model.

CLAIM-DOCUMENTS

Documents constitute evidence. It is well known fact that the purpose of documentation is essentially to prove that the loss actually happened; it happened to the subject-matter of insurance, the cause of the loss was an insured peril, the amount of loss incurred tallies with the amount claimed and there was no fraudulent intention or negligence on the part of the insured. The details of the requirements would vary depending on the type of insurance, details of the cover and based on the market practices.

(1) *Claim Forms*: These are pre-designed forms prescribed for each type of portfolio/policy type and the contents may vary.
   (a) Structured formats are devised to capture maximum information on the loss that happened.
   (b) Claim forms are considered compulsory in most classes of insurance, such as fire and accident insurance. However, in some markets, claim-forms are not used in some types of insurances, such as marine cargo insurance.

(c) Issuance or acceptance of claim-forms do not place the insurer under any obligation to accept the claim or to settle it. In other words, it is not to be construed as an admission of liability on the insurer's part. This is usually clarified on the claim form itself.

(2) *Survey Report*: Independent report of the surveyor is required in cases where applicable, such as large fire losses. The surveyors with qualifications relevant to the claim are usually appointed by the insurers. For example, surveyors with mechanical engineering qualifications for machinery break-down losses, with marine engineering back-ground are sent for hull claims, or with accounting knowledge for fidelity guarantee claims.

(3) *Legal Opinion*: Views on legalities are taken where disputes are expected, especially in matters of liability.

(4) *Specialists' Opinion*: In some cases, other specialists' views are also taken. In case of health and personal accident claims, sometimes, doctor's opinions are taken. Where TPAs are involved, the doctors in the TPAs service take care of this requirement. For cattle claims, veterinarians' reports are called for.

(5) *For Fire Claims*: Report from the Fire Brigade is required.

(6) *For Burglary Claims*: Report from the Police is to be submitted.

(7) *For Fatal W.C. Claims and other Fatal Claims*: Post-mortem report, reports from the Coroner and the Police are to be submitted. The legal heirs may have to produce probate or letters of Administration or Succession Certificates.

(8) *For Motor Claims*: The report from the police, driving licence, and registration book are required.

(9) *For Marine Cargo Total Loss Claims*: The invoice, bill of lading, bill of entry, copy of protest made by the captain of the vessel on the loss, non-delivery or short-landing certificate, landed but missing certificate, letter of subrogation and correspondence

with carriers, port trust, etc. on claims filed against them, need to be submitted.

(10) *Other Evidences*: Supporting Bills/vouchers, bank statements, etc. can be asked for as required to prove the claim or the amount of settlement.

(11) *Other Documents*: In case of hire purchase, hypothecation, mortgaged properties, etc. relevant documentation would be needed, as per the situation.

(12) Original policy and other documents for identity and address proof are also required for claim-settlements.

An impression need not be formed that the above list is exhaustive. It only indicates the wide range of documenting needs of the insurance company to satisfy itself on the validity and amount of the claims to be paid. It also helps in proving the reasons and justification for reducing claims, in case the insured pursues litigation. Documentation also helps the insurer in pursuing subrogation claims effectively and securing rights for hassle-free disposal of cargo. Many insurers post the documentation requirements on their websites for preferring claims so that the insured are clear in the matter. A few examples are given below.

Documents Required for Vehicle Insurance Claims

For Accident Claims

(1) Claim form duly signed.

(2) Registration copy (RC) of the vehicle.

(3) Driving license copy.

(4) Copy of FIR on a case to case basis.

(5) Original estimate.

(6) Original repair invoice and payment receipt from the service centre.

(7) Transfer papers for Regional Transport Office, duly signed, mentioning that the vehicle can not be located (for theft of vehicle cases).

For Third Party Claims

(1) Claim form duly signed.
(2) Copy of FIR lodged with police.
(3) Driving license copy.
(4) RC copy of the vehicle.
(5) Original policy document.

Documents Required for Industrial Insurance Claims

(1) Copy of FIR.
(2) List of loss/damage of stock/equipment.
(3) Claim form duly signed.

Documents Required for Fire Insurance Claims

(1) True copy of the policy along with the schedule.
(2) Report of the fire brigade.
(3) Claim form.
(4) Photographs.
(5) Past claims experience.

Documents required for Agriculture Insurance Claims

(1) Farmers must approach the designated branch of bank or Primary Agriculture Co-operative Society (PACS) and submit the proposal form is in the prescribed format.
(2) Farmers must provide documentary evidence in regard to the possession of cultivable land, copy of the revenue passbook and its extract.
(3) Land revenue receipt should be enclosed.
(4) Farmers must furnish area sown confirmation certificate, if required.

Documents Required for Travel Insurance Claims

(1) Duly completed and signed claim form.
(2) Policy document (copy).
(3) Air ticket jacket/boarding pass.
(4) Copy of the passport showing the travel dates.
(5) Original bills/vouchers.

Documents Required for Home Insurance Claims

(1) Duly completed and singed claim form.
(2) Copy of policy document.
(3) Copy of FIR lodged with police.
(4) Final report from police.
(5) Copy of all invoices, price lists and repair estimates.

CLAIM-SETTLEMENT

It should be borne in mind that the admissibility of claim and amount of claim have to be decided based on the above procedure and documents. The insurer has to settle the claim. The due deductions by way of excesses and under insurances would be adjusted from the claims. Sometimes, partial or *ad hoc* payments may be effected to mitigate the insured's immediate financial difficulties, pending the final settlement. Rights of subrogation and disposal of salvage have to be secured in favour of the insurer through proper documentation and/or against future legal action. After making all the due deductions, and securing all relevant rights, claim settlement is done by way of a cheque drawn representing payment. The details of the payment are entered in the claims register along with the cheque number, etc.

The identity of the insured and to confirm the eligibility of the recipient can sometimes be a matter of concern in policies where the recipient is an assignee or legal heir. Legal heirs may have to produce proof of their eligibility/legal right, such as succession certificate, probate of will or letters of administration. In cargo claim, the policy has to be endorsed in favour of the recipient.

Claim-payments are made against discharge vouchers, with standard wordings within the company with minor portfolio-wise changes. For example, the components of a discharge form for Personal Accident Claim settlement are as follows:

Discharge Form—Specimen-1

Discharge form for Personal Accident claim (Illustrative)
Name of the insured:

Claim No.
Policy No.

Received from ____________________________ General Insurance Co. Ltd., the sum of Rs. _____________ in full and final settlement of compensation due to me on account of injuries sustained by me on account of the accident which occurred on (or about the) ____________________ .

I give this discharge receipt to the said insurance company in full and final settlement of all my claims, both present or future, arising directly or indirectly out of the said claim.

Place

Date

Signature

Discharge Form—Specimen-2

Discharge Form for Third Party Liability claim (Illustrative)

I, ___________________ (Name of the Claimant), son/daughter/wife of ___________________, residing at _____________ hereby acknowledge to have received the sum of Rs. ________ (Rs. ....) which amount is paid by __________ (Name of the insurer), in respect of the claim made by me upon him for bodily injuries and other losses sustained through an accident which occurred to me on (or about) __________ (the date of accident) at ___________ (place of accident) and I agree that the sum is paid with a denial of liability on the part of the said _______ (Name of the Insurer), in respect of the said credence and for damage whether now or hereafter to become manifest, and to the intent that the said and all other persons be absolutely and finally discharged from the further and other claims of every nature and kind whatsoever by me or on my behalf arising out of the said occurrence.

Place

Date

Signature

Witness

Sometimes, the insurers make Ex-Gratia Settlement of claims. This term refers to a claim settlement made by an insurer even when the loss is not covered under the policy. Such settlements are usually made for commercial reasons where the claims experience has otherwise been good or as an exercise for improving the company's good will.

CLAIMS DISPUTED

There are many occasions where there are disputes over claims. Some cases such as third party liability usually takes the legal channel. The Motor Vehicles Act, 1988 provides that third party victim can proceed against the insurers directly. In the court, if the insurer accepts his liability to pay the claim and the amount asked for as compensation, the matter ends at that stage. Otherwise, the legal process continues.

In most cases, disputes usually occur when the insurer does not admit liability to settle the claim or the amount of settlement is not acceptable to the insured.

(1) If the insurer admits his liability under the contract to pay the claim and dispute is limited only to the quantum of loss, the matter can be referred to an arbitrator as an alternative dispute redressal (ADR) mechanism to avoid the delays in the legal procedure.

(2) When the dispute is due to claim acceptance or any other reason, the insured can approach the court for a legal settlement.

(3) Another forum to settle insurance-related disputes/ grievances is the Insurance Ombudsman System established under the Redressal of Public Grievances Rules (1988). Ombudsmen are empowered to entertain complaints on the following aspects in respect of personal life insurance:
   (a) Any partial or total repudiation of claims by an insurer,
   (b) Any dispute in regard to premium paid or payable according to the terms of the policy,
   (c) Any dispute on the legal construction of the policies in so far as such disputes related to claims,
   (d) Delay in settlement of claims, and
   (e) Non-issue of any insurance document to customers after receipt of premium.

Ombudsman's powers are restricted to insurance contract of value not exceeding Rs. 20 lakh. The insurance companies are required to honour the awards passed by an Insurance Ombudsman within three months. If the ombudsman deems fit, he may award an *ex-gratia* payment. The Ombudsman shall pass an Award within a period of three months from the receipt of the complaint. The Awards are binding on the insurance companies. If the policyholder is not satisfied with the Award of the Ombudsman, he can approach other venues, such as the Consumer Forums and Courts of Law, for redressal of his grievances. As per the policyholder protection regulations, every insurer shall inform the policyholder, along with the policy documents, in respect of the Insurance Ombudsman, in whose jurisdiction his office falls, for the purpose of grievances redressal arising, if any, subsequently. There has been a steady increase in the number of complaints received by various Ombudsmen. This shows that the policyholders are reposing their confidence in the institution of Insurance Ombudsman and preferring this route over the legal recourse.

POST-SETTLEMENT ISSUES

From the point of view of the insured, the transaction with the insurance company often ends with the claim payment and discharge voucher. However, there are cases where the insurer has to take care of a few things after the loss.

As intermediaries are involved in assessment of loss, some payments may have to be made to those intermediaries such as surveyors and advocates. These have to be settled/corresponding entries made in the books of account/claims files, etc. There may be direct claim settlements or a system of floats or running accounts maintained with some hospitals, TPAs or garages. The necessary updating has to be done in the accounting records.

There are instances when payments may be recoverable from co-insurers. These have to be intimated to them and the necessary postings made in the books of accounts as per the practice followed. There may be recoveries to be made from the reinsurers. These have to be done through the applicable reinsurance arrangements.

We have seen that the insurer secures subrogation rights and rights to disposal of salvage in his favour through proper documentation and/or legal action before settlement of the claim. The necessary follow up actions have to be done through legal proceedings against third parties to ensure that any dues/ payment rights on account of the loss are made good to the insurer. There may be some insured property, which has been saved from a loss but usually in a damaged condition. The wreck of a car after a total loss or the damaged copper wires of an electrical circuit after a fire loss are such examples. The insurers will sell salvage to off-set at least some part of their losses on the claim payment. As part of the disposal plan, salvage may have to be stored safely for some period of time, for evaluating its market value, inviting quotations and disposal, and for the best possible price. All these are among the post settlement concerns of the insurers.

It is not only routine matter but the truth in this changing world is that settlement of claim can help the insurers in their learning process. Indian companies have a system of surveying major fire losses to find out from a knowledge point of view the causes due to which a loss happened, the risk management lapse, the failure in the systems, and the situations that aggravated the loss event. From the inspection reports, the insurers are supposed to find out as to what went wrong and what preventive action that could be initiated to avoid a recurrence of such a loss at the same site or elsewhere. In some cases, at least, valuable information can be gathered from the loss. These lessons are highly useful for re-designing the loss management and loss prevention strategies for the company. They can also help in designing better underwriting strategies for the company.

SUMMARY

After studying this chapter, it is expected that the readers have built up a fair degree of awareness about the basic concepts of claim-settlement. They should have acquired familiarity with the claim-documentation and procedures. They should also be able to appreciate post-claim settlement concerns of the insurers.

(1) The insurer needs to look into the claims professionally enough to ensure that the claims are payable within the framework of the contract, that the quantum of the amounts claimed does not exceed the amounts stipulated under the contract, and that there is no moral or other hazards involved in the claims.

(2) The consumer of the insurance product (insured), having fulfilled his part of the obligation of the insurance contract by paying the premium, is worried as to how the big insurance company will react to his loss and whether it will fulfil its part of the promise. He is weak as an individual or as a corporate entity, pitted against an insurance company that is strong/ robust, and further weakened by the disaster.

(3) In definite loss, the events that caused the loss should have taken place at a known time, in a known place, and from a known cause. In definite losses, the time, place and cause of risk also are clear enough that a reasonable person, with sufficient information can objectively verify all the three elements. The classic example is death of an insured on the life insurance policy.

(4) For accidental loss, the event that constituted the trigger of a claim would be fortuitous, or at least outside the control of the beneficiary of the insurance. The loss would be pure in the sense that it resulted from an event for which there is only the opportunity for cost. Events that contain speculative elements, such as ordinary business risks do not fall in this category.

(5) A calculable loss is one in which there are two elements that are estimateable or calculable, namely, the probability of loss, and the attendant cost. Probability of loss is generally an empirical exercise, while cost has more to do with the ability of a reasonable person in possession of a copy of the insurance policy, and a proof of loss associated with a claim presented under that policy, to make a reasonably definite and objective evaluation of the amount of the loss recoverable as a result of the claim.

(6) Aggregation is often the essential risk in the limited risk of catastrophically large losses. In this type, sometimes, by the factors commonly applicable to all the policyholders responded (not by factors relating to the individual characteristics of a given policyholder), the same event can cause losses to numerous policyholders of the same insurer. In such a case, the ability of the insurer to issue policies becomes constrained. The classic example is earthquake insurance where the ability of an underwriter to issue a new policy depends on the number and size of the policies that it has already underwritten to arrive at the aggregate position to take decision on exposure.

(7) There are basically three groups of activities involved in claim-settlement—preliminary procedure, investigation procedure and settlement procedure.

   (a) Preliminary Procedure includes notice of loss, effort to minimizing losses and procedural formalities.

   (b) Investigation Procedure involves investigation and assessment, survey report, re-survey, and documentary proof.

(c) Settlement Procedure involves establishing admissibility and handling disputed claims.

(8) It is important that the insured informs the insurer of the loss. The time limit for intimation varies from product to product and from company to company. The promptness of intimation is important for the insurers to investigate and assess the loss. Assessment of claims becomes difficult with passage of time. In some policies such as burglary or road accidents, the insured may have to inform the police.

(9) Motor Vehicle claim procedure involves the following steps:

(a) The insured should write the number of the other vehicle in case of an accident or third party claim.

(b) Names of witness should also be written down.

(c) File an FIR with the nearest police station.

(d) The insured should then contact the insurance company and get a claim number.

(e) The notice of accident should be filed with the insurers.

(f) A surveyor is appointed who calculates and reports the approximate value of loss or damage.

(10) Fire insurance claim procedure involves the following things:

(a) The individuals/corporate entities must inform the insurer as early as possible, in no case later than 24 hours.

(b) The insured should provide relevant information to the surveyor/claim representative appointed by the insurers.

(c) The surveyor then analyses the extent of value of loss or damage.

(d) The claim process takes anywhere between one to three weeks.

(11) Claim-Forms are carefully pre-designed forms prescribed for each type of portfolio/policy type, and the content may vary. These are structured to capture maximum information on the loss that happened.

(12) *Surveyor's Report*: Surveyors having qualifications

relevant to the claim are usually appointed by the insurers either on roll or on retainership basis. For example, surveyors with mechanical engineering qualifications for machinery breakdown losses, with marine engineering background for hull claims, or with accounting knowledge for fidelity guarantee claims.

(13) *Specialists' Opinion*: In some cases, other specialists' views are taken and considered. In health and personal accident claims, sometimes, doctors' opinions are taken. Where TPAs are involved, the doctors in the TPAs' service take care of this requirement. For cattle claims, veterinarians' reports are called for.

(14) Documents required for a Travel Insurance claims are the following:
   (a) Duly completed and signed claim form.
   (b) Policy copy.
   (c) Air ticket jacket/boarding pass.
   (d) Copy of the passport showing the travel dates.
   (e) Original bills/vouchers.

(15) Documents required for a Home Insurance claim are as under:
   (a) Duly completed and signed claim form.
   (b) Copy of policy.
   (c) Copy of FIR.
   (d) Final report from police.
   (e) Copy of all invoices, price lists and repair estimates.

(16) *Ex-gratia* settlement of claim refers to a claim settlement made by an insurer even when the loss is not covered under the policy. Such settlements are usually made for commercial reasons where the claim-experience has otherwise been good, or as an exercise for improving the company's goodwill and to project its image well.

(17) The Ombudsmen are empowered to entertain complaints on the following aspects in respect of personal life insurances:

(a) Any partial or total repudiation of claim by an insurer,
(b) Any dispute in regard to premium paid or payable in terms of the policy.
(c) Any dispute on the legal construction of the policies in so far as such disputes relate to claims.
(d) Delay in settlement of claims.
(e) Non-issue of any insurance document to the customers after receipt of premium.

SAMPLE CLAIM FORM USED BY AN INDIAN INSURER
CLAIM FORM FOR BURGLARY INSURANCE
NOTIFICATION OF PHYSICAL LOSS OR DAMAGE

(The issue of this form is not to be taken as an Admission of Liability)

Please Answer All Questions Fully

1	DETAILS OF INSURED	
1. (i)	Name	
1. (ii)	Address	
1. (iii)	Contact Number	
2.	State the address of premises at which is affected	
3. (i)	Date and time of losses	
3. (ii)	When discovered and by whom?	
4. (i)	How were entry to/exit from the premises affected?	
4. (ii)	Which portion of the premises was affected by the entry or exit?	
4. (iii)	Give brief detail of how exactly the loss occurred. (Specially the articles stolen and property damaged)	
5. (i)	Has a complaint been lodged with the police? If so, by whom and when and at which police station? (Attach a copy of the complaint), if so, this may be done immediately and a copy thereof should be furnished to the company.	
6. (i)	Were the premises occupied at the time of loss?	Yes/No
6. (ii)	If not, on what date and at what hour were they last occupied?	
7.	Is anybody suspected of theft? If so, state full details.	
8. (i)	Is the insured the sole owner of	
8. (a)	The property lost or damaged?	

8. (b)	The premises?	
8. (ii)	Is the insured responsible for repairs to the premises?	
9. (i)	State the total value of property upon the premise at the time of loss.	
9. (ii)	State the amount of the insurance upon such property and name(s) of the insurer(s).	
10.	Is there any other insurance against the present loss under any other policy? If so, give full particulars.	
11	Any other information relevant to processing of claim.	

I/We hereby agree, affirm and declare that:

(1) The statements/information given/stated by me/us in this claim form is/are true, correct and complete.

(2) The details of all persons having an interest in the property in respect of which the claim is being made are provided as per the proposal form or by way of an endorsement in the policy. Furthermore, save and except as provided or disclosed in this claim form, no claim made hereunder (or the same/similar claim) has been made or lodged with any other insurance company.

(3) No material information which is relevant to the processing of the claim or which in any manner has a bearing on the claim has been withheld or not disclosed.

(4) If I/we have given/made any false or fraudulent statement/information, or suppressed or concealed or in any manner failed to disclose material information, the policy shall be void and that I/we shall not be entitled to all/any rights to recover hereunder in respect of any or all claims, past, present or future.

(5) The receipt of this claim form/other supporting/related documents does not constitute or be deemed to constitute an agreement by the company of the claim and the company reserves the right to process or reject or require further/additional information in respect of the claim.

Place:

Date: Signature of Insured

Organisational Structure of a General Insurance Company

INTRODUCTION

Readers must by now have found that in the earlier chapters, we have discussed about general insurance as a separate stream of knowledge, its specialities, its intricacies and the day-today functioning of various key insurance professionals. This chapter gives the readers an idea of how the total set-up works as a collective and cohesive unit functioning as an organization in unison. We will be discussing an insurance company's model organizational set-up. It will familiarize the readers with the various departments of an insurers' organization. It gives readers an understanding of the multifarious functions handled by an insurer through various internal systems. It also attempts to introduce the readers to the basic concept of managing an organization professionally.

ORGANISATIONAL STRUCTURE OF AN INSURANCE COMPANY

Structure and systems as well as staff are the backbone of an organization. Therefore, the organizational structure of any organization gives it the cohesive force that makes it work as a single entity and successful as a team. Large organizations employ thousands of employees. Each one of the four Indian public sector insurance companies has a work-force of around twenty thousand employees. The set-up makes these thousands of individuals develop a corporate identity helping them to identity themselves as part of the company, and share its mission, vision and values. Employees in every cadre should ideally feel that they belong to the organization and form part of the collective entity. They should work for the organization's success, oppose anything that weakens it, and in the process keep their individual interests and personal identities to the background. They should develop a feeling of loyalty towards the company, feel responsible for its fortunes, and form part of the organizational future. The structure of the organization, structure of functions, and the employment structure all try to create an organizational climate, high morale and culture conducive for developing team spirit and achieving collective corporate success.

At the establishment level, under the corporate office (or Head Office), where the Chairman sits and is regarded as the seat of the Board of Directors, there are around twenty Regional Offices (for every one of the public sector insurers) situated in the four metros and all important cities. Some large cities have more than one Regional Office. Under every Regional Office, there are many Divisional Offices and below them are the Branch Offices. All the public sector insurers have around a thousand offices spread all over the country. The agents are attached to the Branches and the Divisions.

DEPARTMENTALIZATION OF AN INSURANCE COMPANY

It can be observed that insurance organizations have the typical organizational pyramidal structure. To look closely at the public sector insurance companies, the Chairman of the Board of Directors acts as the Chairman of the organization. Below him are three or four General Managers, who have the Deputy General Managers reporting to them. Then reporting to them are the Managers, Assistant Managers and the Administrative Officers, all belonging to the Class I cadre. Below this level comes the Class II cadre of Development Officers who are essentially counted as field staff and report to Officers-in-charge of marketing and business development functions. Class III employees form the next two layers. The higher layer consists of Stenographers, Programmers and Senior Assistants, and the lower layer comprises Assistants, Typists, Draughtsmen, Data Entry and Telephone Operators, operators of lifts, operators of Xerox machines and/or Cyclostyling machines, and various support staff consist of such people as peons (messengers) and cleaners (scavengers). Although the agents of the company give external support to its functioning yet they do not strictly form part of the organizational set-up as they are not employees on the payroll, and not related to the regular promotion sachems and other staff benefits. In all, a public sector insurer would have around twenty thousand employees working for it in various capacities.

While communication channels serve as nerves, the staff is like flesh and blood in an organization. Insurance organization is no exception in this regard. The employees are grouped into/ assigned to various departments. The departments generally go by the basic functions of the organization and the different branches of insurance that are handled.

The broadest classification can be technical and non-technical where insurance-related matters are considered technical (operations or line functions) and the rest non-technical (we may call them administrative or staff functions). Non-technical aspects include departments such as accounts, administration, estate and establishment, human resources development and personnel, audit, information technology and data management, language, legal, vigilance, right to information, actuarial, etc. Technical departments include core insurance areas such as fire, marine, aviation, motor/auto, health, re-insurance and miscellaneous. Departments such as technical audit and risk management exist for certain specific functions.

Non-Technical Areas

Book-keeping and accounts is an essential activity of a business organization. As such, Accounts Department of the insurer keeps an account of the money that comes into the insurance company and that goes out. This department deals directly with almost all departments, and records all financial transactions, such as incoming premium, claim-payments, agency commission, management expenses, advertisement expenses, legal charges, surveyors' fees, as well as staff salaries and benefits, loan schemes, etc. at all levels of the offices. At the corporate level, it prepares the company's financial statements to be presented to the company's Board of Directors and shared with other stakeholders, the regulator (IRDA) and the Government. The accounts department finalizes accounts of the provident fund, pension fund, gratuity fund and other staff welfare schemes. It has to present the company's accounts for audit to internal and external auditors, and clarify their queries. It takes care of the company's tax liabilities, such as income tax, professional tax, service tax, etc.

Administration Department extends support to the operating departments and it exists in all offices, and takes care of the various office services, stationery, miscellaneous purchases, office up-keep, maintenance, staff decorum, attendance, leave, benefits, travel, hospitality, car pools, etc., it makes payments for electricity, telephones and other services.

Assets/landed property and equipment have to be maintained and kept in good condition so that work does not get hampered. Therefore, Estate and Establishment Departments take care of the landed assets of the company including purchase, lease, renting and maintenance of office and residential premises. They look after repairs and renovation of buildings, liaison with building societies, civic authorities, and legal matters relating to eviction of tenancy and protecting the insurance company's rights on the building. The department exists at different levels where property is there, but is usually full-fledged only at the Head Office and Regional Office levels.

Vigilance Department of the company not only looks into major frauds and serious lapses having a financial bearing on the company but also it keeps vigil on deviations of practices which may be fraught with danger of being hot-beds of potential mal-practices, embezzlements and frauds. It also maintains confidential dossiers of all employees on complaints and integrity-related issues. A Chief Vigilance Officer, usually on deputation from another company or government, who has to be in touch with the Chief Vigilance Commissioner's Office of the

Government of India and liaises with him in case of major frauds, heads the vigilance department. Although the department exists at the Regional Office levels yet it is fully functional only at the Head Office level.

Audit (Internal Audit or concurrent audit) Department works as the eyes and the ears of the management, and finds out errors/irregularities, frauds, slackness, etc. in the preparation of the financial statements. Auditors visit different offices of the insurers and check the records. They go through the accounts in detail and understand the necessity and legitimacy of the expense from a perspective of prudence, integrity and diligence. Normally, people of good knowledge of accounting and possessing high/undoubted integrity only are posted for audit functions. The department exists at the Regional Office levels, but it is full-fledged only at the Head Office level.

Information Technology and Data Department takes care of the company's IT needs. In many cases, it makes the computer hardware and software purchases, and maintains the IT and network set-up of the office. This department looks after the database management, data mining, data analysis, web-hosting, content development, intranet, remote server locations, etc. It is responsible for data security also. Full-fledged departments exist only at the Regional Office and the Head Office levels.

Right to information (RTI) Department is a relatively new department responsible to answer queries made under the RTI Act to outside entities. It consists of Information/Chief Information officer and an Appellate Authority.

Language Department exists at the Regional Office and the Head Office levels. It tries to popularize the national language in all non-Hindi speaking states. It translates the contents of all circulars and public documents into the national language. In some states, the content of documents in English may not be intelligible to the rural population. Here, documents are translated into the vernacular.

Legal Department takes care of the company's litigation, mostly related to third party and other liabilities, property related matters, and other insurance matters. It liaises with advocates, drafts deeds and documents, and certifies policy and public documents from the legal point of view.

Actuarial Department goes through the financial

statements, the company's assets and liabilities, provisions for future losses, etc. It looks into the transactional data and reserves and makes projections on the solvency margins required of the company to meet its liabilities. It uses actuarial methods and calculates the company's solvency and various probability-based estimates, as well as makes various projections and forecasting that the company would require from time to time.

Technical Areas

Technical audit looks into the different operational areas of the technical departments, including underwriting and claims to find out whether the company's underwriting and claims management policies have been compromised by these departments during their daily working.

Risk management and Inspection Department takes care of the inspection of risks, report its findings to the underwriters, helps them in assessing the risk, suggests risk improvement measures, etc.

Portfolio Department deals with the underwriting, claims and related matters of the different portfolios, usually at the Regional Office or the Head Office level. For example, the Fire Department deals with underwriting and claims under the fire portfolio, marine cargo department with cargo matters, motor department with all motor vehicle-related matters, etc. Likewise, there are departments covering major portfolios, such as Marine Hull, Aviation Hull, Health, and Miscellaneous. There is a separate re-insurance department that looks into the company's re-insurance policy and needs.

FUNCTIONAL STRUCTURE OF AN INSURANCE COMPANY

Apart from the above-mentioned department-wise structure, insurance companies have a functional structure also, that does not strictly follow the departmental structure. In public sector companies, though functional segregation is not very rigid, at the branch and division levels, where there is more of multi-tasking than at the Regional Office and the Head Office levels, functions are practically given top priority. The functional set-up of the organization is more pronounced in the private sector companies that are now operating in India and other countries,

where there is more of man to function matching. In such companies, recruitments and trainings are designed to suit specific roles or functions.

The functional set-up is more of an inter-dependent set-up, with every function complementing the other functions. Prominent function-based departments are sales and marketing strategy, underwriting and re-insurance, business system and IT application, operations and customer services, finance, claims, and compliance.

Sales and Marketing Department decides upon the following matters:

(1) Business-mix and Spread of business.
(2) Training inputs to sales staff as regards policy terms, exclusions, and claim procedures.
(3) Acquisition channels, such as Bancasurance, support/involvement in claims.

This department will have the appropriate personnel reporting to a Sales and Marketing Head or Department in charge who will be responsible for the functioning of the teams under him.

Strategy, underwriting and re-insurance department decides upon the following matters:

(1) Overall business strategy and objectives.
(2) Customers' proposals and risk inspection reports.
(3) Product development, policy working, endorsements and clauses.
(4) Response to cash calls and other recoveries from re-insurers.

This department has experts in the particular areas who work separately with their own teams in their individual areas, and report to an overall department in charge of strategy, underwriting and re-insurance who will be the point of convergence for them and be responsible for the functioning of the teams under him.

Business system and IT Application Department looks into specific functions such as:

(1) Providing a robust technology platform for the company.
(2) Setting up and managing data warehousing and mining capabilities.
(3) Defining all IT processes.
(4) Reporting to the management, as required.
(5) Implementing document management and imaging solutions.

This department's personnel will ensure that the specific areas allotted to them are taken care of and report to overall Business Systems and IT application Department Head who will be responsible for the entire IT needs of the company.

Operations and Customer Services Department is supposed to look into targeted functions, which include:

(1) Creating and maintaining error-free policy document and schedule.
(2) Easy retrieval of proposal and policy documents in soft and hard copies.
(3) Keeping systemic and accurate records of customer interaction.
(4) Doing the needful for customer guidance, surveyors' deputation and other necessary notifications.
(5) Training of staff in customer service, more as regards claims procedures and policy terms.

This department will report to the Head of Operations and Customers' Services who will be responsible to the company for delivering of the quality functions allotted to him.

Finance Department looks into specific functions such as the following:

(1) Ensuring compliance of 'Cash Before Cover' policy through the system.
(2) Accurate and timely release of claim payments.
(3) Hassle-free transactions with accurate recordings.

This department will report to the Head of Finance department or Chief Finance Officer who will be responsible to the company for all aspects of finance.

In the interest of business, Claims Department tries to create a customer-centric culture, balance delivery channels, and ensure regulatory and internal compliance by adoption of the best practices in the market.

(1) Reduce end-to-end claims cycle time through efficient and automated processes.
(2) Enrich customer-claims experience, and help attract and retain the best customers.
(3) Identify and control fraudulent claims and leakages.
(4) Improve claim-costs through good relationships/ negotiated rates with managed care partners and other service providers.
(5) Hiring, developing and retaining the best claims people.

The head of claims will have to interact with all departments and get their support (to the extent required) in claims processing and settlement so that the company's overall organizational goals are met.

The above functional areas are not exhaustive but indicative. Functions such as ensuring legal compliances, conducting of meetings, advertising, etc. can be done through separate teams. The concept of personal functionality by way of assigning detailed responsibilities is being practised in the modern day insurance market. A few examples of specific responsibilities that are given to people in a Claims Department (Motor-specific) are given below:

Motor Claims Coordinator (at the Regional Level)

(1) Liaison with panel surveyors, workshops, and customers.
(2) Documentation management and claim registration.

Claims Officer

(1) Notify, register, reserve, monitor, evaluate, investigate, negotiate, and settle claims within own authority in accordance with company standards and policy.

(2) Recommend to claims manager on claims that are above own authority. Discuss with him/her about complaints, breach of policy conditions, suspected frauds, legal proceedings, and cases requiring technical guidance.

In-house Motor Surveyor at the Regional Level

(1) Survey, re-inspection and assessment.
(2) Empanel and negotiate best rates/terms with network garages.
(3) Empanel and monitor performance of external surveyors.
(4) Handle total loss/cash loss cases, negotiate best salvage value.

Motor Technical Officer: Functions

(1) Organizes technical updates, reference material, and catalogues.
(2) Organizes training on assessment practices, faulty repair techniques, and billing practices of garages.
(3) Maintains and updates the latest information on spare part prices, and repair costs.
(4) Maintains liaison with regions on high value claims.

Claims Manager (this post would be usually common for all portfolios)

(1) Develop strategy and structure for managing department specific claims.
(2) Establish best practices, efficient processes, and claims manual.
(3) Lead, motivate, and develop claim-teams with appropriate business focus.
(4) Develop and implement training and development programmes for the teams.
(5) Benchmark and monitor service levels and turn-around times.
(6) Conduct due diligence, negotiate terms and

discounts, sign up service level agreements with service providers, such as workshops, hospitals, investigators and advocates, and monitor performance.

(7) Approval of high-value claims.
(8) Monitor claim-cost and reserve movement.
(9) Feedback to underwriting, actuary and marketing for developing future policies.
(10) Support to sales and marketing teams during acquisitions.
(11) Audit and reviews.
(12) Monitor leakages and develop fraud alerts.

As we have seen above, the work profiles and functions have been very specifically drawn in these cases, and performance can be effectively monitored in the functional hierarchical models.

INSURANCE AND ENTERPRISE RISK MANAGEMENT (ERM)

Enterprise Risk Management (ERM) is being talked over, of late, in the context of insurance. ERM can be described as a risk focused approach to managing an enterprise, and integrating various concepts such as strategic planning, operations management and internal control. ERM is actually used in the business context to refer to the methods and processes used by organizations to manage risks (or optimize opportunities) related to the achievement of their objectives. The ERM approach includes identifying, analyzing, reponding to and monitoring risks or opportunities, within the internal and external environment facing the enterprises. By identifying and proactively addressing risks and opportunities, business enterprise protects and creates value for their stakeholders, including owners, employees, customers, regulators, and society—overall. When other companies resort to ERM, insurance can be selected as a response to risk management, which can increase business opportunity for the insurers. But this is just one aspect of ERM. The thrust of this section is on the use of ERM for managing an insurance company's risk.

The current view-point that is taking the rounds in the

insurance circles is that, if ERM can be used by other organizations for managing their risk, why insurance companies, which themselves are in the business of risk, should not use ERM and manage their own business risks. This logic is finding favour with many insurers on the international scene, and the risk-based approach used by them is at least being talked about in the Indian market hence this topic has been included in this chapter.

As defined by the composite of sponsoring organization of the red way commission (COSO) of USA, ERM is "a process, effected by an entity's board of directors, management, and other personnel, applied in strategy setting and across the enterprise, designed to identify potential events that may affect the entity, and manage risk to be within its risk appetite, to provide reasonable assurance regarding the achievement of entity objectives".

Presently, the term is evolving itself to address the needs of various stakeholders who want to understand the broad spectrum of risks facing complex organizations to ensure that they are appropriately managed. Regulators and debt providers (lenders) and debt rating agencies have also increased their scrutiny regarding the risk management processes of companies.

The framework that ERM provides for risk management includes the following:

(1) Identification includes identifying particular events or circumstances relevant to the organization's objectives (risks and opportunities). This can be broken up as:
   (a) Understanding the internal environment
   (b) Objective setting
   (c) Event identification

(2) Analysis and analyzing the identified objectives of the organization, i.e. the risks and opportunities in terms of likelihood and magnitude of impact.

(3) Response strategy to respond to the situation. This risk response strategy selected by the management for the specific risk identified and analyzed may include:
   (a) Avoidance, i.e. existing activities giving rise to risk.

(b) Reduction, i.e. taking action to reduce the likelihood or impact related to the risk.

(c) Share or insure, i.e. transferring or sharing a portion of the risk to reduce it.

(d) Accept, i.e. no action is taken due to cost/benefit decisions.

The strategy mentioned above, indicates high level goals aligned with and supporting the organization's mission, and involves effective and efficient use of resources.

(4) Monitoring of the progress is typically performed by the management as part of its internal control activities to understand how the risk-response strategy is working and whether the objectives are being achieved. Monitoring includes information, communication and control activities as well. Monitoring is done through activities such as:

(a) Checking feedback forms.

(b) Review of analytical reports.

(c) Discussions with relevant experts.

(d) Discussions at management committee meetings.

(e) Checking compliance with applicable laws and regulations.

(f) Checking the reliability of operational and financial reporting, and the like.

ERM indicates a comprehensive view of risk from both operational and strategic perspectives, and is a process that supports the reduction of uncertainty and promotes the exploitation of opportunities.

Enterprise risk management is defined by the Risk and Insurance Management Society (RIMS) as the culture, processes and tools to identify strategic opportunities and reduce uncertainty. As per the RIMS risk maturity model for ERM, seven core competencies, or attributes, measure the extent to which the management is committed to ERM. Each attribute carries a maturity level and ERM maturity is determined by the weakest link.

(1) ERM -based Approach: Degree of executive support for an ERM-based approach within the corporate culture. This goes beyond regulatory compliance across all processes, functions, business lines, roles and geographies, degree of integration, communication and coordination of internal audit, information technology, compliance, control and risk management.

(2) **ERM Process Management:** Degree of weaving the ERM process into business processes and using the ERM process steps to identify, assess, evaluate, mitigate and monitor. Degree of incorporating qualitative methods supported by quantitative methods, analysis, tools and models.

(3) **Risk Appetite Management:** Degree of understanding the risk-reward trade-offs within the business. Accountability within leadership, policy to guide decision-making and attack gaps between perceived and actual risk. Risk appetite defines the boundary of acceptable risk, and risk tolerance defines the variation of measuring risk appetite that management deems acceptable.

(4) **Root Cause Discipline:** Degree of discipline applied to measuring a problem's root cause and binding event with their process sources to drive the reduction of uncertainty, collection of information and measurement of the control-effectiveness. The degree of risk from people, external environment, systems, processes and relationships is explored.

(5) **Uncovering Risks:** It means degree of quality and penetration coverage of risk assessment activities in documenting risk and opportunities. It depends on the degree of collecting knowledge from employee expertise, database and other electronic files (such as Microsoft Word, Excel, etc.) to uncover dependencies and correlation across the enterprise.

(6) **Performance Management:** It envisages degree of executing vision and strategy, working from financial, customers, business process and learning and growth perspectives, such as Kaplan's balanced

scorecard, or similar approach. It also involves degree of exposure to uncertainty or potential deviations from plans or expectations.

(7) **Business resiliency and sustainability:** It is the extent to which the ERM process-sustainability aspects are integrated into operational planning. This includes evaluating how planning supports resiliency and value and the degree of ownership and planning beyond recovering technology platforms. Examples include vendor and distribution dependencies, supply chain disruptions, dramatic market pricing changes, cash flow volatility, business liquidity, etc.

The challenges of implanting ERM are many. There are many consulting firms which offer suggestions on implementing ERM programmes. Some of the recognized challenges are common concerns that have been voiced at the Wikipedia website, are given below:

(1) Identifying Board level/Executive sponsors for ERM.
(2) Establishing a common risk language or glossary.
(3) Identifying and describing the risks in a risk inventory.
(4) Implementing a risk ranking methodology to prioritize risks within and across functions.
(5) Establishing an internal risk committee and/or Chief Risk Officer (CRO) to co-ordinate certain activities of the risk functions.
(6) Establishing ownership for particular risk and responses.
(7) Demonstrating the cost benefit of the risk management efforts.
(8) Developing action plans to ensure the risks are appropriately managed.
(9) Monitoring the results of actions taken to mitigate risk.
(10) Ensuring efficient risk coverage by internal auditors, consulting teams and other evaluating entities.

SUMMARY

After studying this chapter, the readers are expected to be familiar with an insurer's organizational set-up and be able to identify the various departments of an insurance organization. They should be reasonably aware of the functions handled by the insurance company through on-roll functionaries and outsourcing. They are also expected to appreciate the concept of managing an insurance company using the ERM approach.

(1) The organization structure helps the employees to identify themselves as part of the company, keep in mind its vision, share its mission and values, and feel that they belong to the organization. Necessary training is imparted for Company citizenship and to be effective workers with cultural/ethical ethos at the back.

(2) Insurance companies have general departments, such as accounts, administration, estate and establishment, human resources development and personnel, audit, information technology and data management, language, legal matters, vigilance, right to information, actuarial, etc. Technical departments include core insurance areas, such as fire, marine, aviation, motor, health, re-insurance and miscellaneous. Also, there are departments such as technical audit and risk management for certain specific functions.

(3) The functions are as follows:
   (a) Business-mix and spread of business.
   (b) Training inputs to sales staff as regards policy terms, exclusions and claim-procedures.
   (c) Acquisition channels, e.g. bancassurance, support/involvement in claims.

(4) The functions are as follows:
   (a) Overall Business strategy and objectives.
   (b) Customer's proposal and risk inspection reports.
   (c) Product development policy wordings, endorsements and clauses.
   (d) Response to cash calls and other recoveries from re-insurers.

(5) The functions of the finance department are as follows:
   (a) Ensuring compliance of Cash Before Cover Policy through the systems.
   (b) Accurate and timely release of claim-payments.
   (c) Hassle-free transactions with accurate recordings.

(6) The functions of the Claims Department are as follows:
   (a) Reduce end-to-end claims-cycle time through efficient and automated processes.
   (b) Enrich customers' claims experience, and help attract and retain best customers.
   (c) Identify and control fraudulent claims and leakages.
   (d) Improve claim-costs through good relationship/ negotiated rates with managed care partners and other service providers.
   (e) Hiring, developing and retaining the best claims people.

(7) The ERM approach includes the following four points:
   (a) Identifying,
   (b) Analyzing,
   (c) Responding to, and
   (d) Monitoring risks or opportunities, within the internal and external environment facing the enterprise.

(8) This risk-response strategy may include:
   (a) Avoidance, i.e. the exiting activities, giving rise to risk.
   (b) Reduction, i.e. taking action to reduce the likelihood or impact related to the risks.
   (c) Share or insure, i.e. transferring or sharing a portion of the risk, to reduce it.
   (d) Accept, i.e. no action is taken, due to a cost/ benefit decision.

Privatisation of Insurance Sector

INTRODUCTION

It has been observed that the Public Sector Enterprises (PSEs) cannot perform their economic and business activities effectively and efficiently in any country due to political considerations. It is observed that the public enterprises have not been discharging their full responsibilities even in a socialist country. The total nationalization of business industry will lead to serfdom or anarchism. Democracy demands full freedom in all matters with people's choice, not forced. But, it is stark reality that it is difficult for every enterprise to compete in the market. The government has to restructure society and economy in such a manner that the poor, the unemployed, can be profitably employed. Entrepreneurship has to be developed and all the educated persons have to set-up their ventures with the latest technology and under franchisee system or through ancilliarization in the industrial sector, if not independently.

India has been planning for development using the Nehruvian-Mahalanobis economic model of mixed economy. Too much expectation from public enterprises will distort the economy and will ultimately lead towards wastage of precious and valuable scarce resources. Therefore, the government is going to re-cast the industrial policy considering the productivity and efficiency as criteria to continue particular units whether as public enterprises or private enterprises. It is a matter of satisfaction that the government has started taking pragmatic approach-based criteria for the development of enterprises. The restriction on the use of full capacity by private enterprises is being removed to increase the output and productivity of the economy.

Time has come when the public enterprises will have to compete with the private enterprises in the level-playing field. If the public enterprises are losing in the efficiency and productivity criteria, they should be closed down. If the private enterprises have more efficiency and higher productivity, those should be encouraged to increase production and output in the economy. It is universally agreed that the government cannot perform all the functions with equal efficiency. It should have nothing to do with business or industry as far as the ownership is concerned. Ownership should pass on to the private hands as the private sector has entrepreneurship. The regulatory role, promotional role, entrepreneurial role and planning role have not been fully performed by any government with the level of efficiency of the private sector. The government should concentrate more on regulatory and planning roles at the macro-level. The entrepreneurial role should be confined only to those areas where the private entrepreneurs are hesitant and cannot discharge their functions satisfactorily at national level. Non-profitable business activities like defense, transport, education, communication and other such types of activities concerning general welfare and national security should only be undertaken by the Government.

According to W.A. Lewis: The nationalization of industry is not essential to planning. A government can do anything it wants to do by way of controlling industry without resorting to nationalization or ownership.

There should not be a state monopoly in the country in all fields. Competition is the backbone of an economy and it pushes up productivity. Therefore, competition should be encouraged to promote production and productivity in the economy. Competition may even be between the public and private enterprises. The public enterprises should be preferred in some areas than private sector, and so, they should be permitted to continue to accelerate the growth of the economy. On the other hand, many public sector enterprises are wasting public money because of continuous losses or less than optimal production. Such enterprises should be handed over to the competent private entrepreneurs.

However, privatization may be done after analyzing the efficiency of the organizations and their role in the economy. Insurance industry along with other financial institutions has been constantly under pressure of privatization without going into the grass-root level problems and their potential consequences. Many Committees and government agencies have been arguing in favour of privatization, de-nationalization and permitting foreign institutions to conduct insurance business in India.

Privatization of Insurance Industry in India—Steps Taken by the Government to Privatize the Insurance Sector

In 1993, the government of India had set-up a high powered committee under the Chairmanship of R.N. Malhotra, former Governor of Reserve Bank of India, to examine the structure of the insurance industry and to recommend changes to make it more efficient and competitive, keeping in view the structural changes taking place in other parts of the financial system of the country.

Objectives of Malhotra Committee

The following were the purposes of the Committee:

In terms of the objectives before the Malhotra Committee, it had surveyed, studied and analysed in its report the structure of insurance industry, to asses the strengths and weaknesses of insurance companies in terms of the objectives of creating an efficient and viable insurance industry, to have a wide coverage of insurance services, to have a variety of insurance products with a high quality services component, and to develop an effective instrument for mobilization of financial resources for development. The report also contained the arguments and made recommendations for changing the structure of insurance industry, for changing the general policy framework, etc. The Committee had the task of making suggestions regarding the following:

(a) To make specific suggestions regarding Life Insurance Corporation of India (LIC) and General Insurance Corporation of India (GIC) with a view to improve their functioning.
(b) To make recommendations on regulations and supervision of the insurance sector in India.
(c) To make recommendations on the role and functions of surveyors, intermediaries like agents, etc. in the insurance sector.
(d) To make recommendations on any other matters which are relevant for development of the insurance industry in India.

Malhotra Committee's Recommendations

Let us be briefed about the recommendations of the Malhotra Committee. The Committee submitted its report in January 1994 recommending that private insurers be allowed to co-exist along with government companies like LIC and GIC. This recommendation had been supported by several factors, the most important being the need for wide insurance coverage in the economy. Major recommendations of Malhotra Committee are as follows:

(i) Raising the capital base of LIC and GIC up to Rs. 200 crores each, half to be retained by the government and rest sold to the public at large with suitable reservations for employees.
(ii) Private sector be granted permission to enter insurance industry with a minimum paid up capital of Rs. 100 crores.
(iii) Foreign insurance companies be allowed to enter by floating an Indian company preferably joint venture with Indian partners.
(iv) Steps to be taken to set-up a strong and effective insurance regulatory body in the form of statutory autonomous board on the lines of SEBI.
(v) Limited number of private companies to be allowed in the sector. But no firm be allowed to operate in both lines of insurance (Life and non-Life).
(vi) Tariff Advisory Committee (TAC) is to be de-linked

from GIC to function as a separate statutory body under necessary supervision by the Insurance Regulatory Authority.

(vii) All the insurance companies be treated on equal footing and governed by the provisions of the Insurance Act. No special dispensation is to be given to government companies.

(viii) Setting up of a strong and effective regulatory body with independent source for financing before allowing private companies into this sector.

(ix) The committee suggested that settlement of claims was to be done within a specific time frame (without delay).

(x) The committee has made several recommendations on product pricing, vigilance, systems and procedures, improving customer service and use of technology.

(xi) It also made a number of recommendations to change the existing structures of the LIC and GIC.

(xii) The committee insisted that insurance companies should pay special attention to the rural insurance business (rural coverage).

Impact of Privatization and Liberalization on Insurance Industry

The opening up of insurance sector for competition offers ample opportunities to both existing as well as new players to penetrate into untapped areas, sectors and sub-sectors and unexploited segments of population as presently both insurance density and penetration are at low level. Both indices being at very low level in the country, even compared to the countries with the same level of economic development and per capita income, are indicative of the vast potential of the growth of this sector in future.

The impact of privatization can be studied under three heads:

Opportunities; challenges or threats; and strategies

(I) Opportunities

The privatization of insurance industry will provide the following opportunities:

(1) Untapped Market

New comers in insurance industry will get the advantage of untapped market. The untapped potential market for insurance products is quite large in spite of the efforts made by general insurance companies and LIC to extend their services throughout the country. But the choices available to the insuring public are inadequate in terms of services, products and prices. The Malhotra Committee estimated that in life insurance, 22% of the insurable population has been tapped so far. Premium per capita is only 2% in India. Premium percentage of GDP is 0.55% which is very less in comparison to the USA where premium per capita is equivalent of Rs. 1381 and premium as percentage of GDP is 4.80%. This huge gap from the global benchmark is itself indicative of huge untapped potential.

(2) Mandatory Insurance

In disaster prone areas, Government of India is going to make insurance mandatory. The interim report of the high powered committee set-up by the centre on disaster management has proposed mandatory insurance of life and property by people residing in a disaster prone area such as coastal belts, flood prone areas, site near nuclear, chemical and hazardous industries and thickly populated areas.

(3) More Products Offered

A state monopoly has little incentive to offer a wide range of products. It can be seen by a lack of certain products from LIC's portfolio and lack of extensive categorization in several GIC products such as health insurance. More competition in this business will spur firms to offer several new products with more complex and extensive risk categorization.

(4) Growth of Economy

With the allowing of holding of equity shares by foreign company either itself or through its subsidiary company or nominee, not exceeding 26% of paid-up capital of insurance company, various joint ventures between foreign investors and Indian partners will be operated resulting into supplementing domestic savings and economic progress of the nation.

(5) Opportunity for Banks

Banks, with their wide area network with branches in all parts of the country, will have good opportunity to enter in insurance business or industry. Banks will succeed in this sector because they have data of customers, trained staff, a good network

(6) Better Customer Services

Privatization would result in better customer services and would help in improving the variety and price of insurance products. Competition will compel the players to bring new and innovative products, wider choice of prices and quality service to the policyholders (consumers).

(II) Challenges

Whether the insurer is old or new, private or public, expansion and extension of market will present multitude of challenges, as described hereunder:

(1) New Insurers

New insurance will have to invest a minimum capital of Rs. 100 crore. The normal gestation period is of five years. Hence, the new insurers will have to lock up their capital for at least five years before earning any profits. Besides, they will face problems of shortage of trained manpower for the insurance industry. The setting up of various offices and distribution of network is a time-consuming process. Further, the new insurer-companies will have to compete with the established insurance companies like LIC and GIC, which have a corporate image and market presence for several years.

(2) Expectations of the Consumers

Today, LIC has more than 60 products and GIC has more than 180 products to offer in the insurance market. But most of them are outdated, as they are not suitable to the needs of the present-day consumers. Hence, all the insurance companies will have to offer innovative products to the consumers. The consumers are particularly expecting good pension plans, health insurance, term insurance, and investment products like unit linked insurance from the life insurance companies. Similarly, the consumers expect innovative products from the general insurance for managing health care, property insurance, accident insurance and other products on an attractive terms and competitive premium. The consumers also expect reduction in the premium of the insurance products for another reason; that the mortality rate in India has come down three times in the last five years.

(3) Premium on Customer Service

The days of giving fixed insurance products are over. Now the customers need insurance solutions that match their needs or wants. The large-scale of operations, public sector bureaucratic and cumbersome procedures hamper nationalized insurers. Therefore, potential private entrants expect to score in the areas of customer service, speed and flexibility. It may mean better products and wider choice for the customers. For extending better service, insurance companies will have to build call centres to provide call-free telephone-based sales and services. The call centres will provide product-related information, customers' accounts' information, queries and complaint handling. These call centres can be used for outbound sales and marketing companies.

(4) Distribution Channel

In the privatized insurance market, there will be multiple distribution channels which will include agents, brokers, corporate intermediaries, bank branches, affinity groups and direct marketing through tele-sales and internet. There will be competition among the channels also. Intense competitions will grow among the old and new insurers in the liberalized insurance market.

There would be substantial shift in the distribution of insurance in India. Many of these changes are due to international trends. World-wide insurance products move from pure service produces to pure commodity products. Then they could be sold through the medical shops, groceries, novelty stores, etc. Once the products gain awareness and popularity, then they can move to remote channels such as telephone or direct mail.

(5) Consumer Education

The existing level of consumers' education and awareness about insurance products is very low. Only 62% of the Indian population is educated and less than 10% are well educated. Even the educated are ignorant about the various products of insurance. Hence, it is necessary that all the insurance companies should undertake the executive plan and policy for education and awareness of consumers about insurance policies. The consumer organizations and media can also play very important role in education of the consumers. This will result in expansion and depth of the insurance market and will also enable the needy consumers to purchase appropriate policies. In fact, the private new comer- insurers have already started putting a lot more emphasis on advertising and using creative tactics to educate the consumers.

(6) Consumer Grievance Redressal Mechanism

The insurance companies have to face an acute problem of the redressal of grievances of consumers for deficiency in products and services. The IRDA has already appointed ombudsman for looking into the grievances of the policyholders and its judgment will be binding on insurers. In the competitive market, awareness level of consumers will increase and it will help consumers to fight for their legal right in case of deficiency in services. Therefore, the number of legal cases filed by the consumers against the insurance companies is likely to increase substantially in future. This will be a challenge to the insurers.

(7) New Product Innovations Needed

In India, only two products of LIC dominate with majority share out of 52 products. With more competition, good products will become an important differentiator among the various competing insurance products. A lot will depend on the kind of products that these outfits would launch. Initially, after launching simple products, the multinationals will shift to specialized products, e.g. Royal Sundaram Alliance will launch a mix of personal and commercial insurance policies. This will cover fire, marine, motor, personal accident and health insurance. HDFC Standard Life will launch two core life insurance products and then another dozen of the same type.

(8) Positioning of Insurance Products in the Market

First of all, the biggest challenge for the insurance companies will be the change in the mindset of people, especially in regard to life insurance. Life insurance is seen more as a tax saving mechanism rather than safety net in case of death, in India, e.g. ICICI Prudential Life Insurance's Chief Marketing Officer, Saugata Gupta says that "Working on consumer attitude will be the greatest challenge". New types of products should be futuristic in outlook. To start with, low premium high cover policies should be introduced and better savings products at later stage.

(9) Rural Area Exploitation the Best Bet

Life insurance business in India suffers from high premium and low returns. A normally competitive industry should be able to increase coverage, mobile large savings, and provide high returns. In terms of mobilizing savings in the form of insurance, India is ranked at 27th in the world. In developed countries like the U.K., the USA and South Africa, life insurance premium accounts for over population only. Now with the entry of numerous private companies in rural areas, it is expected that rural sector will be tapped as well. IRDA has made it mandatory for life insurance companies to sell 5% of their aggregated policies in the rural areas during the first year of operation and that will be progressively increased to 15% by the fifth year. But with gestation period being long and investment required being large, new entrants will feel very difficult to achieve it.

(10) Information Technology the Highly Facilitating Factor

Information technology has become an integral part of the insurance industry worldwide from general accounting to customer service, re-insurance, underwriting and risk management. These have integrated application and are decision-oriented. In the Indian insurance industry, information technology is used as a reporting tool whereas overseas it is used more as a decision-making instrument. The policyholders would be able to check policy details make/change to nominee, to identify schemes, the type of loans available and the amount in their investment accounts on-line and through Internet connectivity. The insurers' advisors can also check accounts of their customers as well as their own accounts.

(III) Strategies

The insurance players would be required to concentrate on the following main strategies to become more competitive and responsive to the needs of the societies:

(1) Environmental Analysis

The companies should concentrate on environmental change, its direction, magnitude and its short-term and long-term impact, formulating strategies to meet the challenges of high competition, preparing contingency plans and then designing action plans for effective implementation of formulated strategies.

(2) Restructuring Organization will Help

The traditional hierarchy system is very slow in making decisions due to several levels of management involved, its procedural inflexibility and slow communication process/ system. A manager in the privatized scenario is required to be an organizational specialist, country specialist and global specialist.

(3) Speed, Cost Effectiveness and Innovations Required

The private insurance companies will have to make substantial investments in customer relationship management technologies. They will be required to have wide area network (WAN), connecting branches spread across wide geographical locations and work out modalities for facilitating premium payment through the Internet. LIC is setting up an interactive response system in more cities so that a policyholder need not travel to the office of company for information. After all, the customer should have the choice of getting work done in the shortest possible time without having to visit the office of insurance companies.

(4) Human Resources Development the Key to Business Development and Client Servicing

Human resource is important for any organization, more especially for organizations activities of which revolve around special human interactions. The new private insurance companies need people with the right set of knowledge, skills and aptitude for insurance alongwith right type of products and services. The persons who are involved in selling the product and those who are doing the back office work need to equip themselves with newer skills and insights into every aspect of functioning of the company. They have a daunting task of exploiting potential in the industry and at the same time bring down risk level to the company for providing insurance coverage. They have to retain the existing customers for which they need to have better understanding of products and services by creating healthy internal environment with group harmony. Existing companies will have to frame their human resource policies to retain the competent personnel and motivate staff continuously since new companies entering insurance business will be eyeing them by offering lucrative salaries.

(5) Efficiency in Distribution to be Assured

It is very important factor and may prove bottleneck to the new players. Insurance companies are making the products available through the ready distribution channels of banks, non-banking finance companies and housing companies. One has to be careful doing this, since creating distribution with distances does not automatically mean controlling them. There will be more places from where customer can purchase insurance polices with the starting of corporate agencies besides the consultants and agents currently selling these policies. Due to this, a new concept of Bancassurance has emerged which is defined as a kind of service that the insurance companies use to offer their products through the distribution channels of banking industry. There is need to augment sources of revenues for survival. Bancassurance has promoted two big classes of financial institutions to combine their strengths and create a new means of marketing and servicing their products. Convergence of banking sector traditionally considered being more competitive and insurance sector having a vast untapped potential of growth has resulted into bancassurance.

(6) Risk Management

Insurance companies will have to bring new approach and sophistication in market research techniques, future portfolio expansion like all intermediaries in financial markets do.

(7) Efficient Marketing Strategies

Marketing strategies for insurance products in the emerging scenario could be understood in the following steps:

$R \rightarrow STP \rightarrow MM \rightarrow I \rightarrow C$

where

R	= Market Research,
STP	= Segmentation, Targeting, Positioning,
MM	= Marketing Mix,
I	= Implementation, and
C	= Control.

The focus of emerging marketing strategies would centre on the prepositions like reduced costs, increased profitability, reduced time to market, improved customer intimacy, retained customers for life, establishing strong partnership. Formulation of a marketing strategy is more a process than an event. Environmental factors like macro-economic parameters, regulatory norms and theme, technology, infrastructure, legal set-up, competition by way of new entry, degree of globalization, etc. need to be scanned and considered in framing the likely scenarios. The competitive advantage of a company may stem from the many discrete activities in value chains. Each of these activities can contribute to a company's relative cost position or create a basis for differentiation.

(8) Ethical Issues

The governance problems in service industry like insurance have been raised time and again as well as risk management techniques. Companies will need to leverage this sophistication backed by information technology to select good risks and rate them. On the other hand, insurance companies invest the funds of policyholders and owned capital and accumulate surpluses and reserves. Companies try to earn the highest rate of return possible on investments consistent with risk objectives, because pre-eminence is related to investment performance. As the rate of return on investments increases, the insurance companies can lower the premiums they charge on new policies. Higher rate of return provides higher earnings on cash values and lesser the need for premium revenues. Premium rates are a competitive factor and high investment returns are crucial in maintaining and improving an insurance company's sales position. Strong investment performance supports growth in policy sales and sets aside the sense of helplessness among the employees and customers alike. Companies must realize this particularly in the emerging scenario of intense competition wherein customers will have a range of options for investments and insurance. At the same time, the regulators and companies will have to be cautious of customers who indulge in unethical practices by manipulating or hiding vital information in their dealings with companies and inflict losses, resulting in increase in cost of insurance. Ethics will have to be ensured in every activity of the company.

Scenario of Insurance Industry in India as it Obtains Today

Seventeen new players have entered the field of insurance, both life and non-life business, after opening up of insurance industry to private sector in India. Some of these are:

Tata AIG Life Insurance Company Ltd.
Birla Sunlife Insurance Company Ltd.
HDFC Standard Life Insurance Company Ltd.
Kotak Mahindra Old Mutual Life Insurance Company Ltd.
Reliance General Insurance Company Ltd.
ICICI Prudential Life Insurance Company Ltd.
Royal Sundaram Alliance Insurance Company Ltd.
Bajaj Auto Alliance Insurance Company Limited.
IFFCO Tokyo General Insurance Company Ltd.
ING Vysya Life Insurance Company (Pvt.) Ltd.
SBI Life Insurance Company Ltd.
Dabur CJU Life Insurance Company Ltd.
Max New York Life Insurance Company Ltd.

SBI Life Insurance has lunched three products: Sanjeevan, Sukhjeevan and Young Sanjeevan and so far, it has sold more than 300 policies under its plans. Various insurance companies have tied up with banks to market their products, e.g. HDFC Standard Life has tied up with Indian bank and UCO Bank in the Eastern region. It has also entered into an MOU with Peerless Bank as the latter's branches will help a rural reach for insurance company. Proposed joint venture Dabur CJU Life Insurance where Dabur group holds 74% and UK-based CJU life's 26% stake would be started with an equity capital of Rs. 110 crore. CGNU group being UK's largest insurer and one of the world's sixty largest insurers with assets worth $ 300 bn under its management and Dabur being India's leading FMCG Company, this venture may emerge as a leading player in insurance industry. Kotak Mahindra is likely to get approval for two more products, which include term insurance and equity-linked policy in a bid to offer wider range of products.

In India, till now, only 20% of the insurable population is covered under insurance while the remaining population is yet to be insured. As the insurance sector has been opened up, the monopoly of government companies has broken and many new private players have entered into the insurance sector and thus the sector has become highly competitive, full of challenges. The insurance and the economic growth of the country mutually influence each other. As the economy grows, the standard of living of people also improves.

In fact, as the economy widens, the demand for insurance products emerges. A well developed insurance sector promotes economic growth by encouraging risk taking. The average annual rate of growth of the country in the first three decades after independence was 3.5%. In the nineties, the average annual rate of growth of income has been 5.8% per annum. Life expectancy has also increased from 32 years in fifties to 61 years now. As life expectancy increases, there will be a need to take care of long retired life. So, the Indian life insurance market along with general insurance market is full of potential. The only need is to frame suitable strategies to tap the whole market in more efficient and effective manner.

10

Asset-Liability Management (ALM)

INTRODUCTION

This (ALM) started with banks under Basel prudential norms, applicable throughout the world. Traditionally and previously banks were concerned only with increasing the size of their balance sheets. They were focusing on few specific items of the balance sheet like deposits, credit to priority sector and reducing the size of NPAs – recovery of bad and doubtful loans and advances (Assets). After the introduction of prudential accounting norms, deregulation of interest rates, globalization and economic liberalization, Indian banks began facing serious problem of mismatch between their assets and liabilities due to volatility in the interest rates and foreign exchange rates. Emergence of new instruments, new players and new products at highly competitive rates in the market increased banks' risks. Now in a fairly deregulated environment, interest rates on all money market instruments are determined for most part, and often, by the market forces. All the banks are now allowed to determine own interest rates on domestic deposits and loans and advances over rupees 2 lakh.

The changes in interest rates affect the banks in two ways as under:

(1) Since assets (loans and advances) and liabilities (deposits and borrowings) are not realised simultaneously, the mismatch affects the interest income.

(2) It affects the market value of assets like treasury bills, commercial paper and certificate of deposits, etc.

Therefore, it is no longer the case that banks shall be asset-driven and primarily concerned to find resources to finance lending. Rather banks are moving progressively to the stage of not only adjusting liabilities in accordance with potential assets but also adjusting assets in accordance with potential liabilities.

MEANING OF ALM

The various types of risks faced by the banks can be managed through the management process known as Asset-Liability Management (ALM). Asset-Liability Management refers to the policy of the banks with regard to mix of assets and liabilities. In the context of RBI guidelines to the banks, 'asset-liability' management can be defined as a continuous process of planning, organizing and controlling asset/liability volume, maturities, yields and rates. In other words, asset-liability management can be defined as a function which involves planning, directing and controlling the flow, level, mix and rates on the bank assets and liabilities.

OBJECTIVES OF ASSET-LIABILITY MANAGEMENT (ALM)

An effective Asset-liability management of banks should encompass:

(a) Review of interest-rate outlook.

(b) Fixation of interest, product pricing of both assets and liabilities.

(c) Review of credit-risk management and credit portfolio.

(d) Review of investment portfolio and risk management.

(e) Review of liquidity risk and management of liquidity risk.

(f) Review of policy of foreign exchange operations and risk management.

BALANCE SHEET STRUCTURE: IMPLICATIONS FOR ASSET-LIABILITY MANAGEMENT (ALM)

The subject of assets (especially advances and investments) and liability (especially deposits and borrowings) management revolves around balance sheet. The ALM requires that assets and liabilities should be planned, organized and controlled so that profitability is managed and liquidity is managed.

The analysis of balance sheet of a bank reveals that among the liabilities, a significant portion comes from deposits (savings, term deposits and current account deposits) and among these deposits, term deposits bear a fixed rate of interest for a specified period but carry a risk of pre-mature encashments. The savings bank deposits have no maturity period. Borrowings (from RBI and other banks) are also among liabilities which carry interest at market rate but repayment is generally known.

The analysis of assets side reveals that the most significant portion of advances is liked to prime lending rate (PLR) which is a floating rate. Once the PLR changes, the rate on the loans and advances would change instantly without any time lag. An overwhelming majority of the investment portfolio is in the form of fixed rate government and other securities.

Balance Sheet Structure

(A) Liabilities Side

(a) Deposits

Savings Fund Accounts and Current Accounts

The features of both the deposits are that there is no maturity date and the clients are free to deposit or withdraw any amount at any point of time.

Term Deposits

The term deposits may be in the form of cumulative term

deposits, non-cumulative term deposits and recurring deposits. As regards liquidity, the client has the freedom to encash them at a pre-matured date if he needs money urgently. In case of recurring deposits, the instalment amount may not be paid in time.

In case, interest rates increase, the customers can decide in their favour.

(b) Borrowing

Terms of Borrowings are clear as regards liquidity and interest rates.

(B) Assets Side

Investment

The investment may be for medium and long-term and there is little flexibility for reshuffling. Major portion of investments carries fixed rate of interest.

Advances

The repayment of advances by customers is no doubt pre-determined but repayment still depends upon host of factors. Some part of cash credit and overdraft may not be availed of by the borrowing units leading to uncertainty in liquidity management.

SCOPE OF ASSET- LIABILITY MANAGEMENT

Asset-liability management of a bank, earlier known as Treasury Management, is a part of overall risk management. Risk is defined as, "Risk is uncertainty as to the outcome of an event when two or more possibilities exist." The aim of asset-liability management is to manage risk exposures so that they are kept within the acceptable levels and at the same time help to generate income and maintain profitability. Efficient asset-liability management procedures should enable a bank to control and limit risks associated with maturity mismatching, Interest rate gaps and foreign exchange exposure and so on. ALM addresses the following risks:

Liquidity Risk; Interest Rate Risk; and Market Risk.

(I) Liquidity Risk

Liquidity Risk refers to the ability of a concern to meet its commitment when due and to undertake new transactions if profitable. Liquidity risk can emanate in any of the following situations:

(a) Conversion of contingent liabilities into fund-based commitment.
(b) Non-receipt of expected cash flows from recovery of loans.
(c) Increased availment of sanctioned limits.
(d) Disproportionate outflow of funds arising out of non-renewal/withdrawal of deposits.

Liquidity Risk is Categorised into Two Types:
(i) Trading Liquidity Risk, and (ii) Funding Liquidity Risk.

Trading Liquidity Risk

Trading liquidity risk arises as a result of liquidity of securities in the trading portfolio of the bank. Liquidity and return are negatively correlated. So higher returns can be expected by accepting an illiquid investment in the portfolio and should be monitored on frequent basis. In reality, one of the important considerations for the inclusion of investment in the trading portfolio is on the basis of its liquidity status. As the trading portfolio is short-term in nature with regulator-constrained maximum holding period of 90 days, it is better to include only those securities which are not only liquid at the time of creation but are expected to be liquid over the holding period of portfolio.

Funding Liquidity Risk

Funding liquidity risk arises as a result of mismatch between the timing of the cash flow of assets and liabilities; funding liquidity risk that arises due to mismatch is the outcome of difference in balance sheet strategies followed by different institutions in the same industry. It is possible that a few banks may suffer from shortage of liquidity while others may have excess funding liquidity.

Measurement of Liquidity Risk

There are two approaches to measure liquidity risk at balance sheet level. These are: Liquidity Gap Analysis and Structural Balance Sheet Ratios.

(I) Liquidity Gap Analysis

The liquidity gap at a particular level of maturity is the difference between maturity of assets and maturing liabilities. When maturing liabilities exceed maturing assets, a negative gap is created and when maturing assets exceed maturing liabilities, a positive gap is created.

Reserve Bank of India, in its guidelines, has instructed the banks to classify maturing assets (cash inflows) and maturing liabilities (cash flows) in eight maturity periods (called tie buckets). The cash flows from assets and liabilities include both principal and interest cash flows.

The liability gap analysis is illustrated through an example of "Liquidity Gap Statement" of PRS Bank:

Liquidity Gap Statement of PRS Bank as on 25-06-2011

(Rs. In Crores)

Maturity	*Assets*	*Liabilities*	*Gap*	*Cumulative Gap*
01 day – 14 days	2,000	2,300	(300)	(300)
15 days – 28 days	3,000	3,600	(600)	(900)
29 days – 03 months	4,000	5,000	(1,000)	(1,900)
3 months – 06 months	4,000	5,600	(1,600)	(3,500)
6 months – 12 months	2,000	2,000	0	(3,500)
1 year – 02 years	3,000	2,600	400	(3,100)
2 years – 05 years	6,000	4,000	2,000	1,100
Over 5 years	2,000	3,100	(1,100)	0

It can be observed from the above statement that the liability maturing over the next three months from 25-06-2011 exceed maturing assets by Rs. 1900 crores (cumulative gap). The total maturing liabilities at Rs. 10, 900 crores (2300 + 3600 + 5000) over the first three months requires to be met by (a) fresh deposits, (b) renewal of deposits, and (c) borrowings from other banks and RBI. At the end, the liquidity gap will always be nil because assets always equal to liability plus equity.

Banks generally do not and can not maintain 'NIL' gap in all maturities. The objective of this liquidity gap analysis is to determine the tolerable gap. These gaps are also called mismatches. The RBI desires that the gap in the maturity buckets of 1-14 days and 15-28 days should be limited to 20% of the maturing liabilities of cash outflows in the respective maturity buckets.

With the information available in the liquidity gap statement, the banks can evolve prudential limits for the gaps according to their risk taking capacities and as per guidelines/ norms fixed by the RBI from time to time.

Structural Balance Sheet Ratios

The liquidity position of the banks can be assessed through structural balance sheet ratios.

Some of the ratios are discussed below:

Purchased Funds to Liquid Assets

Purchased funds, for example, are call money borrowings including short-term refinance, etc. These funds should not constitute a significant portion of liquid assets. It is important and urgent to specify a tolerance limit for that purpose so that outflow of funds on account of purchased funds is controlled.

Core Deposits to Core Assets

Outstanding in loan books and the statutory reserves constituted core assets are considered for this ratio. The ratio of core deposits to core assets should be specified to maintain a stable liquid position.

Call Borrowing to Total Borrowing

This ratio reflects the dependence of a bank on call borrowings to honour its commitments. Call borrowings are generally costly.

Liquid Investments to Total Investments

Liquid investments are convertible into cash at any time. More the liquidity lesser the profits, so the banks are to trade off between liquidity and profitability.

Liquid Assets to Total Assets

Extent of liquid assets available to meet outflows on account of deposits in normal/abnormal circumstances is shown by this ratio.

As banks deal in money, major part of money must be in the form of investment and liquid assets.

Liquidity Risk Management

A rational idea that emerges after liquidity analysis is liquidity risk management. The issues which are relevant in managing liquidity risks are:

To keep constant watch over the fact whether the liquidity-asset mis-match (surplus or deficit), under consideration, is within tolerable limits as per the policy of the management of the bank. If yes, it is OK. If not, what should be various measures or strategies to be employed to ensure that the imbalance is within the tolerance limit.

Financial experts suggest that even if liquidity mismatch is within the tolerance range, the management should adhere to strategies which maximize benefits in a given market environment. However, keeping in mind the tolerance limits to be strictly followed, the management must be proactive rather than passive. Among the numerous strategies available are: trading portfolio, refinance facilities, market borrowing, wholesale deposits, securitization, loan sales, etc. Every strategy has to be evaluated in terms of cost and the intended benefit before implementation for managing the A-L mismatch.

(2) Interest Rate Risk (IRR)

Interest affects all financial transactions. Banks' profits accrue from interest income more than non-interest income. The interest rate risk is the risk of decline of earnings owing to change in interest rates. The profitability of the bank is largely dependent on the interest spread (interest spread is the difference between interest earned and interest expended). A sizable chunk of banks revenues and costs are indexed to interest rates. Since interest rates are unstable, so are the earrings.

The following kinds of risks will either individually or cumulatively result in interest rate risks:

Rate Level Risk

There is always a possibility of resetting interest rate levels either due to market forces or due to regulatory intervention. Suppose that RBI lowers Cash Reserve Ratio (CRR) by 2%, the result would be that the market would be flooded with excess liquidity which shall result in lowering interest rates.

Pre-Payment Risk

The decline in interest rates at times leads to pre-payment of loans. When interest rates are declining, customers who had taken loan at higher rates would like to substitute a cheaper debt or pre-pay the costly loan. The pre-paid cash in-flows will have to be re-deployed at a lower rate, which shall invariably affect profitability.

Basic Risk

It is quite possible to link liabilities and assets to two different bench-marks resulting in floating rate. Suppose that these two base rates do not move in tandem with each other, the net interest income either increases or decreases.

Real Interest Rate Risk

The level of inflation also plays a critical role in determining the real interest yield/cost.

Volatility Risk

The frequent changes in interest rates affect the business volume as well as pricing of the products. The effect or fluctuation in the short-term will have a greater impact on cash flows since the adjustment period is very short.

Measurement of Interest Rate Risk

There are three approaches available to measure interest rate risk, these are:

Earnings Approach; Interest Rate Gap analysis; and Economic Value Approach.

(1) *Earning Approach to IRR:* The earnings approaches which is an important top line performance indicator is expressed either as net interest income or net interst margin.

(a) *Net Interest Income (NII):* Net interest income is the excess of interest income over interest expenses. Mathematically NII is expressed as:

$$NII = \text{Interest Income} - \text{Interest Expenses}$$

Interest income includes interest income from advances plus interest income from investment.

Note: Interest for the purpose of interest income also includes dividend received from equity portfolio of mutual fund investments, etc.

Interest Expenses include: Interest paid on deposits plus interest paid on borrowings.

(b) *Net Interest Margin (NIM):* When NII is expressed in percentage as the basis of total assets or earning assets, it is called as NIM. Mathematically the formula is expressed as:

$$\text{Net Interest Margin} = \frac{NII}{\text{Earning Assets}} \times 100$$

$$\text{Or} \qquad = \frac{NII}{\text{Total Assets}} \times 100$$

(2) *Interest Rate Gap Analysis:* Interest rate gap analysis technique is similar to liquidity gap analysis technique. In interest rate gap analysis, the assets and liabilities are placed in the buckets on the basis of timing of change or expected change in interest rates on the assets and liabilities and not on the basis of cash inflows and outflows as in the case of statement of liquidity gap. The RBI has prescribed a statement of interest rate sensitivity for regulatory reporting.

Total liabilities and total assets, i.e. column A and B refer to rate sensitive assets and rate sensitive liabilities.

All the assets and all the liabilities are categorized into rate sensitive and rate non-sensitivity groups. Equity capital on the liabilities side and cash on the assets side are non-sensitive. Any change in interest rates would not have any impact on cash and equity. Equity in itself is not sensitive to interest rate changes; it is sensitive through other liabilities and assets.

Statement of Interest Rate Gap Analysis

(Amount in Crores Rs.)

Time Buckets	*Total Liabilities (A)*	*Total Assets (B)*	*Net Gap (C)*	*Cumulative Gap (D)*
1 day–28 days	4,198	4,324	126	126
29 days–3 months	5,186	2,960	(2,226)	(2,100)
3 months–6 months	21,860	21,302	(558)	(2,658)
6 months–12 months	5,460	2,850	(2,660)	(5,268)
1 year–3 years	13,202	5,972	(7,230)	(12,496)
3 years–5 years	7,584	7,786	202	12,296
Over 5 years	2,344	24,756	22,412	10,116
Non-sensitive	20,684	11,210	(9,474)	642
Total	80,518	81,160	642	-

The assets and liabilities are rate sensitive if—

The cash flows from them are on their maturity.

The cash flows represent an interim, or part principal repayment.

The interest rate applicable to the outstanding principal, changes contractually during the period under consideration.

The outstanding principal can be re-priced when some base rate or index changes.

Interest is payable on liabilities and interest is receivable on assets. If rate sensitive liabilities exceed assets, this will have negative effect on net interest income and *vice-versa*.

(3) *Economic Value Approach*: The economic value approach takes into consideration the long-term impact of interest rate changes by covering the entire life of all rate sensitive assets and liabilities. Under this approach, the effect of interest rate changes are studied on an important variable called "Economic Value of Equity". Mathematically Economic Value of Equity is:

Economic Value of Equity = Economic Value of Assets –
Economic Value of Liabilities

It may be understood that the essence of the equation reflects the residuary nature of the claims of the equity shareholders who are the ultimate owners. The term economic value is preferred to the market value as number of assets and liabilities in the balance sheet of a bank do not have a ready market. Economic value of equity approach also removes the problem of different bases for valuation of items in the balance sheet. The balance sheet of a bank recognizes the changes in the value of few items while other assets and liabilities are reflected at historical cost despite the change in value. This approach is also superior to earnings approach. A higher accounting profit does not necessarily mean better performance unless the degree of risk attached to such profits is taken into considerations.

The economic value of equity approach is based on the present value of money which is the basic foundation of the subject of finance. The value of assets and liabilities is inversely related to the interest rates.

The interest rates of assets and liabilities influence the value as:

(a) When the rates of interest on assets and liabilities go up from the present level, the value of the assets would fall and *vice-versa.*

(b) When the value of assets increases or value of liabilities decreases, the economic value of equity increases and *vice-versa.*

(3) Market Risk

The Basel Committee on Banking Supervision (BCBS) in its publication "amendment to Capital Accord to incorporate Market Risks", published in January 1996, has defined market risk as, "The risk of losses in and off balance sheet position arising from movements in market price".

Market risks can arise out of the following:

Interest rate risk; Equity position risk; Foreign exchange risk; and Commodities risk.

Approaches to Measure Market Risk

Measures for market risk are broadly categorized as under:

(1) Factor-based Measures.
(2) Volatility-based Measures.

(1) *Factor Sensitivity Measures*: Factor sensitivity measures assess the impact of change in the major factors on the market value of the portfolio. The most important factor sensitivity measure is the modified duration. Modified duration is the direct measure of sensitivity in value of a security or a portfolio of bonds for a change in interest rates. In duration method, the duration of an asset or liability is calculated as the weighted average maturity of the resultant cash flows, the weights being the present value of cash flows. Duration is less than the maturity of the coupon bond. Greater the duration of duration gap, higher is the interest rate risk exposure of the assets and liabilities.

One of the significant applications of the factor sensitivity measures is to use them for setting limits.

Example: a bank may set the maximum modified duration of its bond portfolio as (say) 8. This means that the price sensitivity that the bank is willing to accept in case of the bond portfolio is maximum 8% of the value of the portfolio for 1% change in interest rates. A loss more than 8% will not be tolerated by the bank. This limit is a caution to the trading manager in order to discourage them to earn higher commission (being percentage of trading profits) due to higher risk. There is higher risk if trading manager goes against the situation; it may lead to closure of banks as it has happened in case of Barings Bank of the U.K.

(2) *Volatility-based Measures*: Volatility-based measure, popularly known as value at risk (VAR), has gained a lot of prominence. The most favourbale advantage of value at risk is its uniformity in measuring trading risk across various positions such as interest rates, equity, commodity and currency which is the weakest thing as far as factor sensitivity measures are concerned. As a result of uniformity of measurement, it is possible to aggregate risk across completely different positions (compare and contrast) among various positions to assess the relative riskiness.

The following example will make the VAR clearer:

Market value of Security: Rs. 400 crores

Confidence Level used for VAR computation 98%
Value at Risk = 8 crores
Holding period used for VAR competitions 2 days
VAR = Rs. 8 crores

The example states that out of 400 crores of security Rs. 8 crores is value at risk. The maximum loss that bank will suffer on 2 trading days would not exceed Rs. 8 crores on 98% of the trading days (confidence level used for VAR computation is 98%). Only on 2% of the days, the loss would exceed the VAR of Rs. 8 crores. If we assume 200 trading days in a period, the above interpretation means that 196 trading days out of 200 days would have losses less than Rs. 8 crore. Only on 4 days out of 200 days, the losses would exceed the VAR computed.

Methods for Computation of VAR

There are three main methods for the computation of VAR:

Historical Simulation: Historical simulation which is based on historical/past data is non-parametric in nature. The main assumption of this method is that the past trends and volatilities in price would repeat in future also.

Variance Co-variance VAR: This is widely accepted and practised method at present. This method was popularized by the investment bank, J.P. Morgan, in the 90s. This method is parametric as it assumes that the prices follow normal distribution. This method is based on correlation, standard deviation, arithmetic mean and co-variance etc. for the estimation of VAR.

Monte Carlo VAR: The term Monte Carlo is a technique of research operation. This approach is not based on the assumption of distribution of properties or assets prices but involves empirical estimation and the statistical distribution from the prices which is then applied to simulate the prices leading to the estimation of VAR.

SOME CASES THAT ARE INTEGRAL TO THE EVOLUTION OF GENERAL INSURANCE

Case I: Principles – Non-Disclosure

Joel Vs. Law Union and Crown Insurance Company—(1908) 99 LT 712, CA.

(Dispute on what should be disclosed and what would be treated as non-disclosure)

Finding: There is no duty on the insured to disclose facts which he could not reasonably be expected to know.

Fletcher Moulton, L.J. (at 718)

The duty is a duty to disclose, and you cannot disclose what you do not know. The obligation to disclose, therefore, necessarily depends on the knowledge you possess. If a reasonable man would have recognized that the knowledge in question was material to disclose, it is no excuse that you did not recognize. But the question always is was the knowledge you possessed such that you ought to have disclosed it?

Let me take an example. I will suppose that a man has occasionally had a headache. It may be that a particular one of these headaches would have told a brain specialist of hidden mischief, but to the man it was an ordinary headache indistinguishable from the rest. Now, no reasonable man would deem it material to tell an insurance company of all the casual headaches he had in his life, and if he knew no more as to this particular headache, there would be no breach of his duty towards the insurance company in not disclosing it. He possessed no knowledge that it was incumbent on him to disclose, because he knew of nothing which a reasonable man would deem material or of a character of influence on the insurers in their action. (He) can not be held liable for non-disclosure in respect of facts which he did not know. Insurers are ... (entitled) to full disclosure of all knowledge possessed by the applicant that is material to the risk.

Source: E.R. Hardy Ivamy, 'Casebook on Insurance Law', London, Butterworths, 4th Edition, (pp. 5-6, 1984).

Case 2: Motor-Damage to Insured Vehicle

Seaton Vs. London General Insurance Company Ltd. (1932)43 LLL Rep 398.

[The engine of an insured lorry was removed for repair to the insured's workshop at a distance of nearly 150 yards away from the garage where the lorry was kept. There, the engine was destroyed by fire. Insurer repudiated liability stating that the vehicle was covered only when it was in a complete condition].

Finding by the King's Bench Division: Where a vehicle is dismantled into two pieces, and one piece is removed for the purpose of repair, it is still a vehicle for the purpose of a motor insurance policy.

Du Parcq, J. (at 399)

(If) he had taken the engine for the purpose of repair, he would still have been insured in respect whole of the vehicle into his yard or any other place to repair it, and then would of the motor vehicle ..... and any damage to it would have been covered. But he left the vehicle bereft of its engine in the garage and took the engine to another part of the premises .... the engine was burned. .... while it was in the carpenter's shop.

It is said ....(that the company) .... Did not insure against loss of two vehicles, and that if he is going to be allowed to divide up his vehicles in two or more sections, it seems hard on the company .... (it) seems to be almost beyond dispute that the mere fact that he has taken the engine out of the vehicle does not prevent the vehicle as a whole from being insured .... Therefore, ... in my opinion that at the time when the fire occurred, Mr. Seaton still had a motor vehicle although it was in two pieces.

I think, therefore, it is impossible to say that Mr. Seaton was not covered by his policy because he divided the lorry into two and took the engine to another part of the premises.

Source: E.R. Hardy Ivamy, 'Casebook on Insurance Law', London, Butterworths, 4th Edition, (pp. 85-87, 1984).

Case 3: *Yorkshire Insurance Co. Ltd.* Vs. *Nisbet Shipping Co. Ltd. (1961) 2 (All ER 487*

[Whether under the doctrine of subrogation, an insurer can recover from insured any more than what they had paid].

Finding by the Queen's Bench Division: Under the doctrine of subrogation embodied in the Marine Insurance Act, 1905, the insurer could not recover from the assured anything more than he has paid to the assured.

[A vessel insured for pound 72, 000 became a total loss after colliding with a Canadian Government ship. The insurers paid pound 72, 000 to the assured, who then claimed damages from the Canadian Government. Meanwhile, as the Pound Sterling had been devalued in 1949, the loss (when converted into English currency) came to nearly pound 127, 000 which was paid by the Canadian government to the assured. The assured repaid the pound 72, 000 to the insurers, and claimed that they were entitled to keep the excess sum of pound 55, 000.]

It follows that in my view the insurer's rights in this case were limited to recovering from the assured the amount paid, that is to say, pound 72, 000. He is entitled to no more. The principle, I think, is a simple one; it renders irrelevant any consideration of the particular concatenation of circumstances which enable the assured to recover from the Canadian Government a sum in sterling in excess of the value of the ship at the time of the casualty. The fact that the policy was a valid policy, with, as it transpired, a policy value somewhat less than the real value is also irrelevant. The simple principle which I apply is that the insurer can not recover under the doctrine of subrogation now embodied in Section 79 of the Marine Insurance Act, 1906, anything more than he has paid.

Source: E.R. Hardy Ivamy, 'Casebook on Insurance Law', London, Butterworths, 4th Edition, (p. 224, 1984).

Case 4: Householders' Comprehensive Policy—Definition of Flood

Young Vs. *Sun Alliance and London Insurance Ltd. (1976) 2 Lloyd's Rep 189.*

[*Definition*: The meaning of the word 'flood' in a Householder's Comprehensive Insurance policy covering storm, tempest or flood"].

Finding of the Court of Appeal: 'Flood as used in the phrase in the policy referred to something that is violent and abnormal, and not seepage'.

Lawton, L.J. (at 191)

[A house was insured to cover (*inter alia*) damage by storm, tempest or flood. Seepage of water from an underground water course damaged a lavatory on the ground floor of the house. The insured made a claim on the ground that the damage was caused by flood].

This appeal raises a semantic problem which has troubled many philosophers for centuries, and it can, I think, be expressed in the aphorism that an elephant is difficult to define but easy to recognize. I find difficulty in defining the word flood as used in this policy, I have no difficulty in looking at the evidence in this case and coming to the conclusion, as do, that the water in the lavatory was not a flood within the meaning of Para 8 of this policy.

(Counsel) pointed out to the court that the phrase in the policy is storm, tempest or flood, and that the word flood is used as a word in ordinary English usage to cover a situation which may be very different from the situations to which the words flooded or flooding are appropriate. I agree. It is not without reference that Para 9 in the next paragraph in the policy, refers to the Escape of water from or frost damage to any water, drainage or heating installation, so flood is something different for the purposes of this policy from an escape of water.

I agree with Shaw, L.J. that the essence of flood in ordinary English is some abnormal, violent situation. It may not necessarily have to be sudden, but it does, in my judgment, have to be violent and abnormal. This seepage of water through a rise in the water level was not violent, and it was not all that abnormal, it was the sort of incident which householders sometimes have to suffer as a result of rising damp. I, too, would dismiss the appeal.

Source: E.R. Hardy Ivamy, 'Casebook on Insurance Law', London, Butterworths, 4th Edition, (pp. 266-67, 1984).

Case 5: Liability – Negligence and Fraud

West Wake Price and Co. Vs. *Ching—(1956) 3 All ER 621.*

[Whether a claim due to a mix of 'negligence and fraud' is covered under a liability insurance covering 'negligence'].

Finding of the Queen's Beach Division: The 'claim' was limited to an unmixed claim relating only to an 'act of neglect, default or error'.

Devlin, J. (at 831)

[A firm of accountants had affected a Lloyd's Accountants indemnity policy against claims arising out of an act of neglect, default or error on the part of the assured or their servants in the conduct of their business as accountants. One of the clerks employed by the insured converted a client's money to his own use. The client made a claim partly on the grounds of negligence and partly on dishonesty. The accountants' firm, in turn, claimed an indemnity from their insurers, who repudiated liability stating that the loss was not covered under the policy].

I have reached the conclusion that there is in fact a simpler and more effective test, which is the correct one. It depends simply on the true construction of the policy. Businessmen often want to write into document words which they think will amplify its meaning, but which lawyers reject as superfluous, nevertheless, the writing of superfluities sometimes helps to clarify questions of construction. If a layman wanted a phrase such as claim in respect of negligence only or claims in respect of the negligence but not in respect of fraud, a lawyer would tell him that his additions were superfluous, since negligence meant negligence and nothing else and did not include fraud .... if words such as these were there, however, they would serve to show that a claim in respect of negligence alone. Applying this test, which I think is the right one, the claim in this clause is outside the policy.

Source: E.R. Hardy Ivamy, 'Casebook on Insurance Law', London, Butterworths, 4th Edition, (pp. 257-58, 1984).

Bibliography

C. Arthur Williams (Jr.) and Richard M. Heins, Risk Management and Insurance (1950).

G. Hart, R.A, Buchanan and B.A. Howe, The Actuarial Practice of General Insurance, Institute of Actuaries of Australia, Fire Insurance in India by P.A.S. Mani, Hindustan Advertisers, Bombay (1952).

Henery Kete and L. Gurney, Guide to Marine Insurance, Sir Isaac Pitman and Sons, London (1948).

IRDA Circulars on File and use Guidelines and Data Collection post-Detariffing, website: http://www.irdaindia.org.

IRDA Regulations, website: http://www.irdaindia.org.

Organization of Indian Insurance by Prof. S.P. Sharma, Allied Publishers Pvt. Ltd. 1967.

P.A.S. Mani, Fire Insurance in India, Hindustan Advertisers, Bombay (1952-62).

Report of the Committee Reforms in the Insurance Sector by R.N. Malhotra and others.

Report of the K.P. Narasimhan Committee on Provisions of the Insurance Act, 1938 by Mr. K.P. Narasimhan (and 10 other members) submitted to the IRDA, (July 26, 2005).

Standing Committee on International Financial Standards and Codes—Report of the Advisory Group on Insurance Regulation by R. Ramakrishnan, T.G. Menon and others, DEAP, Reserve Bank of India (2000).

Standing Committee on International Financial Standards and Codes Report of the Advisory Group on Insurance Regulation by R. Ramakrishana, T.G. Menon and others, DEAP, Reserve Bank of India (2000:30) (*ibid.*: 31-32).

The Actuarial Practice of General Insurance, D.G. Hart, R.A. Buchanan, and B.A. Howe, Institute of Actuaries of Australia Motor Accidents Authority (MAA) the regulatory body of the New South Wales State of Australia. Utah State Insurance Rules, Definitions, website http://www.Insurance.utah.gov/rules/590-121.htm

The India Motor Tariffs Published by the TAC, website: http://www.tac.org.in

The Insurance Act, 1938.

The Insurance Act, 1938. All tariffs published by TAC, website http://www.tac.org.in. Website of Wikipedia.

The Royal exchange Assurance—A History of British Insurance (1720-1970) by Barry Supple, Cambridge University Press (1970).

The Sarbanes-Oxley Act of 2002 of USA, also known as the Public Company Accounting Reform and Investor Protection Act of 2002 and commonly called SOX or Sarbox.

Website of Agriculture Corporation of India Ltd., Website of General Insurance Corporation of India Ltd.

Website of Bajaj Alliance Insurance Co. Ltd.

Website of ICICI Lombard Insurance Co. Ltd.

Website of Insurance Information Institute http://www.iii.org

Website of International Association of Insurance Supervisors: http://www.iaisweb.org.

Website of IRDA http:///www.irdaindia.org

Website of National Insurance Co. Ltd., Website of Oriental Insurance Co. Ltd.

Website of New India Insurance Co. Ltd.

Website of the Governing Body of Insurance Council, http://ombudmanindia.org.

Website of the Risk and Insurance Management Society (RIMS): ERM for Financial Institutions, Rating Criteria and Best Practices by Standard and Poor, website: http://www.mgt.ncsu.edu/pdfs/erm/sp_erm_busdevbk.pdf.

Website of United India Insurance Co. Ltd.

Website of Wikipedia: Website of the Committee of Sponsoring Organizations of the Treadway Commission.

Index